How to Build & Modify

FORD

Fuel-Injected 5.0-Liter V-8 Engines

Tom Wilson

First published in 1998 by MBI Publishing Company, 729 Prospect Avenue, PO Box 1, Osceola, WI 54020-0001 USA

The information in this book is true and complete to the best of our knowledge. All recommendations are made without any guarantee on the part of the author or Publisher, who also disclaim any liability incurred in connection with the use of this data or specific details.

We recognize that some words, model names and designations, for example, mentioned herein are the property of the trademark holder. We use them for identification purposes only. This is not an official publication.

MBI Publishing Company books are also available at discounts in bulk quantity for industrial or sales-promotional use. For details write to Special Sales Manager at Motorbooks International Wholesalers & Distributors, 729 Prospect Avenue, Osceola, WI 54020-0001 USA.

Library of Congress Cataloging-in-Publication Data
Wilson, Tom.
    How to build & modify Ford fuel-injected 5.0-liter V-8 engines/ Tom Wilson.
      p. cm.–(MBI Publishing Company PowerTech Series)
    Includes index.
    ISBN 0-7603-0201-4 (pbk.)
    1. Ford automobile—Motors—Maintenance and repair—Handbooks, manuals, etc. I. Title. II. Title: How to build and modify Ford fuel-injected 5.0-liter V-8 engines. III. Series.
TL215.F7W55   1998
629.25'04--dc21   98-31680

On the front cover: All dressed up and polished to go, the cover engine epitomizes the versatility of the 5.0 HO V-8. Whether made up for Saturday night cruising or rigged for race track battle, the Ford 5.0 HO has proven more powerful, more durable, and more easily modified than any other modern production engine. *Harvey Hester, courtesy* Super Ford *magazine.*

On the back cover: (top)Light, powerful, inexpensive, and easy to work on, the 5.0 HO proved to be the ultimate Mustang engine for the common man. Key to the 5.0 HO's personality is its long intake path that promotes torque. This is the 1994–1995 version with the low-profile upper intake manifold and stamped steel valve covers. (bottom) Nitrous oxide is known by many nicknames, but whether you call it spray, juice, or squeeze, the kick is still the same. Nitrous is probably the most explosive, and fun, of the power-adders, and for a street-strip car it is ideal. Commuting to work can be done with absolute stock drivability and fuel mileage, then at the strip you can easily enjoy up to 150 extra horsepower. Many 5.0s run in the 12s with 150 horsepower from spray and little else.

Edited by John Adams-Graf
Designed by Katie L. Sonmor

Printed in the United States of America

CONTENTS

Acknowledgments 4
Introduction 5

CHAPTER 1
The 5.0 HO Engine 7
General Description
1986–1993 Engines
1994–1995 Engines
1996 5.0 HO
Engines

CHAPTER 2
Understanding and Modifying
EEC-IV 18
System Description
Working with EEC-IV
Speed/Density Leaning
Computer "Chips"
Piggybacks
EPEC
Carburetion

CHAPTER 3
Induction 32
Intake Air Silencer
Air Filters
Mass Air Meter
Throttle Body and EGR Spacer
Intake Manifolds
Long Runner
Box Intakes
Cowl Induction
Installation Tips
Phenolic Spacers
Trick Stuff
Dyno Testing

CHAPTER 4
Exhaust 46
Intake Air Silencer
The Stock Exhaust
Short-Tube Headers
Street or Race?
Long-Tube Headers
H-Pipes
X-Pipes
Cat-Back
Cat-Back Installation

CHAPTER 5
Ignition 59
Inductive vs. Capacitor
Maintenance
Forced Induction Requirements
Aftermarket Ignitions
Installation Tips
Distributors
Drive Gear
Battery

CHAPTER 6
Fuel 67
The 5.0 Fuel System
Definition of Terms

CHAPTER 7
Power Adders 74
Power Adding as a Kit
Street, Strip, or Track?
Convenience
Future Increases
Cost

CHAPTER 8
Nitrous Oxide 78
Theory of Operation
System Description
Wet vs. Dry
Nitrous Accessories
Fuel and Driveline Requirements

CHAPTER 9
Superchargers 84
Centrifugal vs. Positive Displacement
Centrifugals
Positive Displacement
Accessories
Fuel
Air Filters
Low Restriction
Air Inlet
Cat-Back Exhaust
Boost Retards
Octane Boosters
Bypass Kits
Drive Belts and
Pulleys
Blower Braces
Intercoolers

CHAPTER 10
Turbocharging 97
5.0 Turbo Kits
Turbo Technology

CHAPTER 11
Strokers 103
Why a Stroker?
Stroker Blocks
Stroker Crankshafts
Damper and Flywheel
Stroker Connecting Rods and Pistons
Stroker Tradeoffs
Stroker Tuning
Why Not a 351?

CHAPTER 12
Short Block Preparation 108
Why a Stroker?
Cylinder Block
Boring
Sonic Checking
Honing with Block Plates
Align Boring and Honing
Decking
Lightening
Crankshaft
Balancing
Rear Main Seal
Knife-Edging

Oiling
Oil Pans
Connecting Rods
Deburring and Shot
Peening
Aftermarket
Connecting Rods
Pistons
Dome Shape and Deburring
Balancing
Head Bolts and Studs
Crate Engines
Crank Kit
New vs. Rebuilt
Stock vs. Modified
Cost

CHAPTER 13
Cylinder Heads 118
Stock Cylinder Heads
Odds and Ends
Cylinder Head Preparation
Porting
Screw-In Studs and Guide Plates

CHAPTER 14
Camshafts and Valvetrain 134
Camshaft Terminology
Camshaft Strategy
Normally Aspirated
Supercharged Engine
Turbocharged Engines
Nitrous Oxide
Popular Camshafts
5.0 Lifters
5.0 Pushrods and Rocker Geometry
Rocker Arms
Rocker Installation and Adjustment
Rocker Arm Adjustment

CHAPTER 15
5.0 Trucks 147
The Basic Engine
Truck Speed/Density
Camshaft
Mass Air Conversion
Induction
Forced Induction
Exhaust

CHAPTER 16
Running the 5.0 151
Driving
Timing and Fuel
Electronic Tuning
Cooling Down
Short Belts
Head Gaskets

Appendix Sources 157

Index 158

ACKNOWLEDGMENTS

Because it represents a decade's accumulation of knowledge, it is impossible to list the hundreds of enthusiasts and professionals who have assisted in writing this book. Even in the course of researching specific points, I have spoken with far too many people to mention all of them by name here. However, at the definite risk of excluding a deserving individual, the following made major contributions to this work.

Doug Baker at ESI/JBA Racing Engines deserves special mention for his engineering talents throughout, but especially in Chapter 6, where his mastery of fuel system design provided the core of the chapter, and Chapter 14, where Doug's daily immersion in machine shop practices is also the backbone of the chapter.

Steve Turner, Senior Editor at *Super Ford* and my chief accomplice, was also instrumental in the creation of this book. His as-yet unruined memory and special interest with 5.0s were crucial in seeing this project through to completion. Steve has also authored his own book on the subject, *How to Tune & Modify Your Ford 5.0-Liter Mustangs.*

Dan Nowak was another individual who willingly lent a big hand. Numerous parts and procedures were photographed at Nowak and Company, along with a few stories being told while the strobes flashed.

J. Bittle of JBA Racing Headers provided considerable support, with special emphasis on headers and exhaust.

Obtaining just the right photos is always something of a chore, and Brian Murphy of BBK was extra helpful in providing BBK's in-house studio and huge parts inventory for my use, along with some of his own photos.

Vern Bowen, an ace technician at Drew Ford in San Diego, and not quite incidentally also an accomplished 5.0 road racer and slalomist, answered more than his share of dumb questions from me at all hours, while Don Emory lent his 5.0 pickup for the camera.

Plus you'd never get anywhere without your friends. Luckily I didn't have to bug too many buddies on this project, but local Ford man Bill Atkins did get the call and was generous in lending his clean SN-95 for photography.

I must say that almost without exception, the thoughts contained in this book have all been borrowed from others in the industry. It's their endless hours developing new parts at the track and in dyno cells that have proven the concepts and made possible the fun we enjoy with 5.0s today.

Furthermore, while this book is independent of Dobbs Publishing Group and *Super Ford* magazine, it would not have been possible without my association with that title since 1987. Underlaying all of my 5.0 knowledge, I'm pleased to acknowledge the editorially sound environment Larry Dobbs, owner and Publisher of Dobbs Publishing Group, has provided *Super Ford*, and thus to myself. Also, the patient understanding of Donald Farr, Editorial Director at DPG, is kindly acknowledged, a debt I have not been able to publicly pay for 10 years. I'd also like to thank my friend Steve Statham, former managing editor at *Super Ford*, for his help with the earlier 5.0 Mustangs.

Ultimately, those at home pay by far the largest price for projects of this size. To Jan, Mark, and Scott, I can only say thank you for your loving support and untiring patience.

INTRODUCTION

Occasionally a car is so right for its time it redefines the performance scene. The electronically fuel-injected 5.0 Mustang is such a car.

The foundation was laid in 1979 when the Fox-chassised Mustang replaced the unloved Mustang II subcompact platform. By 1982, the time was right for Ford to introduce a GT version. With its marine camshaft and Holley carburetor, the '82 GT signaled a performance renaissance after the automotive dark ages of the '70s. Although the '82's technical specifications seem quaint today, they warmed the carb and mechanical cam crowd to the new body style and to modern cars in general.

The carbureted Mustang reached its zenith in 1985 before being replaced by the first EFI GT the following year. Initially, this first fuel-injected effort confirmed the worst rumblings of pit rail pundits. The car made less power than the previously carbureted version, it was more expensive, and worst of all, no one could work on it. There were no points, no jets, no accelerator pumps. Instead, there were wires, injectors, throttle bodies, and (worse yet) a computer. If one did anything to the engine, the computer did its best to undo it. No one outside of Ford, and precious few inside, knew how to work with the infuriating black box. Pioneering enthusiasts paid dearly for their efforts. In exchange for hours and hours of work, they gained horrid hunting idles, impossible drivability, and at least as much backtracking as horsepower progress.

Ford continued to develop the Mustang. After one year, the '86 GT's cylinder heads were ditched in favor of better flowing castings taken from the '85 GT. Also in 1987, the 5.0 LX was introduced, a brilliant combination of the GT's mechanical goodies clothed in base bodywork for less money. Then, most importantly, on the 1987 California, and then on all 1988 models, mass air metering was introduced. This final development flung open the door to performance modifications—the computer could finally accept performance modifications.

Then an unusual thing happened. Ford, busy with emission and quality concerns, plus unsure of what direction to take with its pony car, left the Mustang alone. As the archrival Camaro became more expensive without offering a performance advantage, the Mustang continued on with its old, but paid for, chassis. Enthusiasts complained about rear drum brakes and wished for more power from the factory, but nevertheless snapped up the fast and affordable Mustang. They recognized the 5.0 as the best 7/8 finished car in history; it was like an assembled kit car that wanted only the final performance customizing from its owner.

This combination of established chassis, modern engine, and continued production formed a critical mass of Mustangs. Hot rodders had learned the mass air Mustangs could be tuned for great power with excellent drivability. Ford Special Vehicle Operations (SVO) introduced the mass air retrofit kit for earlier EFI Mustangs and suddenly there was a huge crowd of power-hungry Mustang owners ready to buy parts. It didn't take the speed industry long to discover this ready market and the 5.0 phenomenon was on. Either you had a 5.0 Mustang and were taking part in a new age of performance discovery, or you simply weren't with it.

The 5.0 HO engine continued for two years in the revamped '94–'95 body style, finally bowing to the all-new modular V-8 in 1996. Still, hundreds of thousands of 5.0s prowl America's highways, and 5.0 performance will continue to evolve for decades to come.

Since 1987 I've been documenting the 5.0's rise to dominance in the pages of *Super Ford* magazine. Up to 1990 I was West Coast Editor, when I moved up to Editor, a position I still hold. While I claim no personal expertise in tuning these exciting cars, I've been involved on a daily basis with those who most certainly know how. It's from this army of experts I've drawn the material for this book.

Between these covers I address the most popular aspects of 5.0 hot rodding. Commonly referred to as "bolt-on" modifications, the parts and work described here involve the entire engine, with special emphasis on those parts above the short block. Hot street enthusiasts, drag racers, slalomists, road racers, anyone short of all-out professional racers, should find all the power they can use here. I've attempted to straddle that difficult line where both first-time and old-hand 5.0 owners will find the book useful, but above all, it's a book to lead the neophyte to a good solid beginning in 5.0 tuning.

As you improve your Mustang, keep a few general thoughts in mind. First, the 5.0 engine was balanced from air filter to tailpipes to work as a unit. Excitedly changing a few items in the engine because those parts were on sale that week—in other words, without a plan—won't work. If you haphazardly add performance equipment, it's possible to spend a fortune changing parts on a 5.0 and have it run like a dog. You must change parts so they work in unison, a concept I've tried to incorporate throughout this book.

From a power viewpoint, the exhaust ports of the stock cylinder heads are the choke point. Improved street performance is possible without touching the stock heads, but the sooner you either port the stock heads or replace them with any of the many excellent aftermarket pieces, the sooner you'll be on the road to significantly increased power.

As you make more power, you'll need to improve the chassis accordingly. While chassis modifications are beyond the scope of this book, I must state '93 and earlier stock 5.0 brakes are not up to extremely hard street driving, much less competition. Invest in premium front brake pads immediately and definitely consider larger front brakes. The PBR brake as offered by Baer Racing is

a wise choice; SVO and others have good, upgraded packages, too.

If you are modifying your Mustang for street performance, remember, you have a street car. That means running catalytic converters and no street racing. It is easier to make horsepower without catalytic converters, but removing cats is ethically and legally wrong. We all like to breathe, and the 10–15 horsepower gained on a hot street engine just at the top end of the tach is no justification for spewing pollutants into the atmosphere. There are other ways of making that 15 horsepower and remaining clean. As for street racing, in today's crowded world, racing on the street is incredibly stupid and dangerous. Put your energies into track competition where consistent timing equipment lets you learn so much more anyway.

Finally, spend your money wisely. Decide on what type of 5.0 Mustang you want to end up with before you start. Map out your strategy on paper, and plan your parts purchases. While it's smart to shop, remember your local speed shop is more than a place to inspect parts before purchasing by mail order. A good local shop is a huge help, but you've got to support him occasionally if you want him to stay in business.

See you at the races,

Tom Wilson

C
O
N
T
E
N
T
S

General Description 8

1986–1993 Engines 8

1994–1995 Engines 16

1996 5.0 HO
Engines 17

Light, powerful, inexpensive, and easy to work on, the 5.0 HO proved the ultimate Mustang engine for the common man. Key to the 5.0 HO's personality is its long intake path, which promotes torque. This is the 1994–1995 version, with the low-profile upper intake manifold and stamped steel valve covers.

THE 5.0 HO ENGINE

From the 1986 introduction of electronic fuel injection to the end of Fox-chassised Mustang production in 1995, the 5.0 HO engine remained relatively unchanged. The notable differences were to the cylinder head, fuel injection, and pistons. Less important modifications concerned the camshaft and power rating.

The basic 5.0 engine is part of the great small-block Ford family, which began in 1962 with the 260. Soon upped to 289 and then 302 displacements, the small-block family was designed as a light, compact sedan engine. The nonskirted block (the block ends at the main-bearing parting line) and thin-wall casting technique were aimed at reducing weight and conserving package size, not providing large overbore capacity. This limits displacement potential, as witnessed by Ford's own 302, or 5.0-liter maximum size

before going to the physically larger, more robust 351 Windsor, or 5.8, to call it by its modern designation.

The small block has seen tremendous competition success in everything from local drag racing to Carroll Shelby's Cobras and Ford's own GT-40s at the 24 Hours of Le Mans. Carbureted, the oversquare small block is a natural high-rpm screamer, not a torquer. Old carbureted small-blocks were built to work with deep rear axle gears and to rev to the moon. The gears were necessary to cover up the engine's lack of low- and mid-range torque; the hideous fuel mileage that resulted was something everyone simply lived with.

All that changed with electronic fuel injection (EFI). It isn't that fuel injection by itself builds torque. Rather, it is the long intake manifold runners made possible by port fuel injection that promote torque. Squirt fuel in the late

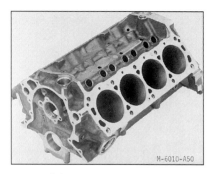

Heart of the 5.0 HO engine is its light, compact block. Strong enough for all typical bolt-on modifications, the modern Mustang block is good for over 400 horsepower, but as power rises, longevity goes down in a hurry. The stock block is offered by Motorsport as the M-6010-A50; its racing and extreme duty 5.0 block was the A4; is now the R302.

5.0 engine at the throttle body and the tortuous intake manifold would fill to dripping with puddled fuel. However, only dry air flows through the vast majority of the 5.0's intake tract, and this is what makes the long, complicated 5.0 intake path possible. It's those lengthy, somewhat narrow intake runners and relatively small cylinder head ports that transformed the small-block Ford from high-rpm screamer to low- and mid-rpm torquer. The result is that street-driven 5.0s can be improved by increasing the size and shape of the ports and runners to gain top-end breathing, while retaining the long-runner manifold design to retain as much torque as possible for good street manners and fuel economy. Only when dedicating a 5.0 to the racetrack should high-rpm, shorter runner, unrestricted breathing intakes be considered.

General Description

Like its 260/289/302 forerunners, the 5.0 HO uses a lightweight, compact engine block that has a cylinder deck height of only 8.206 inches. Ford's philosophy with its smallest V-8 back in the early 1960s was compact power, and this philosophy has stayed with the 302/5.0 engine throughout its life span. The 5.0 HO is built for power, yes, but not in an extremely robust way like the 460 big block. Fuel economy and cost concerns drove Ford to lighten the 5.0

block, right up to the end of Mustang production. Thin-wall block casting techniques on the 5.0 save weight, which limits radical boring for displacement increases. Late 1960s blocks, especially the Boss 302 version, are stronger foundations for truly high-output 5.0 engines, although the best choice is SVO's M-6010-A4 or R302 racing block. It's a strong block, ready for huge power outputs or a long life at more moderate power levels. For the typical street bolt-on power adders discussed in this book, the stock block is fine.

Just don't be amazed when, after upgrading the entire top half of the engine, bolting on a blower or nitrous, and turning all the screws until it runs low 11s at the strip, the stock block gives up pretty quickly. Ford designed it for standard longevity at a bit over 200 horsepower; stuffing 400 horsepower into it means it won't make 200,000 miles.

Crankshafts in the EFI 5.0 engine are the same throughout the production span discussed in this book. A lightweight crankshaft by high-performance standards, it has proven durable in all bolt-on uses. Likewise, 5.0 oiling is of no concern to the bolt-on enthusiast. High-pressure oil pumps are not necessary as long as the stock 6,250-rpm rev limit is maintained.

What causes long-time hot rodders the most wonderment is the 5.0's connecting rods, especially their puny 5/16 bolts. Again, these items live, thanks to the limited rpm available, so for bolt-on power, even supercharging and nitrous, they're fine. However, if you are rebuilding a 5.0 engine and stepping up the power, then moving to an upgraded connecting rod bolt, if not the entire rod, along with forged pistons, would be your first hot rodding step.

Once past the short block, not much else matters in the 5.0 HO, as eventually everything else gets changed by eager performance fans. There is certainly nothing inherently wrong with the engine. Its valvetrain has proven durable, and its induction/exhaust flow is reasonably well balanced, but in the search for power, the top of the engine is easily and practically replaced.

If you are looking for parts not to replace, consider the camshaft. Tuners often remark that the bolt-on type of cars do very well with the stock cam, which offers easy street manners, the best possible street torque, and no hassle when you go for a smog test. Many cars run in the 12s at the strip on the stock cam, so until you've exhausted all other breathing possibilities, stay with the original bump stick.

While the 5.0 engine changed little in the period covered by this book, the detail modifications listed below are worth knowing about.

1986–1993 Engines
Mustang-Based

From its inception in 1982 until through 1993, the 5.0 HO engine in the Mustang was built as a Mustang engine. That means it was not sourced from another Ford chassis and given a few tweaks to work in the pony car. Thus the intake manifold layout, header configuration, and other details were

Blue Oval Alphabet Soup

Ford fans eventually pick up the differences among the several acronyms and names used to denote Ford performance entities. Heading the list is SVO, or Special Vehicle Operations. Special vehicle is the corporate euphemism for racing, thus SVO is the group at Ford charged with supporting Ford's various racing programs, such as Indy car, Trans Am, and NASCAR.

SVO also sells performance parts under the Ford Motorsport name. Thus you hear people talking about "Motorsport valve covers." SVO and Motorsport are the same group of people, and SVO and Motorsport are used interchangeably by enthusiasts.

Then there are SVT and SVE. Special Vehicle Team is the well-known group that markets limited-edition Ford automobiles, like the SVT Mustang Cobra or SVT Contour. SVT people are essentially salesmen, but they also handle the market research and business end of promoting these cars. The Special Vehicle Engineering (SVE) group is the team of engineers who design and put those cars together.

Another lightweight piece is the 5.0 crankshaft. Like the block, it is not really suitable for killer rpm or horsepower in stock form, but it handles bolt-on power beautifully. Ford machinists refer to this as a "2M" or "lightweight" crank because of its casting number and reduced weight, compared to previous small-block crankshafts. Also, before 1981, 302 cranks used full counterweighting, but since 1981 a 50-ounce imbalance on the flywheel was fitted, and one of the rear counterweights was greatly reduced, as can be seen here. All EFI 5.0s use this crank.

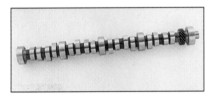

While there have been minor changes to it, the EFI 5.0 HO camshaft has been essentially the same since 1987. Built from steel to work with roller lifters, the stock cam is a low-friction, surprisingly good power builder. It can't be beat for streetable torque and fuel economy, and still provides good high-rpm horsepower when augmented by bolt-on breathing aids such as intakes.

Starting in 1985, the 5.0 HO got a roller hydraulic lifter cam as seen at left. The older, flat tappet cam caused more power-robbing friction and could not support valve action as radical as the roller. The taller roller lifter means the 1984 and earlier blocks with lower lifter bores cannot use roller lifter cams without the help of a conversion, sold by Crane Cams.

built around the Mustang chassis and not shared with any other Ford.

During this period, the 5.0 was also used in the F-150/250 pickup truck, Bronco, Thunderbird, Crown Victoria, Mercury Grand Marquis and Cougar, Lincoln Town Car, Lincoln Mark VII and Mark VII LSC. The pickups and Bronco used a truck version of the 5.0, which differed in intake manifolding and by using speed/density engine management. Most of the non-Mustang car engines also differed from the Mustang's 5.0 HO. Cars other than Mustang used the standard 5.0 engine, which Ford engineers refer to as the "mom and pop" engine. It has less aggressive camming, electronics calibration, exhaust manifolding, compression ratio, and other detail differences. The standard 5.0 is not as good a high-performance foundation as the HO engine, but it is fine as a core engine for pan-up engine build.

1986

When first released for EFI duty in 1986, the 5.0 HO was rated at 200 horsepower and fitted with speed/density fuel injection, along with restrictive cylinder heads. The 1986 GT heads do not breathe as well as the carbureted 1985 castings or the 1987 and later parts. The culprit is a swirl-inducing shroud curled tightly around the intake valve side of the combustion chamber; additionally, the piston crown is flat, which limits valve lift.

You'd think porting these heads would help, but it is really far better to replace them. An aftermarket head is easily the best choice, but even a set of the 1987 and later E7TE stock castings would be a step up. Still, the economies of head preparation make a prepped E7TE casting more expensive than several of the aluminum aftermarket heads, so aftermarket heads are the way to go. Eventually, the stock heads should be very inexpensive, as people create a pool of discarded E7TE head castings in their move to aftermarket parts. Because the E7TE casting was used from 1987 to the end of 5.0 HO Mustang production in 1998, there are plenty of them around.

Additionally, the 1986 5.0s used a smaller, 58-millimeter throttle body and a more restrictive small-port, small-plenum upper intake than later EFI 5.0s. If you're changing these items anyway, it really doesn't matter, but if you are looking for a near-stock driver, a 1987 or later is a better choice. Otherwise you have to change the heads and intake just to keep up with the 1987 and later cars. On the positive side, the 1986 cylinder block has Siamesed bores and thicker cylinder walls and decks than 1985 and earlier blocks, so it's a good short block to build an engine around.

Camshaft

Few people know the 5.0 camshaft was changed at some time in 1990. The change was small, and was to eliminate a harmonic problem at 5,750 rpm. Apparently, bedlam broke loose in the valvetrain exactly at, and only at, 5,750 rpm with the early cam. Because this rpm is so high and brief in duration, the only time the engine ever sees it is while being revved to redline, so valvetrain wear was never a real-world problem. Nevertheless, Ford elected to change the camshaft slightly to eliminate any possibility of harmonically induced valvetrain failure. The new camshaft superseded the original 5.0 EFI cam, meaning the old cam is completely sold out and replaced with the new one. Thus, if you ask for a replacement cam for a 1987 5.0 from your Ford dealer's parts counter, you'll get the new cam.

It's worth noting the new cam is not quite as aggressive as the old one. Although Ford says the cam changes were minute and should not have cost any power, they had an effect on the engine's perceived power and responsiveness. How much is debated by enthusiasts. Some say it cost 3 horsepower, but whatever it is, if you've sensed the late 1980s 5.0s ran a bit harder than the 1990s cars, you're probably right. Again, the change is very small, so it's not anything to lose any sleep over. Besides, the stock 5.0 cam, in either form, has been proven time and again to be a surprisingly eager power builder, but also smooth running and

The 5.0 Engine Compartment

LEGEND

1. Thermactor Air Diverter (TAD) solenoid—Directs thermactor air from the rear of the cylinder heads to the exhaust "H" pipe after warm-up.
2. Thermactor Air Bypass (TAB) solenoid—Vents thermactor air when not needed (normally cold starts).
3. Vacuum Storage Canister—Stores vacuum to prevent interruption of services during wide-open throttle operation.
4. Throttle Body—Regulates the amount of air entering the engine.
5. Air Inlet Hose—Directs air into the throttle body from the mass air meter (mass air system) or the air cleaner housing (speed density system).
6. Idle Air Bypass Valve—Regulates the amount of air needed to maintain a smooth idle.
7. Engine Coolant Temperature (ECT) sensor—Reports the coolant temperature to the computer.
8. Injectors—Delivers fuel sequentially to each cylinder.
9. Oil Filter Cap
10. WOT Cutout Relay—Takes air conditioning compressor off-line during wide open throttle operation.
11. Fuel Pump Relay—EEC-IV activates the fuel pump through this relay.
12. Mass Air Flow Sensor—The electronic portion of the mass air flow meter.
13. Mass Air Flow Meter—Electrically measures the mass of air entering the engine and reports the information to the computer.
14. Thermactor Air Bypass Valve—Directs the flow of air supplied by the thermactor (fresh air) pump.
15. Alternator
16. Belt Tensioner
17. Air Silencer—Used to muffle pulsation noise emitted by the induction system (located behind fender apron).
18. Canister Purge Solenoid—Allows fuel vapors from the carbon canister to enter intake manifold.
19. Air Cleaner Housing—Contains rectangular panel air filter.
20. Thermactor Air Pump—Delivers high volume, low pressure fresh air to the exhaust system.
21. Water Pump, Fan, and Fan Clutch
22. Air Conditioning Condenser Connections—Attaches refrigerant lines to the air conditioner condenser.
23. Center Line Crash Sensor — Air bag-equipped vehicles only.
24. Radiator
25. Radiator Cap
26. Coolant Reservoir and Low Coolant Switch (if so equipped)
27. Power Steering Pump
28. Battery
29. Air Conditioning Compressor
30. Spout Connector—Must be unplugged when checking initial ignition timing.
31. Windshield Washer Reservoir

32. Vacuum Hose Diagram
33. Ignition Coil—Under plastic cover.
34. Starter Relay—Under plastic cover.
35. Coolant Temperature Sender—Relays coolant temperature to the gauge in the instrument panel.
36. Engine Oil Dipstick
37. Electronic Distributor—Controlled by the computer.
38. Front Strut Insulator and Camber Adjustment Plate
39. Upper Intake Plenum
40. Brake Master Cylinder and Booster
41. VIP Test Connectors—Computer test ports.
42. Windshield Wiper Motor
43. Vacuum Distribution Tee—From left to right the connections are: vacuum source (intake manifold), unused port (plugged), vacuum reservoir (#18), speed control servo (if so equipped), power brake booster.
44. Air Charge Temperature (ACT) sensor—Reports the temperature of the air in the intake manifold to the computer.
45. Barometric Absolute Pressure (BAP) sensor—Reports barometric pressure to the computer.
46. Positive Crankcase Ventilation Valve (PCV Valve)—Relieves crankcase pressure.
47. Fuel Pressure Regulator—Uses intake manifold vacuum to lower the fuel rail pressure during low rpm operation.
48. 10-Pin Connectors—Mates the engine wiring harness with the main wiring harness and the EEC computer.
49. Exhaust-Gas Recirculation (EGR) Vacuum Regulator Solenoid—Controls the vacuum that opens the EGR valve.
50. EGR Valve and EGR Position Sensor—Allows exhaust gases to enter the intake passage during various engine speeds. Reports valve position to computer.
51. EGR Spacer—Provides a hot gas passage to and from the EGR valve.
52. EGR Coolant Hoses—Circulates coolant through the EGR spacer.
53. Throttle Position Sensor—Relays the percentage of throttle opening to the computer.
54. Transmission Dipstick Tube—Automatic transmission only.
55. Crankcase Vent Tube—Allows crankcase fumes to enter the intake system.
56. Wiring Harness—Electrical wiring connecting all of the engine's electrical components to the computer located under the right-side kick panel.
57. AC Accumulator—Provides a storage area for the refrigerant in the AC system and houses a chemical drier that removes moisture from the refrigerant.
58. Vacuum Check Valve—Allows airflow in only one direction in order to keep vacuum storage canister fully charged.
59. Hood Ground Strap
60. AC Low Pressure Switch—Will not allow the air conditioner compressor clutch to energize if refrigerant pressure drops to

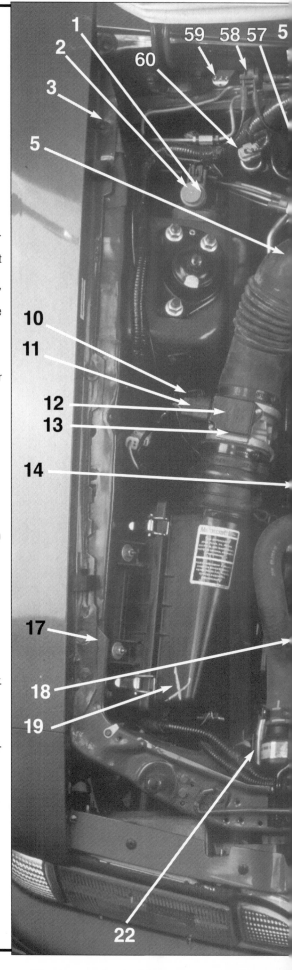

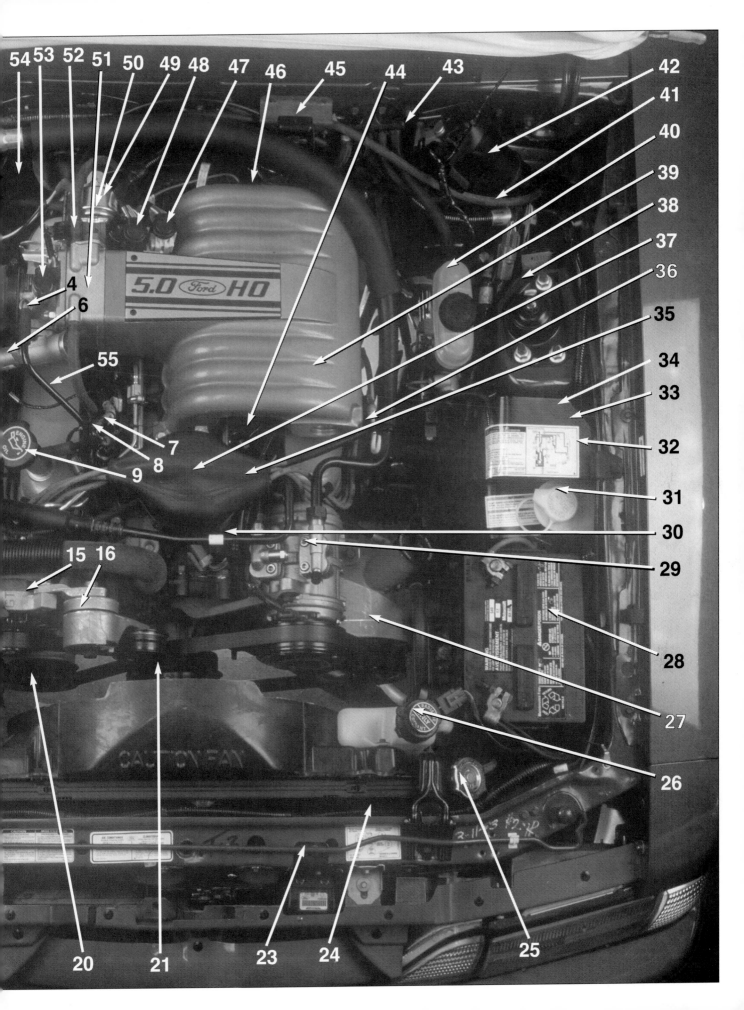

Lack of a mass air meter between the air filter and throttle body denotes a speed/density car. The less restricted air path means more power, in stock configuration, than with mass air metering. This stock engine ran 12.87/103.87 at the strip just before this photo was taken, in a chassis with extensive racing preparation. Once past stock, however, only mass air metering can adapt to the engine's changing air, fuel, and spark needs.

emissions legal when combined with the usual bolt-on power parts.

Let's also note all 1985 and later 5.0 Mustang camshafts are built from billet steel and work with hydraulic roller lifters. Until 1985, Ford cams were cast iron, and the ignition distributors used cast-iron gears. Also, the earlier cams were flat tappet (nonroller) cams. Because all EFI 5.0s use steel cams and roller lifters, you shouldn't have any concerns when buying aftermarket parts designed for these engines, but be aware that the steel cam requires a steel drive gear on the distributor. An earlier 302 cast-iron gear distributor will fit in the engine, but the iron drive gear will wear out extremely rapidly, filling the engine with metal shavings.

MSD and others offer bronze distributor drive gears that wear the same with iron or steel cams. These are fine for race engines that are rebuilt often, but their life of approximately 10,000 miles is too short for the street. SVO offers the necessary replacement steel gears.

As for the roller lifters, it's possible to use a flat tappet cam in a late-model block, but why? There are plenty of hydraulic roller cams available for the 5.0, so stick with them. For the record, roller cams will not work in flat tappet blocks, a situation typically found when hot rodding 5.0 and 5.8 truck engines.

Forged vs. Hypereutectic Pistons

One of the beauties of the mid-1980s 5.0s was their bulletproof forged piston. Enthusiastic supercharger boost and silly amounts of nitrous had a difficult time killing the forged pistons. Head gaskets were lifted left and right, but the pistons lived on. Unfortunately, to save costs, Ford went to a hypereutectic piston with the 1993 and later engines. These are fine in normal duty, and their lighter weight can be thought of as an advantage, but they don't offer the brute strength of a forging.

Again, as long as your fuel and spark are correct, you shouldn't hurt a hypereutectic piston with light bolt-on power. It's just that their safety margin is smaller than a forging. For six, maybe eight, pounds. of boost, 70 horsepower worth of nitrous, and that sort of bolt-on modification, hypereutectics are acceptable, but at the first rebuild, replace them with forgings. Also, don't expect Ford's hypereutectic pistons to live through big boost or nitrous, at least not for long. Somewhere above eight pounds of boost, they are on the edge.

Also, apparently some hypereutectic pistons are considerably better than others. The word is the Ford piston is so-so, but the Keith Black hypereutectics are considerably stronger. And, as always, all of these hypereutectic pistons are lighter and can be fitted more tightly to the cylinder for quieter running than a forging. Thus, high-quality hypereutectics are still a good choice in moderate, normally aspirated applications, although blowers, turbos, and nitrous really demand forgings.

Speed/Density vs. Mass Air Metering

The other major change was the move from the original speed/density

While it looks like just another accessory under the Mustang hood, the mass air meter revolutionized 5.0 performance tuning, with its accurate, adaptable air measuring capability. All meter electronics are concentrated under the plastic cover seen here atop the meter; the rest is a simple cast-aluminum tube.

Pre-1992 Mustangs can use this reduced-diameter, lightweight starter from SVO. It offers less vehicle weight, faster cranking, less current draw and a touch more room for headers. The 1992 and later cars come stock with this starter.

fuel injection to mass air metering. This is the single most important development in 5.0 performance.

Speed/density fuel injection does not measure the amount of air entering the engine. Instead, it infers the density of the air (one-half of the speed/density equation), and thus its mass, from the throttle opening and manifold pressure. There is no mass air meter, just the Throttle Position Sensor (TPS) and a Manifold Absolute Pressure (MAP) sensor, plus an rpm signal from the distributor, of course. You might want to think of a MAP sensor as a vacuum gauge, because that is basically what it is, a vacuum gauge calibrated to report to the EEC-IV computer in electronic units. Like any vacuum gauge, the MAP sensor signal is an excellent indication of the load the engine is under.

By knowing how wide the throttle is open, what sort of load the engine is experiencing, and how fast the engine is revving (the other half of the equation), speed/density EEC-IV can go to tables and look up how much fuel to inject and the ignition timing to administer. It's a good system that requires relatively little mathematical calculating by the computer. Therefore, speed/density responds very quickly. It easily has the time to guesstimate where the engine will be next (higher or lower rpm, more or less load) and therefore what to expect next.

Speed/density has another advantage; its air path is unobstructed by a mass air meter, so the engine can

Ford's new Special Vehicle Team came in with a winner when they introduced the 1993 Mustang Cobra. It's GT-40 spec 5.0 engine gave the 5.0 a much more satisfying personality, thanks to an extra 1,000 usable rpm and willingness to rev.

Reading Ford Part Numbers

Ford part numbers come in two varieties, those from mainstream production and those from SVO. Additionally, a handful of casting numbers are in common use.

Production Part Numbers

Behind Ford part numbers is a long story, suitable for telling on rainy days when there is no racing. For now, simply being able to read the year in a regular production part number may help smooth things for you at the parts counter.

A typical Ford number is: F0ZZ-3A674-C. To read the year, start at the beginning, an F in our example. It stands for the decade in which the part was released for production. Ford started its numbering program in the 1940s, so C stands for the 1960s, D the 1970s, E the 1980s, and F the 1990s. The second digit in the four-digit prefix is a 0 (zero), which is the second digit in the year the part was released. Thus this part was released in 1990. Most of the time, just knowing this much will help you identify what you are looking at.

Next is the letter Z, which stands for the car line the part was designed for; Z decodes into Mustang. The second Z stands for Ford (as opposed to Lincoln or Mercury), although this position can also stand for the division of Ford Motor Company, such as Engine, Electronic, Chassis, and so on.

Next is the basic part number—the type of part in question. This happens to be a power steering pump, so the 3A674 part of the number really means "power steering pump assembly." Finally, the C suffix gives the change level, or the version, of that part. The C suffix means the part has been modified twice.

SVO Part Numbers

SVO numbers are similar to regular Ford part numbers, but simpler. All begin with an M to denote Motorsport. This is followed by a four-digit number, which denotes the type of part, using the same codes as regular part numbers. A 6010 is an engine block, cylinder heads are 6049, and so on. You just have to know what these numbers are, but the more you cruise the Motorsport catalog, the more you'll recognize these identifiers.

With SVO part numbers, the suffix simply completes the identification of the basic part. Most of the time these alphanumeric suffixes readily identify the part, but not all can. Thus, M-6049-J302 denotes a Motorsport cylinder head that fits a 302 (5.0) engine. The "J head," as some Ford types refer to it, happens to be the old aluminum street/strip head cast by Alan Root, but you had to read the catalog to find that out.

It's a good idea to learn as many of these part numbers as possible. It helps sort out in your head the many available parts, and it's just the thing to impress your friends.

Casting Numbers

Ford cast what amount to modified part numbers into some parts. All you really need to know is that the number cast into a part is not the exact part number of that part, but it is usually close. Also, the central part of the part number is left out. Thus the E7TE casting number found on 1987–1995 5.0 cylinder heads is pretty easily identified as having started originally in 1987. The E at the end signifies the Engine division.

Just to show you can't rely on casting numbers to order parts, there is also an E7TE cylinder head on late 460 truck engines. Clearly it won't work on a 5.0!

Besides giving a neat factory look, the emission-certified GT-40 package makes a fine daily driver. Ongoing development in blower technology has made the best centrifugal superchargers more powerful, easier to bolt on, and likely less expensive alternatives than the full GT-40 combination, but the two together are still a great way to go on the street.

Ideally suited for real-world street driving, the slightly heavier, quieter, more rigid, and better handling 1994–1995 Mustang GTs are best tuned for torquey street performance, although they can be turned into fearsome track warriors if desired. The lighter 1993 and earlier cars are the better choice if track action is your main intent.

Other cars have used the High Output version of the 5.0 engine, including the Thunderbird and Explorer. From the enthusiast's perspective, the meaningful differences in these engines lay in the intake manifolding, oil pan, and pump pick-up and other details. The short blocks and cylinder heads are all the same.

breathe unimpeded. This is a major reason Ford still uses speed/density on its Formula One engines.

However, speed/density has one major disadvantage. It doesn't adapt to changes in the engine's hardware. At first this isn't a problem. Change the air filter, bump up the timing, add a set of headers and rocker arms, and a speed/density engine will usually respond enthusiastically with crisper throttle response and more power. What has happened is the modest breathing aids have eaten into the small cushion of slightly rich mixtures Ford programmed into the speed/density computer to protect against detonation. Because the speed/density computer can't tell more air is moving through the engine, the air/fuel mixture leans out and power goes up . . . to a point.

Things are different once enough parts are added to improve breathing significantly. Say you change the camshaft. The computer can't tell and instantly its carefully programmed air/fuel and spark tables are rubbish. The first thing the hot rodder notices is

that drivability has gone to pot. The idle hunts around the tach in a maddening series of stumbles, dead spots appear, throttle response goes soft, and fuel economy drops. Power drops, too. Get a bit extreme with too radical a cam and the engine will barely start and run, much less make power. As speed/density

owners probably know by now, it doesn't take much cam to bring on the tilt sign. Certainly an E303 will do it.

This is not a problem for Ford's race teams. They simply program another chip in the pits and pop it in the race car's computer. In fact, Ford's pro teams in series like Formula One

M-6007-C50
M-6007-C51

A low-profile intake manifold with a built-in, curving air inlet are the instant visual clues to the Thunderbird-based 1994–1995 5.0 HO engines. Nearly identical to the 1993 and earlier 5.0 HO powerplants, all the necessary hot rod pieces are available for this version of the 5.0 HO, so there's no reason to shy away from them.

literally "burn" (program) new chips because the weather changed from the morning practice session. You don't have that kind of flexibility, obviously.

The answer is mass air metering. By fitting a mass airflow (MAF) meter in the intake tract upstream of the throttle, the EEC-IV computer can directly read the weight (mass) of air entering the engine. Ford chose not to fit a MAP sensor to the mass air metering 5.0s because the computer can infer (calculate) engine load by plugging the throttle position and air mass into some formulas and doing the calculations. This requires considerable math processing capability (EEC-IV can perform 2.1 million calculations or so per second), but saved a couple of dollars by not having to fit a MAP sensor.

So, with mass air metering you can change the camshaft, intake manifold, fit headers, even tack on a supercharger, and the EEC-IV pretty much takes it all in stride. There are other factors. Some modifications, such as a supercharger's fuel management unit, take the fuel or spark needs far outside EEC-IVs limits and require their own fuel and spark control units, but by and large, a mass air metering EEC-IV system is an amazingly powerful and adaptable fuel injection system.

Because its engine compartment is too narrow to accept the overly wide modular V-8 engines, the Explorer sport utility carried on the 5.0 HO engine into 1998. The Explorer version of the 5.0 uses several unique exterior parts to fit the Explorer chassis, but these can be changed to fit in a Mustang.

Power Ratings

Even though individual factory-fresh engines often vary by about 5 horsepower, many enthusiasts get excited about factory power ratings. Ford has rated the 1987 and later EFI 5.0 as high as 225 horsepower and then later, with no apparent changes, given it a 210 horsepower rating.

Various explanations float around on why this happened, but the truth is apparently the engine never truly made

225 horsepower when run strictly by Ford's power rating test procedures. Eager types at Ford hung the 225 horsepower rating on the HO engine to promote sales, but then recanted to a more accurate 210 horsepower when so many were sold and the prospect of government wrist slapping had become more probable. So, all the 1987–1993 engines are actually within shouting distance of each other, so don't worry about the ratings. Even if there was a

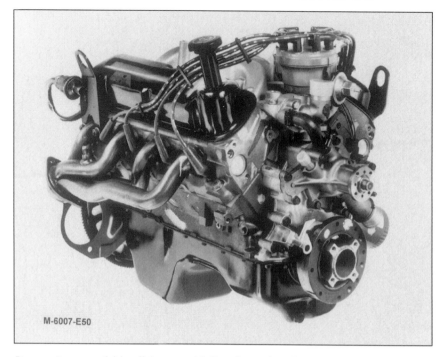

M-6007-E50

Because it was available off the assembly line, the Explorer-based 5.0 HO has been used by SVO as a crate engine. Here it appears dressed for carbureted duty as the M-6007-E50, a great place to start if you are building a track-only 5.0 Mustang for bracket racing, slaloms, or the like. To fit in the Mustang, the front engine dress needs modification, as outlined in the text. Otherwise, the engine internals are identical to the Mustang engine.

couple of horsepower variance, the differences among individual 5.0s, and especially the way they've been maintained, is a greater variable. Plus, if you are changing the intake, heads, and exhaust, you're ahead of the factory anyway.

1993 Mustang Cobra

Easily the best of the 5.0 engines in factory trim, the limited-edition 1993 Mustang Cobra from SVT features the GT-40 induction package. The GT-40 gear was originally designed by mainstream Ford powertrain engineers as the next step, to be introduced at the 25th Mustang anniversary. Management let the birthday slide by without fanfare, so the hardware was picked up by SVT for its first effort, the Mustang Cobra.

The GT-40 package on the 1993 Cobra and the GT-40 kit for the 1993 and earlier 5.0 Mustangs in the SVO catalog are the same thing. The 1994–1995 version of the kit differs only in the throttle body and inlet adapter, which are necessary to fit under the later car's lower hood.

Highlights of the GT-40 package are improved cast-iron cylinder heads, the very good tubular GT-40 intake manifold, 65-millimeter throttle body, SVO short tube headers (in either bare stainless or with a ceramic coating), 1.6 rocker arms, and a 110 liter-per-hour fuel pump.

The rockers are 1.7:1 ratio items on the 1994–1995 kit; 3.55 rear axle gears and a replacement strut tower brace to clear the larger-than-stock upper intake manifold are included.

While not part of the kit in the SVO catalog, the Mustang Cobra cars (all years) used EEC-IV computers with unique software, plus 24-pound injectors. The GT-40 car engine was rated at 235 horsepower; the SVO catalog says the kit gives 270 horsepower using SAE gross measuring criteria (open exhaust, etc.).

While the GT-40 kit is considered a bit tame these days by the blood and guts crowd, it makes a nice driving 5.0. A standard 5.0 HO is torquey, but rpm limited. It feels agricultural, as they say. The GT-40 costs about 18 lb-ft of torque down low, but adds 1,000 usable rpm to the top of the powerband. These extra rpm, and

the extra horsepower made there, give the 5.0 a much sportier feel. Such a Mustang is faster at the track, and feels much more eager when rowed through the gears. Furthermore, because the GT-40 adds top-end breathing, it is a much better than the stock unit as a foundation for a blower or nitrous engine.

1994–1995 Engines

When Ford revamped the Mustang in 1995, it changed the source of the 5.0 HO engine. Instead of being a unique Mustang part, it was based on the Thunderbird version of the 5.0 HO engine. This made sense because one of the challenges presented by the new Mustang was its low cowl height. This brought the hood too low to use the old Mustang intake manifold, so the Thunderbird engine, with its low-profile intake, was a logical choice. Otherwise, the engines were identical internally.

A side effect of the lower, T-Bird–based intake manifold was that the cast-aluminum rocker covers used on the 1993 and earlier cars no longer cleared the intake. Thus the 1994–1995 engines use stamped steel rocker covers, which may pose a clearance issue with bulky aluminum roller rockers, so be sure to ask if the rockers you are considering will clear.

Ford's FEAD (Front Engine Accessory Dress—how the alternator, air pump, drive belt, and so on are attached) was different on the 1994 engine, so there are a few changes with 5.0 Mustangs from the last two production years. The later cars use only a 15

1/2-inch electrically-driven fan; there is no belt-driven radiator fan.

Detail differences in the exhaust headers, H-pipe, and mufflers are also found on the 1994 cars, and parts specific to those years should be used. The AOD-E automatic transmission also made its debut on the 1994 Mustang, so that transmission and EEC-IV processor must be kept together. Also remember that the 1994–1995 cars are heavier than their predecessors, so performance was off just a tad.

1996 5.0 HO Engines

When Ford replaced the Mustang's 5.0 HO with the 4.6 Two-Valve "modular" V-8 in 1996, the only vehicle left using the 5.0 was the Explorer sport utility. This meant the source of car-based 5.0s was gone, so Ford SVO began using Explorer-based powerplants for its 5.0 crate-engine needs.

Luckily, the Explorer was using the 5.0 HO and not the "mom and pop" 5.0. This meant the basic engine was identical to the Mustang/Thunderbird long block, differing mainly in its front engine dress (engine-mounted accessories) and intake manifold. Furthermore, the Explorer used a different oil pan than the Mustang. Hypereutectic pistons were still used in this engine, of course.

Later, around mid-1996, Ford updated the GT-40 cylinder heads used on the Explorer. These are GT-40P heads, which feature detail improvements to the ports and a slightly relo-cated spark plug. They are the best of the GT-40 iron heads.

While Ford never installed this engine in Mustangs, it is the basis of the M-6007-A50 and B-50 SVO crate-engines, and should prove a source of 5.0 HO engines in wrecking yards for years. For one of these engines to be used in a 1986–1995 Mustang, the following items need to be changed from Explorer to Mustang parts:
-oil pan and oil pump pickup
-water pump
-front cover
-flywheel
-damper.

Use the Mustang front engine dress (alternator, air pump, etc.)

Note that these engines, like the Mustang 5.0 HO, use the 351W firing order of 1-3-7-2-6-5-4-8.

SVO Catalog

If you don't have an SVO catalog, get one. Any Motorsport dealer can sell you one for a few dollars. Published by SVO, the Ford Motorsport Performance Equipment catalog is a must-have, because it is jammed with Ford's performance parts, as well as important reference sections. You can answer many questions with the Motorsport catalog. The SVO catalog can be obtained through: Ford Motorsport Performance Equipment, 44050 N. Groesbeck Highway, Clinton Township, MI 48036-1108, or call the Motorsport hotline: (810) 468-1356. For official shop manuals and wiring diagrams, call Helm Publications: (800) 782-4356.

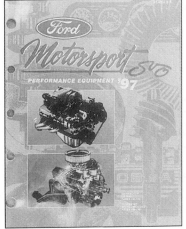

This is also a good place to point out why SVO parts are typically among the best you can buy. This is especially true of major parts, such as cylinder heads, blocks, drive shafts, and so on. Motorsport parts are factory parts, and when they say they'll fit, they fit. If they say it makes 40 horsepower, it makes 40 horsepower, occasionally even more. Best of all, holes that need drilling are drilled, and those that don't aren't—quality control means some-

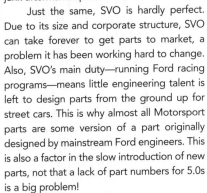

thing at SVO. This is because Motorsport parts must meet certain Ford durability and quality control criteria. This is in stark contrast to the surprisingly large number of junk aftermarket parts.

Just the same, SVO is hardly perfect. Due to its size and corporate structure, SVO can take forever to get parts to market, a problem it has been working hard to change. Also, SVO's main duty—running Ford racing programs—means little engineering talent is left to design parts from the ground up for street cars. This is why almost all Motorsport parts are some version of a part originally designed by mainstream Ford engineers. This is also a factor in the slow introduction of new parts, not that a lack of part numbers for 5.0s is a big problem!

Whatever its limitations, SVO is the 900-pound gorilla of Ford performance. SVO is the only organization with the resources to introduce something as sophisticated and well-engineered as the mass air metering conversion kit. Without SVO, the 5.0 would not have reached half its potential.

C
O
N
T
E
N
T
S

System Description 19

Working with EEC-IV . . .21

Speed/Density Leaning . .21

Computer "Chips" 26

Piggybacks 28

EPEC 29

Carburetion 30

UNDERSTANDING AND MODIFYING EEC-IV

Ford Motor Company moved from carburetors to electronic engine controls using a series of engine control systems. All have been titled Electronic Engine Control, which is invariably shortened to EEC (rhymes with "peek"). First there was EEC-I, then EEC-II, and when the fuel-injected Mustang was introduced in 1986, Ford was up to EEC-IV. This is the system you must master to unlock your Mustang's potential.

As expected, the early EEC systems were quite basic, controlling only a few engine parameters, while the later systems are all-inclusive. EEC-IV is a FADEC system, in engineering-speak. FADEC stands for Full-Authority Digital Engine Control, meaning all aspects of the ignition and fuel systems are controlled by EEC-IV. So are many other engine-related systems and functions, such as the EGR (Exhaust Gas Recirculation) canister purge and some air injection (Thermactor) functions.

Since approximately 1996, Fords have been equipped with EEC-V, which is pretty much EEC-IV with On-Board Diagnostic capability, level II (OBD-II). Thus, EEC-IV is something of a dead language, but one still very powerful from an engine control point of view, and still in use on hundreds of thousands of 5.0 Mustangs. It will remain popular and in the enthusiast's mainstream until 5.0 Mustangs finally fade away in the distant future. Learning EEC-IV is also an excellent step to learning EEC-V, so don't think you're wasting your time learning it.

EEC-IV has several good points. Most importantly, it truly is a powerful engine controller capable of accurately administering fuel and spark for excellent power production. Aftermarket racing engine control systems like DFI and Electromotive are powerful too, but not in the same league as EEC-IV.

EEC-IV is also adaptive; within limits, it modifies its fuel and spark curves depending on the driver's habits and current conditions; also, on the 5.0 Mustang, EEC-IV controls Sequential Electronic Fuel Injection. "Sequential" means the fuel injectors operate in the engine's firing order, spritzing fuel to each cylinder in time with its intake stroke. This gives maximum efficiency and power, as opposed to "batch" or "bank" firing the injectors in groups.

On 1988 California, and all 1989 and later Mustangs, EEC-IV is equipped with mass air metering, as discussed in the previous chapter. This allows seemingly limitless engine modifications, including such radical improvements as supercharging.

One frustrating aspect of EEC remains, however. Unlike other automakers, which use off-the-shelf

With the aid of a nitrous plate system and drag slicks, this street-driven 5.0 coupe can boast 10-second wheelstanding performance when not commuting to work or running to the store. While this 5.0 is obviously biased toward performance and is a bit harder-edged than stock, such a huge range of capabilities is mainly due to EEC-IV engine management, a system all 5.0 tuners must understand to fully develop their cars.

On all 5.0 Mustangs, the EEC-IV computer is housed behind the passenger-side kick panel. Well protected there from the elements, shock, and radio frequency interference, you do have to stand on your head a little to get at it. There is only one screw in the door threshold, and a push-in barbed plastic fastener low and forward holding the kick panel on.

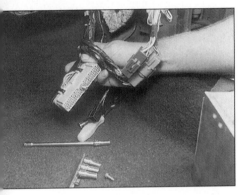

A single 10-millimeter bolt secures the main harness connector to the computer. As with any wiring, don't thrash it, or connectors like these, back and forth when working with them. That only loosens connections and can eventually break wires. To remove the main harness from the computer, loosen the 10-millimeter bolt; to reattach it, start the connector by hand, then use the bolt to draw the connector evenly down against the computer. Avoid bending the computer's pins.

electronics and sensors, Ford built EEC-IV completely in-house, using proprietary (secret) hardware and software. Combined with EEC's imposing software complexity, it's this secrecy that makes EEC a complete pain to work with at times. Very few people, even inside Ford, completely understand EEC-IV at anything other than a basic level, and the people who understand the software and hardware

necessary to fundamentally modify EEC-IV can be counted on one hand.

Luckily, the large majority of 5.0 hot rodding requires no attention to the EEC-IV system. Either the mass air metering version of EEC-IV adapts to the engine modification automatically, or the kits developed for the 5.0 Mustang contain hardware and software to handle the changes. Examples of these are the FMU (Fuel Management Unit) and electronic "chips" used with superchargers or large mass air meters.

Even if you will likely never modify or even really work on the EEC-IV system directly, you are money ahead learning EEC-IV basics for two reasons. First, you need to understand EEC-IV to understand the how and why of sparking and fueling your 5.0. Controlling fuel and spark is basic to all hot rodding, and if you don't know how your engine controls these important functions, you won't make the power you should, or worse, you could end up damaging your engine.

Secondly, because EEC-IV controls so many parts of your 5.0, inevitably you will need to troubleshoot your engine or some modification to it. By learning what all those little black cans, boxes, and wiring are all about, you'll be way ahead of your troubles.

System Description

The heart of EEC-IV is the Electronic Control Unit or Module. Sometimes this is abbreviated ECU or ECM, but mainly it's referred to simply as "the computer." The computer lives in the front passenger's kick panel and is connected to the rest of the system via a 60-pin connector and a rather substantial main wiring harness.

Inside the EEC module is a circuit board that is built at Ford Electronics by first populating the board with chips and then dipping it in a solder bath. Such construction means there is no way to remove a single chip off the circuit board without damaging the surrounding parts, so there is no servicing to be done inside the computer. Even Ford doesn't repair anything inside the computer; replacement is the only

option if the computer goes bad, which happens very rarely.

EEC-IV computers also differ in their software, sometimes rather unexpectedly. There are differences for model years; manual transmission; automatic transmission; high-altitude; convertible; hatchback; and coupe; optional equipment (air conditioning); rear axle ratio; and vehicle weight, among other things. Ford labels each computer with both alphanumeric and bar codes, but there is usually no practical reason to swap computers, other than for testing. Just be aware that what seems to work so well in your buddy's car might not be compatible in yours.

Of course, the EEC system involves plenty of wiring. These are bundled together into harnesses. The main harness does the primary job of connecting the computer to various sensors and relays, some of which are on the engine while some are on the chassis. The engine harness is found atop the engine. It plugs into the main harness and most of the hardware on the engine. There is also a third harness, a smaller one that runs between the main harness and the two oxygen sensors in the H-pipe. These three harnesses and a computer are sold as matched sets by SVO.

Like all modern engine management systems, EEC-IV is a closed loop system. Closed loop means the computer issues commands to the fuel and spark systems (the first half of the loop), the engine burns the fuel delivered, and then the oxygen sensors sniff the exhaust gases, measuring the amount of oxygen present, and report back to the EEC-IV (the other half of the loop). Thus, the EEC knows both how much fuel the engine should have received and how much was burned. It then uses the post-combustion information (oxygen content) to fine-tune the fuel delivery. Such fine control is necessary to keep the air/fuel ratio in the narrow window required by the catalytic converters.

There are many times when EEC-IV operates in open loop, that is, when the computer commands whatever fuel and spark values are stored in its tables, and ignores the oxygen content in the

Mustang computers vary considerably, depending on body style, transmission, rear axle ratio, model year, region sold in, and so on. Ford uses bar and alphanumeric codes to keep things straight at the factory. All you need to do is keep your computer with your car, or use a known replacement when supplied as part of a kit, such as the Cobra kit.

Part of SVO's Main Harness Kit is this installation manual, which has several useful diagrams and recommended procedures for anyone working around a 5.0 HO engine. It is available separately; see the M-12071-C302 description in the Motorsport catalog for ordering information.

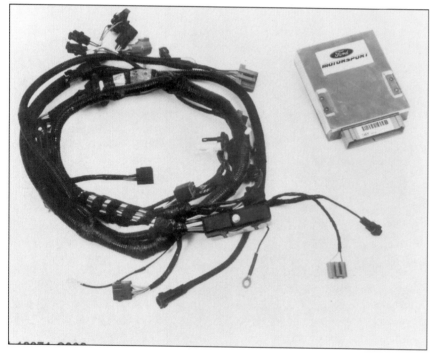

Because Ford changed the computer and wiring harness details for almost every year of EFI 5.0 Mustang production, it's impossible to swap computers and harnesses piecemeal. Instead, either move the entire computer and wiring harnesses from the donor vehicle to the new car, or use the computer and wiring harnesses from the Motorsport catalog. This is smart when building a race car or street rod with an EFI 5.0 engine. SVO's replacement computer and main engine harness are shown here.

any leaded race gas. Also, antiseize compound should be used on the O_2 sensor threads during installation, but take care to not get any anti-seize on the O_2 probes or they'll fail.

Because the computer needs to know how much load the engine is under, and how that load might change, it needs to know how far the throttle is open. The Throttle Position Sensor (TPS) does this job. A small plastic box mounted at the top side of the throttle body at the top end of the throttle shaft, the TPS converts the throttle position into an electric voltage, which is then easily sent to the computer.

The voltage range of the TPS is low, from 0 to about 1.5 volts. It can be adjusted by loosening the TPS mounting screws and slightly changing the relationship between the TPS and the throttle shaft. This adjustment is necessary to take up any slack between throttle shaft movement and the TPS movement, in other words, you don't want the throttle moving without the TPS sensing the movement and failing to inform the computer. Other than that, the TPS needs no adjustment, so it is something that is typically adjusted only when a new throttle body is installed.

With mass air metering, how much air is entering the engine is measured by the mass air flow meter, typically shortened to MAF in writing and referred to as the mass air meter in conversation. Ford's mass air meter is the "hot wire" type, and looks like a short section of tubing from the outside, with a much smaller tube inside the larger one. Most of the air simply passes through the main body of the MAF and does nothing. But a known small percentage of the total air passes through the small tube, where it encounters a small coiled wire. This wire is electrically heated to a preset temperature. The more air moving over the wire, the greater the wire is cooled.

exhaust. Engine start, warm-up, and WOT (wide open throttle) are notable periods of open loop operation.

Numerous sensors and actuators are used to inform the computer or to carry out its wishes. To measure the actual air/fuel mixture during closed loop operation, one oxygen sensor is fit-

ted to the exhaust pipe of each bank of cylinders. Rare metals are necessary in oxygen sensor production, so O_2 sensors, as they are typically called, are fairly pricey units. That's why you don't want to foul them with lead, and it takes only a couple of gallons of leaded race gas to ruin the O_2 sensors. So, don't run

Getting a good look at the injectors and fuel rail means removing the upper intake manifold. The chromed fuel rail bolts to the lower intake manifold, thus providing the holddown for the injectors, which fit loosely into holes in the intake. Always double-check injector and fuel rail security when working in the area; you don't need a fuel-fed fire!

The MAF circuitry is designed to keep the wire at a constant temperature, so as the air cools the wire, more electricity is needed to heat the wire. The voltage used is sensed by the computer, thus telling it directly how much air the engine has ingested. This direct air measurement is a highly accurate way of keeping the computer informed of the engine's fuel and spark needs.

The computer doesn't directly put the mass air meter information to use. In other words, the computer does not say to itself, "There's so much air going into the engine, thus I'll command this much fuel to go with it." Instead, the MAF signal is used in a calculation along with the throttle position signal and rpm to arrive at a load calculation. Then the load figure is used to compute the amount of fuel to inject and how much ignition advance (timing) to use.

This is why swapping mass air meters can have such seemingly unusual consequences. If you change air meters and suddenly get detonation (pinging), and try to compensate by jacking up the fuel pressure, but it doesn't help much, you could be confused and frustrated. But if you understand the pinging could be caused by increased ignition timing

and not just a lean fuel mixture, then you can see why increased fuel pressure might not help. You'll still have your detonation problem, of course, but you'll now know a better trimmed air meter is the solution. Trimming is the electronic engineer's way of saying "tuning" or calibration. The bottom line is, if lean-spots, stumbling, hunting or other drivability problems persist, try another air meter.

This also brings up the idea of computer and meter matching. Because the mass air sensor affects both fuel and spark values dictated by the computer, it is important the meter and computer work as a pair. Experience shows it is difficult to predict which meter, computer, and bolt-on combinations work properly together. Certainly SVO's 70-millimeter Cobra mass air meter, 24-pound injector, and computer kit is perfectly matched, and can handle the airflow and fuel needs of any conventional "bolt-on" car, but then, so do other meters.

Speaking of matching, the mass air meter and the fuel injectors must be matched as well. In other words, the stock air meter is matched to 19-pound injectors. Adding larger injectors, such as 36-pound injectors, requires an air

meter trimmed for 36-pound injectors. Sometimes this can be done electronically, with a chip, rather then having to purchase an entirely new mass air meter.

Working with EEC-IV

As delivered by Ford, the EEC-IV engine management system is programmed to deliver excellent performance, but with a fair safety margin built in against detonation and overheating. The EEC also serves as a rev-limiter by shutting off the fuel supply at 6,250 rpm. As you modify your Mustang, it is necessary to change the fuel and spark values, and because there are no direct knobs to turn to do this on an EEC-IV–equipped vehicle, it is necessary to do it indirectly.

Speed/Density Leaning

One way Ford protects the 5.0 is with a relatively rich engine mixture. With 1986, 1987, and non-California 1988 5.0s, the mild hot rodding possible with the speed/density air metering used in those years will improve airflow, but with no change in fuel delivery. As better exhaust and induction systems are added to these engines, they naturally lean out, as the fuel injection has no way of knowing the air/fuel ratio has changed. This eating into the factory-set safety margin in the fuel mixture naturally improves performance until enough airflow is added to lean the engine past the maximum power point, and then things go downhill in a hurry. This is why speed/density Mustangs will happily accept headers, intake manifolds, air filters, and perhaps even mild cylinder heads, but turn ugly when any appreciable camshaft is tried.

So, speed/density 5.0s do not adapt well (one is tempted to say at all) to change. If you have one and want to step up performance, absolutely your first step is to convert to mass air metering using the kit from the SVO catalog. However, if you are not planning on substantial breathing improvements (perhaps only an air filter, headers, open exhaust, and an intake manifold) then stick with speed/density. You'll save considerable money, and the lack of an air

Throttle Body Installation and TPS adjustment

Installing a throttle body on the 5.0 is 90 percent easy wrench work, followed by a simple electronic adjustment: setting the throttle position sensor (TPS). Calibrating the sensor is easy, provided you have a digital volt meter. These are available from many sources, probably including your buddy's toolbox.

The following procedure was shot at BBK, which offers many throttle bodies in its extensive line of 5.0 parts. The throttle body is a BBK 70-millimeter unit, but the installation procedure is identical for any throttle body. Also, because there is no utility in installing a larger throttle body without also installing a larger exhaust gas recirculation (EGR) spacer to match, both items are covered here.

Follow that reasoning downstream another notch, and you come to the upper intake manifold. Its opening also needs enlarging, which is typically done with a die grinder fitted with an 80-grit sanding roll. Use the EGR spacer as a guide to scribe a line into the intake, then remove material to the line. Stuff a rag thoroughly into the intake's opening and vacuum the intake to capture the metal debris.

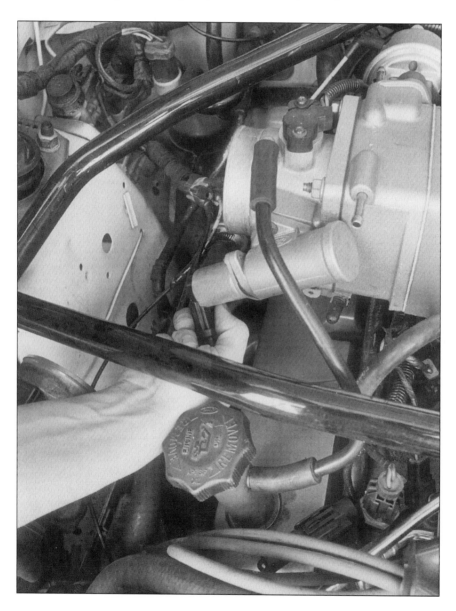

Begin by removing the air intake hose. The round cylinder mounted at an angle on the throttle body is the idle speed control solenoid. Disconnect its wires by looking for small tabs, which must be depressed to free the connector halves. Underneath the throttle body is the throttle linkage. Slip a screwdriver between the linkage and the throttle lever, then lever the ball-joint there apart. Atop the throttle body is the throttle position sensor and EGR water connections; undo both, plus the PCV system's fresh air tube.

Once the four nuts are removed, the throttle body will slide off its studs, with token resistance from its gasket. After you get the throttle body on the workbench, remove the throttle position sensor (the dark piece atop the throttle body) and transfer it to the new throttle body.

With the throttle body out of the way, the two bolts holding the throttle cable bracket become accessible. Remove both of them and lay the cable aside, then undo the EGR valve's electrical connector. Next remove the two bolts holding the EGR valve to the EGR spacer and remove the EGR valve, and finally the spacer itself. A light pry or hammer tap may be necessary to overcome the stuck gasket. At this point, the opening to the upper intake is accessible and can be enlarged to mate with the new EGR spacer.

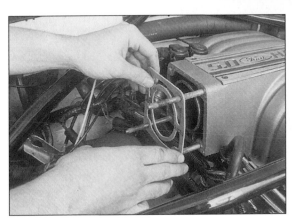

Installing the new EGR spacer and throttle body is little more than retracing your disassembly steps. New gaskets should be used to avoid leaks. A quick scraping off of the old gasket will no doubt be required, and then a new EGR spacer gasket can be slid over the intake's studs. A new EGR valve gasket can also go on, followed by the EGR valve.

With the EGR spacer buttoned up and the throttle cable reinstalled, the throttle body can be slid over the studs and tightened down. These nuts are going on studs that anchor in the aluminum upper intake manifold, so don't make like a gorilla. Torque is only 12–18 lb-ft. Pop the throttle cable back on, followed by all the other connections, such as the PCV tube, EGR hoses, and so on. However, leave the idle speed control wire off.

Lubing the intake air hose makes it much easier to slip it onto the throttle body. Don't get carried away and run the engine without the hose in place, as the air is then unfiltered. Interestingly, the engine runs without running the air through the mass air meter by using the open loop, or "limp-home" mode.

Right: You must check the throttle position sensor adjustment for proper drivability. This is done by measuring between the dark green/light green wire and the black/white wire on the sensor. The voltage must be between 0.8 and 1.0 volts.

To tune the throttle position sensor to the new throttle body, it is necessary to calibrate the throttle position sensor. Start by warming the engine. Do this by disconnecting the idle speed control solenoid wiring, if you hooked it up earlier, then turn the throttle plate stop screw clockwise five turns from its fully closed position (the screwdriver on the stop screw in this photo). Run the engine until it is at operating temperature. Then turn the stop screw until the factory idle speed is obtained (look underhood for a sticker with the idle speed listing). Use a sensitive tachometer on a piece of tune-up equipment for this step, and note that you may need a little extra idle speed with a larger-than-stock cam or other engine mods. Finally, shut the engine off and reconnect the idle speed control solenoid wiring.

If the voltage is out of spec, adjust it by loosening the throttle position sensor's mounting screws and rotating the switch slightly. A small movement should get you a usable voltage reading. If not, elongate the sensor's mounting holes with a small round file until you get in the proper range. Once you've got the position sensor tuned up, you're in business. In case you are wondering, your adjustment calibrates the actual throttle position with the TPS, which, in turn, sends the computer the proper voltage for a fully closed throttle.

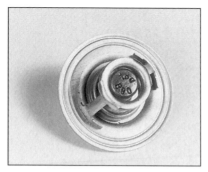

Coolant temperature is monitored by EEC-IV, so if too cold a thermostat is run, the computer will enrich the mixture. This results in poor mileage, high emissions, cylinder wall washing, oil dilution, and rapid cylinder wall wear, so don't do it. A 180 degree thermostat like this one will help in warm climates, and isn't too cold to fool the computer, but don't go any colder. Beware any advice calling for a 160 degree thermostat. Use a replacement or reprogrammed chip, instead.

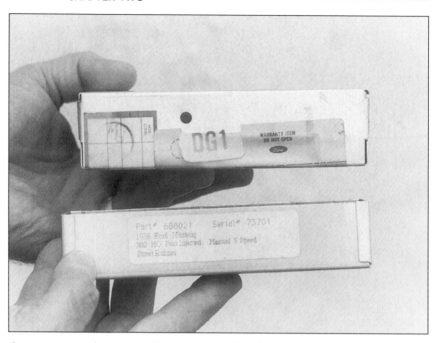

Some computer chips are small, some are fitted into large covers like the one in the bottom of this photo, but all attach to the opposite end of the computer from the cable connector. As the sticker over the computer port says, installing a chip voids the computer warranty.

meter is one less restriction in the air stream. Stock-to-stock, a nice 1987 speed/density 5.0 will likely outrun its 1989 counterpart. In extremely well-prepared chassis with all-out driving, stock speed/density engines have run in the high 12s at the strip.

Computer "Chips"

With the mass air metering used from 1988 to 1995, the slightly rich condition pretty much stays with the engine unless airflow is improved by an order of magnitude, such as with a supercharger. Then the problem is getting enough fuel into the engine, demanding larger fuel pumps and injectors.

However, totally stock and lightly modified 5.0s seem to benefit from a slight leaning of the air/fuel ratio. This is done with computer "chips" fitted to the computer's service port.

The other major way of increasing power is to advance the ignition timing. Again, Ford is relatively conservative in its timing settings. Ford can't have 5.0 Mustangs lined up for warranty work at the dealers, so it is forced to tune for worst-case scenarios. That's why you can take a stock 5.0, fill the tank with 87-octane regular gas, turn on the air conditioning, and rocket off between Phoenix and Atlanta in the blazing heat of summer and not have it overheat or detonate.

Ford could pick up a few more horsepower under more normal conditions by supposing 92 octane premium and an owner who understands that full-throttle acceleration on seriously hot days with the air conditioning blowing ice chips in the cockpit is simply too much to ask of the cooling system.

This is what the aftermarket chip companies do. They bump up the timing, subtract a little fuel, and tell you to use premium gas and keep an eye on the coolant temperature. It's what hot rodding is all about, and it works pretty well most of the time. The trick is, it is difficult for the chip makers to know exactly how much timing to add or fuel to subtract. Ford's computers differ in their calibration, as we've seen, and like Ford, the chip makers can't be adding timing up to the ragged edge and having customer engines blowing up.

This is one reason, until recently, why aftermarket computer chips have traditionally had a spotty record of power improvement. On one 5.0, their computer strategy may offer a significant benefit in timing or fuel. On another 5.0, the stock calibration may

have been more aggressive to begin with, and the improvement will be less, perhaps even imperceptible. Also, because there is no emission certification work done at WOT, Ford has always been able to get aggressive with the fuel and spark at WOT. Thus, computer chips have traditionally been most effective in improving low- and mid-range power, while not being able to do as much with WOT power.

This has changed in the mid- to late-1990s, as the chip makers gained experience with the various Ford tuning strategies and learned they have to ask plenty of questions of each owner to get a chip that will do some good. If you see a chip maker offering a single part number for all manual transmission 5.0s and another for automatics, beware. Seek out the manufacturers who seemingly want to know your grandmother's maiden name. They have to know a tremendous amount about your particular 5.0 before they can burn a chip that will work correctly.

Another huge change has been in the sophistication of the chip makers. At first, the chips were designed to modifying the EEC-IV's computer signals

Relatively powerful electronic control of the fuel and spark with easy interfacing through a simple keypad is what the PMS controller is all about. No separate laptop is necessary, as the PMS keypad is all you need. Quick push-button tuning is easily accomplished, plus the keypad reads out fuel, spark, and EEC-IV parameters (oxygen sensors), of interest to anyone trying to optimize their EEC-IV engine management. It's a great tool for anyone with an ongoing engine development program, where changing hardware calls for changing the electronic trimming.

back to the computer, which then did its best to get the engine back to where it thought it should be, using its adaptive capability.

Currently, custom electronic tuning has replaced mass market, one-size-fits-all chips. Custom tuning got its start when the affordable, relatively accurate Dynojet chassis dynos became available. Around the same time, Autologic and Superchips developed methods of burning custom software for EEC-IV cars. By writing new chips and checking the results on a Dynojet, modern tuners have come to learn EEC-IV in unprecedented detail. Today the more-experienced shops can get close to an optimum chip on the first try given a reasonably popular powertrain combination (say a stock displacement 5.0 with good heads, centrifugal supercharger, improved exhaust, and a decent fuel system). More radical or unique combinations usually require a handful of attempts before everyone is happy.

SVO's Extender was designed for the bolt-on guy who wants simple, easy control over his combination. With stone-simple plug-in connections between the computer and main wiring harness, the Extender is ultra simple to use. The Extender's rev limiter is redundant on a bolt-on car, and the air fuel mixture can be more finely controlled by (the vastly more expensive and complicated) EPEC. Still, crafty tuners have combined an Extender and adjustable fuel pressure regulators to tweak the mixture, especially on blower cars. The computer taped to the rollcage of this drag car is a typical expedient when doing lots of EEC-IV work. Besides, the rollcage blocks the kickpanel access.

as they were sent from the computer to the injectors and ignition module. Sometimes a simple, dirt-cheap strategy of simply multiplying the values by some constant across the rpm range was used and left at that. Other times the "tuning" was more sophisticated, but no matter what, the EEC computer was

left wondering what in the world was going on. After all, it had sent out orders for so much fuel and spark, and figured it could expect so much oxygen in the exhaust gas in exchange. Instead, something substantially different would appear in the exhaust pipe, the oxygen sensors would sniff it, report that value

Not only do the screws attaching air meter electronics use Torx heads, they use a special Torx head with a nipple in the center. It takes a special T20 Torx headed tool to remove these, a move Ford made to keep just anyone from fiddling with the air meter's fragile heated wire and electronics.

Perhaps even more important than peak power improvements, these modern tuners vastly improve drivability and torque at part-throttle operation with their precise electronic tuning. Furthermore, such tuning supports huge injectors, up to the 80-pound range, to run on the street. This eliminates the less accurate mechanical fuel management units (FMU).

So, the bottom line is, excellent drivability, fuel economy, and power are available only with sophisticated electronic tuning. The two outfits catering to the 5.0 custom electronic scene are Autologic and Superchips.

Autologic is the brand name for Mike Wesley's chip writing software. Wesley also does business under the C&M Racing Systems banner (in case that company is more familiar to you). Autologic is marketed to professional tuners or speed shops. A customer brings his car to the speed shop where it is sampled on a Dynojet; then a new chip is written right there, installed in the computer, and the car is re-run on the dyno to verify the results. The software has proven very good at extracting power, although the skill of the person tuning (writing the code being burned into the chip), is critical, as they are the ones making the tough decisions with no backup.

Superchips uses modem-equipped dealers. A customer takes his car to a Superchips modem dealer, who examines the car (again, typically on a Dynojet), and then calls into Superchips home office where another computer has the software to write a new chip. A technician at Superchips enters in the data, and the software writes the new code, which is modemed back to the dealer's chip writing machine. The machine burns the new chip, the tuner installs it in your car, and the results are verified. It sounds complex, but takes just minutes. Superchips allows five trials on the tuner's part before charging for another chip write-up.

Remember, while it is possible to tune for absolute max power, that's not what you want. Subtract a degree or two of ignition timing, and add a hair of fuel to ensure against extremely hot weather or unexpectedly difficult operating conditions.

Furthermore, custom chips are optimized for whatever mechanical package is on the engine. Add a blower, change cams, or the like and a new chip is required. Thus, it might be nice to get all your mechanicals in place while running an FMU, then finish-off the combination with electronic tuning. Alternately, the shop may be willing to work through a set number of chips as you advance through your hardware purchases, all for one price.

An alternative to custom chip tuning is to do it yourself. This is done with Fel Pro, Electromotive, EPEC, or other programmable engine management systems. Too expensive and asking too much knowledge of the individual owner for street use, this strategy is best left to racers who are constantly changing their electronic tuning.

Piggybacks

Various devices have been offered to modify EEC-IV signals, or to give simple, easily understood and adjusted effects. All of them plug into the computer's service port and are collectively referred to as piggyback devices, as they work with the EEC-IV computer rather than replace it. Some of the best known piggyback devices are the Interceptor and Extender.

The Interceptor, now out of production, was developed by Doug Wallis, now operating as EFI Systems, Inc. As the name implies, the Interceptor fits between the computer and the various sensors and actuators. It intercepts and conditions the EEC-IV output signals to change the fuel mixture and spark timing. No computer is needed to communicate with the Interceptor, which uses its own hand-held keypad. Adjustments to the fuel and spark are made over several fixed rpm ranges using standard terms. Compared to later devices, the Interceptor is pretty basic.

Wallis' new offering is commonly called the PMS. It is similar to the old Interceptor, but with considerably more capability. Like the Interceptor, the PMS is entirely self-contained, and commands are entered via a small keypad that rides in the cockpit. All sorts of information is displayed by the PMS, so it is a great learning and tuning tool, all in addition to its ability to modify the fuel and spark. The PMS' huge advantage, besides its affordability, is its ability to work with standard terms, and in units that are understood by the average enthusiast. The more powerful laptop-driven EEC-IV reprogramming tools are complex and require extensive tuning expertise on the tuner's part; the PMS gives less control but is much, much easier to use and I recommend it.

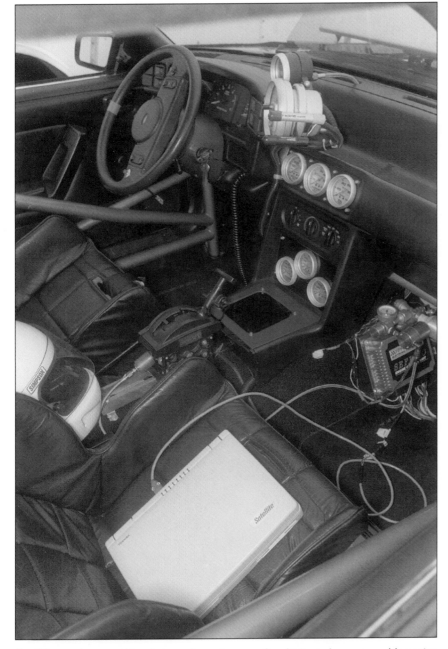

Pro 5.0 racers have traditionally been the main users of sophisticated programmable engine management systems such as this DFI/Fel Pro installation. The cost of these systems and the required laptop computer necessary to interface with them, along with the complexity of the programming, have been the stumbling blocks. However, users of SVO's powerful EPEC and Fel Pro's system have found the data logging and tuning possible with these powerful systems invaluable. Savvy street customers have found working with a shop that knows these systems can result in exceptionally smooth, powerful, and easy to live with 5.0s that produce stupendous power. If a 600-horsepower street car is what you want, programmable electronics are where you'll eventually end up.

above 6,250 rpm requires better connecting rods and bolts, and possibly pistons, so it is an expensive way to go.

Tinkering with the air/fuel ratio is more helpful to most tuners. The Extender's ease of adjustment and relatively low cost makes it a workable tool for the bolt-on enthusiast who may need it. Its usefulness continues today when combined with traditional mechanical tools such as advanced ignition timing and even FMUs. For the most sophisticated racer, it has waned in light of the newer, more powerful computer-based systems.

EPEC

There is another way to deal with EEC-IV, and that is to replace it with another engine management system. Some of the most serious 5.0 racers have done this for years with Haltech, DFI, and Electromotive TEC-II hardware. This requires computer and engine-tuning savvy beyond the scope of this book, and is not a viable option for bolt-on level 5.0 owners. To use this approach effectively you must understand engine fuel and spark tuning at a sophisticated level, plus command a bit of IBM computer expertise. It's pro stuff, but if you've got the inclination to learn the systems, they've got the horsepower to motivate serious 5.0 race machinery.

Ford SVO has a sophisticated system that is at least equal to the DFI/Electromotive/Fel Pro in capability, but is more user friendly. Actually, it's an EEC-IV replacement system the dedicated 5.0 owner could learn to use easily enough. Called Extreme Performance Engine Computer (EPEC, pronounced "epic"), the system was designed and is built by a Ford engineer named Sam Guido, who also invented the Extender.

EPEC shuts off almost all of EEC-IV functions, replacing them with its own. In fact, EPEC is so strong, it can easily run the car on its own, and such a version may eventually be available to racers. Because EPEC was designed to be its own system, one aimed at racers looking for maximum control, it is easily used. Little in the way of computerese

Its ease of use makes it an excellent tool for all but the most ardent 5.0 racers.

Ford SVO's simplified electronic tuner is the Extender, which uses simple screwdriver adjustments to change the air/fuel ratio and raise the rev limiter. For almost every bolt-on 5.0, the ability

to raise or clip (e-speak for remove) the rev limiter is not necessary. The stock 6,250-rpm rev limit is above the useful powerband of all street-driven, supercharged, turbo, nitrous and stroked 5.0s, and most of the normally aspirated cars as well. Besides, running the engine

Carbureted racers say their way is cheaper and less complex than fuel injection, but a look at this Pro 5.0 engine compartment with dual Holley Dominators and a king's ransom in nitrous and fuel plumbing makes you wonder. With the advent of more powerful, less-expensive engine control computers, more racers will move to EFI.

need be known, and the control panels are intuitive, clearly labeled, and use standard terms, such as "air/fuel mixture" rather than more engineering-based terminology such as "injector pulse width." The units are also user-based, such as "12:1" for the air fuel ratio, rather than "milliseconds of pulse width."

It seems the real limitation with the EPEC is not your computer knowledge or your hardware, but rather the tuner's engine know-how. EPEC gives the power to modify air/fuel ratios and timing at any rpm or engine load, so you can both realize tremendous power gains, and blow up the engine if you don't know what you're doing. Get a knowledgeable person to help guide you along to start, and go slowly. It's always best to sneak up on tuning anyway. As the old

racing adage puts it, it's better to foul a plug than burn a piston.

Another important consideration of all tuning, but one especially important with the computerized systems, is a way to quantify how you are doing. The best tool, and the easiest to use, is the Dynojet chassis dyno, because the entire car and all its systems are tested together. Of course, Dynojet time adds up, and there is likely no such dyno anywhere near you. In that case, the drag strip is a good tool, but then you have the extra distraction of driver-induced variation. Consistency at the track is vital when using it as a tuning tool, and most drivers have real trouble repeating their performance accurately enough for development work. Also, the track gives only a rough idea of

what's going on, and lacks the precision of a well-equipped dyno.

Luckily, the EPEC software doubles as a data logger, a real plus for this system. All sorts of parameters can be saved from a run, allowing you to study what is actually happening in the engine management system. This is a huge step forward for 5.0 tuning, as data never before seen is available for scrutiny. Things like TPS voltage can be logged, along with all the usual rpm and time data.

Carburetion

Finally, there is the old-fashioned way of dealing with EEC-IV: take it off and put on a carburetor instead. It's not my intent to get very deep into carburetion; there are plenty of other books available on how to set up a Holley car-

Besides carburetion, some Pro 5.0 racers have opted for aftermarket speed/density fuel injection systems like DFI or the newer version of the same system offered by Fel Pro. This gives them the benefits of EFI with easier tuning than EEC-IV has traditionally offered, but it certainly didn't save any money. Such stand-alone computer systems are also speed/density, so for ultimate race performance, they need occasional tuning to compensate for weather, like jetting a carburetor. Such systems are impractical for street use and not legal there anyway.

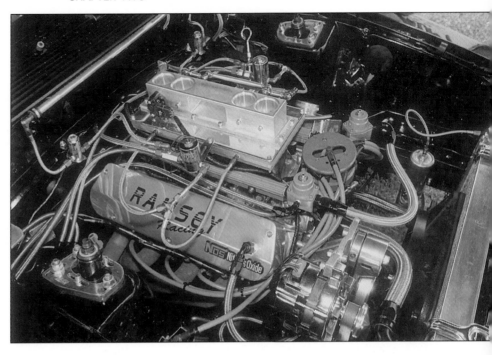

buretor on small-block V-8s. It is worth a look here at the pros and cons of carburetion, however, as there are a fair number of hard-running 5.0s at the drag strip and road racing track that entry-level enthusiasts may mistakenly wish to duplicate on the street.

So, before going any further, let's dispense with the concept of carbureting a late-model Mustang for street use. Just forget it. It's illegal, for starters, as it is clearly tampering with the emission equipment of the 5.0 HO engine, where the EFI is considered part of the emission system. The catalytic converters will fail shortly when carbureted as well. It's also a huge step backward from a power, mileage and drivability standpoint. If EEC-IV is baffling to you, mentally pull over to the side of the road and take the time to seriously study the EEC-IV system. You won't find the innards of a 4150 Holley any easier to work with or understand than EEC-IV. You'll also find the long-runner EEC-IV intake manifolds deliver the torquey response that feels so good on

the street. Today, carburetion is for racing only.

Racers like to say carburetion's largest advantage is simplicity. If you've been fiddling with and racing carburetors for 20 years, then it's natural to carburate a 5.0 race car. Cost is also a factor on a race car where electronic tuning aids may be considered too expensive. Also, there are the types of intake manifolds available for carburetors. The typical, inexpensive, easily obtained single-plane intakes offer easy high-rpm power that long-runner EEC-IV intakes can't match. This works at the track, where deep rear axle ratios make up for the lack of torque, and no one cares about the lousy mileage, but with the advent of short- and medium-length runner intakes, the breathing advantage of carburetion is fast disappearing. Then there are the rules. In SCCA A-sedan, the EEC-IV must be removed and a Holley installed, a rule mandated to simplify tech inspection. Other sanctioning bodies have similar rules.

Downsides to carburetion at the races are actually few, at least for the

average weekend warrior. They include having to re-jet every time the weather changes and packaging difficulties with the popular centrifugal superchargers. Carbureted 5.0s are typically augmented with nitrous oxide, which is the quick and relatively well-beaten path to big horsepower. If you're playing with a bracket 5.0, then the time-honored Holley carb and Edelbrock intake combination could be a way to go. Just remember, you already have the fuel injection, and would have to buy the carburetor and intake.

Don't underestimate the growing knowledge and power of fuel injection, however. It's the way things are going, and EFI racers ultimately enjoy more power. Cylinder-to-cylinder variations are reduced, the power can be tailored precisely, data logged, and less time spent on seemingly endless jet changes. When set up correctly, EFI engines run cleaner, with less fuel dilution or fouling when idling or at light throttle (return road, etc.). It's simply a better way to run an engine.

CONTENTS

Intake Air Silencer 33

Air Filters 33

Mass Air Meter 33

Throttle Body and EGR
Spacer 37

Intake Manifolds 39

Long Runner 39

Box Intakes 43

Cowl Induction 43

Installation Tips 44

Phenolic Spacers 45

Trick Stuff 45

Dyno Testing 45

INDUCTION

Absolutely the first concept to understand when hot rodding the 5.0 engine is the importance of the systems approach. You can buy parts and swap them until your Visa card is smoking wreckage, but if you don't plan which parts to change, and in what order, the only effective result of your action will be charring your plastic.

Like all piston engines, the 5.0 HO is an air pump. Air from the atmosphere is pulled into the engine, compressed, and heated with burning fuel to raise its temperature, and thus its pressure. This pressure is put to work on the top of the piston, and the remainder vented back to the atmosphere. Packing in more air, and adding additional fuel to heat the additional air, increase the energy available. Restricting the airflow through the engine reduces the power that can be generated.

It's important to understand that any air restriction, either in the intake or the exhaust side of the engine, will limit power. If any one part of the air path is a choke, then no matter what you do to all the other parts, it won't make any difference. The airflow must be improved starting at the intake air silencer, moving through the entire intake tract, through the cylinder head and out the exhaust system. It's the gas flow version of a chain being only as strong as its weakest link.

So, to improve breathing, you want to strengthen the weakest link, then the next weakest, and so on. In the 5.0 HO engine, the weakest link is the exhaust port in the cylinder head. You can add big mass air meters and throttle bodies, change the mufflers, and install a set of headers and you won't make a huge difference. Sure, it will help some, and a few people have proven a 5.0 can be put into the 12s at the drag strip running through the stock exhaust port, but it is not easy,

nor is it practical. To make good power, the stock cylinder head must be ported or replaced by a more performance-oriented aftermarket head. This is true even with nitrous or blowers. Power adders give you more of what you already have, but they won't turn the stock 5.0's somewhat rpm-limited powerband into a top-end screamer. Never forget, it's the combination of parts that counts, and the most important power producer is the cylinder head.

Because the systems approach is so important to making power, the better aftermarket tuners have developed packages for the 5.0. The most important of these is SVO's GT-40 kit, if for no other reasons than that it has been available the longest and is widely available and used. There are also packages from Edelbrock, Holley, and Roush Racing, plus BBK, Vortech, and others, if you count their blower kits and associated hardware. You might want to consider these kits as a form of power adder.

Because there are so many parts to talk about, we'll break the airflow path into several chapters. In this chapter,

Hugely popular, the K&N filter is an inexpensive, good first-time bolt-on part. It won't make any power on stock or near-stock engines, but as power builds, it helps. K&N reports that owners tend to wash their K&Ns too frequently. Unless you live on a dirt road, you should not need to clean these filters for about 50,000 miles. Excessive cleaning wears out the fabric element.

K&N packages its conical air filter, mount, cleaner, and oil into an FIPK, or Filtercharger Injection Performance Kit for the 5.0. A filter this size does flow impressive air volume, but the open element is exposed to hot underhood air, which isn't good for horsepower. With any open air filter, beware of fan wash, which is air being blown off the engine cooling fan (engine driven or electric). Fan wash can cause erratic idling and weird drivability problems.

Stock 5.0 air meters are 60 millimeter and feature a wire screen for large foreign object protection. You don't need a degree in aerodynamics to understand that the large flat area and right angle bends do not flow air very well. Inside the small hole above the main air passage are two small, coiled, filament-like wires. They're the business end of the air metering electronics. One coil is the heated sampling wire, the other is a temperature probe, so EEC-IV can tell what the air temperature is. Here the stock meter is shown attached to its mounting bracket.

we'll discuss the intake side of the engine's airflow path. Most tuners spend most of their effort on intake airflow because, until you add forced induction, it has only atmospheric pressure to power it. The exhaust side has leftover combustion energy to assist it out of the engine, and so in some ways it isn't as finicky about supporting power.

Intake Air Silencer

Inside the right front fender is the intake air silencer. A nonmoving piece of blow-molded plastic, it bolts to the air filter box using common bolts, but on the other side of the fender. You can't see it from the engine compartment, but have to look up underneath the fender from the wheel side if you want to see it. Combined with the air filter, the silencer forms a muffler of sorts to practically eliminate intake air noise. In the process of dampening noise, it also restricts airflow, and is best removed. This is especially true on 1993 and earlier cars, and not so critical on SN-95 Mustangs.

This is one of those happy modifications that cost nothing but the time to unbolt the silencer. The tradeoff is a very slight increase in noise, an increase that most owners appreciate, as it adds a

bit of throatiness at WOT. At that, it's not much of an increase, and is completely unnoticed on any Mustang with aftermarket mufflers.

Air Filters

When it comes to air filters, about the only game in town is K&N. If there is a power increase from replacing the stock panel paper air filter with K&N's fabric panel filter, it has to be small. But the K&N is washable, so if nothing else, you won't have to keep buying paper air filters.

K&N also offers conical versions of its filter. They are used with some supercharger applications and K&N's own FIPK (Filtercharger Injection Performance Kit) offering. The FIPK includes a conical filter element and the necessary mounting hardware.

The FIPK is considerably more expensive than the simple panel replacement K&N, but it offers more. It's CARB (California Air Resources Board) exempt, and by eliminating the stock airbox around the flat panel, airflow is improved. Not a huge help on dead stock 5.0s, this helps more as more performance parts are added. It also lets more intake noise out than the panel filter because it is not contained in a box,

and its hot underhood placement negates some of its flow improvement.

Mass Air Meter

Next in the airflow path is the mass air meter. Although a mass air meter looks like little more than a simple tube with a couple of small coiled wires in it, they are, in fact, precision instruments that perform a vital job; it's just that their expensive electronics, very difficult to adjust, don't show.

Because of the difficulty and high cost of building sophisticated air meters, some aftermarket manufacturers have evolved a two-tier approach. When cost is a major factor they offer an inexpensive meter, and then they have their flagship models for when performance is the big concern. Most typically, you get what you pay for, but not always. There are many instances where the inexpensive meters work fine, sometimes even slightly better than their more expensive counterparts. There are also a million stories about how one meter would barely let the car run, while another seemed to free 20 horsepower. The trouble is, these stories conflict, and after a decade of 5.0 tuning, no clear consensus has been developed on which air meter is king. There are a few dogs out there; I've left them out of this book.

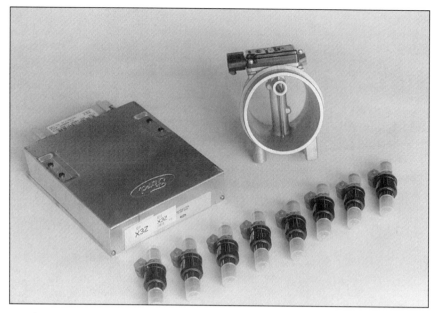

For the average bolt-on car, SVO's "Cobra Kit" is likely the best way of stepping up to 24-pound injectors, and it certainly is a good way of obtaining a matched computer, 65-millimeter air meter, and injectors when scratch-building an EFI engine—components you want matched for drivability. The Ford electronics trimming delivers the best drivability possible.

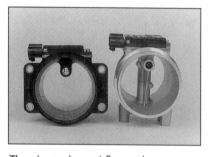

There's a clear airflow advantage to SVO's plastic 70-millimeter meter at left, compared to the 65 millimeters of vaned airflow on SVO's regular production meter at right. The center vane on the aluminum meter may be removed, as it is there to prevent backwashing the signal in 4-cylinder applications and is not needed on a V-8.

The real test of an air meter is in idle and part-throttle operation. Making power at WOT is relatively easy because EEC-IV is in an open loop, but getting the electronics correctly calibrated across the engine's entire operating range is something not everyone can do.

Anyone who's read the mail-order ads knows there is a bewildering variety of air meter sizes available. Of course, the larger the air meter, the more air will flow through it. There is, however, a practical limit to how large you want to go. If a huge air meter is placed on a relatively

As sold, the traditional cast-aluminum Pro-M 77 comes with a black plastic inlet tube and rubber flex coupling. While the meter housing flows around 1,800 cubic feet per minute of air, the turned, narrow discharge tube chokes this way, way down. Fabricating or using another tube with a gentler turn into the throttle body would help considerably. Pro-M trims its meters with a scientific sandblasting process that is surprisingly accurate, if not quite up to what Ford can do, of course.

low-power engine, you are asking a lot of the meter. After all, it can only measure a small percentage of the air flowing through it, and the larger the meter, the smaller that percentage becomes. This harms meter accuracy, and it is not recommended. All but the most serious Mustangs do just fine with a 70–77-millimeter air meter.

Besides, just how much air do you need? Ford SVO says the stock 55-

millimeter mass air meter is a good match for the stock 19-pound per hour (typically shortened to simply "lb.") fuel injectors, because that's what they put on the 5.0. The stock meter allows considerably less than 500 cubic feet per minute of airflow measured at 1.5 inches mercury. The eight injectors, without jacked-up fuel pressure tricks, give 152 pounds of fuel per hour. That means a maximum of 300–310 horsepower from either the airflow or the injectors, although with a Boost-a-Pump or other trick, you can get more power from the stock injectors. The following chart helps put the engine's airflow and mass air meter needs in perspective:

Meter (hp)	Diameter (mm)	Airflow (cfm)
stock 225	55	465
Cobra 425	70*	664
Pro-M	77	808
KB	80	977

*airflow obstructed by center post

Thinking in carburetor terms for those comfortable with those figures, very few racing small blocks can use more than a 750-cubic foot per minute carb, and most street engines are slightly overcarbureted at 650 cubic feet per minute. By that reasoning, a 70-millimeter air meter is plenty for any street car. This implies the reference pressure drop for the cubic foot per minute rating is the same as for four-barrel carburetors, that is, 1.5 inches mercury.

Airflow is just the beginning with air meters, though. Once a large enough meter is selected for the engine's intended power level, matching the air meter's electronics to the rest of the fuel injection system is necessary. Air meters are calibrated to the injector size they'll be used with, and while it's possible to get away with running the injectors and air meters about one step out of phase with each other (19-pound injectors with a meter intended for 24-pound units), it's not a good idea. It will not provide the best power or, especially, the best drivability, and it's an especially

Pro-M's lower-cost alternative, the Bullet, has done as well as its big brother in dyno testing. The aluminum shield on the right edge of the air filter protects against fan wash. Both the filter and shield are supplied with the meter.

risky alternative when forced induction is involved.

What is so tricky with air meters is that their signal is used by the EEC-IV computer to calculate a load figure. Because this load value is plugged into equations to calculate the fuel and spark values, goofing up with the air meter means getting both the air and the fuel fouled up. Unfortunately, the way this usually goes is to get the air meter voltage correct for WOT, but then at less than WOT, it drops and the computer thinks the engine is under less load than it actually is. This leads to leaner mixtures and more timing (the computer is a fuel efficiency nut), and that means detonation. Damaging in normally aspirated engines, detonation is the death rattle in blower motors.

SVO Cobra Kit

Ford SVO offers a cast-aluminum 70-millimeter air meter that's very popular as part of the High Capacity Mass Air Upgrade Kit, M-9000-A50, better known as the "Cobra Kit." This air meter was stock on Thunderbird SCs, and was a popular add-on by itself before SVO packaged it for sale in the Cobra kit.

SVO, however, does not offer it alone because of the need to electronically support it with a recalibrated computer.

This meter casting has been used in many Ford applications besides the T-Bird, including V-6 and inline four-cylinders, so the unit bolts right into the 5.0's stock rubber air hose, and mounts to the stock meter bracket.

Even though it was used as a stand-alone meter by enterprising enthusiasts, Ford says this meter needs a matching computer to use it with the intended 24-pound injectors, hence the Cobra Kit. Word on the street is the Cobra processor is slightly less aggressive than the stock processor, but no one has done any testing to prove it. Supposedly, the Cobra computer reduces ignition timing a bit quicker in response to high coolant temperatures and rpm than a GT computer. If true, this could soften a normally aspirated car slightly at high rpm, and give the typical supercharged Mustang a slightly wider safety margin from detonation. For performance street driving, whatever minor differences exist between the two computers is insignificant and can easily be tuned around with a bit more blower boost, nitrous, camming, ignition timing, cylinder head porting, or whatever you might have that requires 24-pound injectors. At the track, the difference might be 1/10 second.

SVO Plastic

SVO also lists a 70-millimeter plastic meter for the 5.0, M-12579-A70. At press time this meter was available only in 30-pound injector form, but SVO said it might release it in 24-pound configuration. A meter for 30-pound injectors is a bit much except for seriously boosted

With a full range of sizes and popular pricing, the BBK throttle bodies have proven best sellers. In fact, the BBK 70-millimeter seems nearly universal. When Edelbrock got into the 5.0 market, it elected to offer the BBK throttle body to mate with its intake manifolds. Thus both business names are found inscribed on the casting, and the same part is found in both company's catalogs.

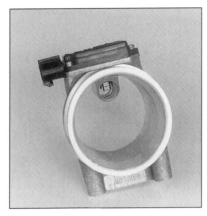

Most controversial of the air meters is the simple, inexpensive C&L. It uses the stock air meter electronics, and trims them with different-sized sampling tubes (the smaller tube inside the main diameter). Vortech offers it under its name, and it seems to work well with Vortech blowers, but more than a few others report part-throttle drivability troubles with positive-displacement blowers or tricky normally aspirated applications.

Kenne Bell offers one air meter, a big 80-millimeter casting, then trims it with a custom computer chip. Shown here with a large open-element air filter, the chip is the small, light gray box below the meter and filter. The piece at lower left is the meter mounting bracket. This combination has made power in dyno tests, no doubt due to ignition timing upgrades in the chip.

Cutting open the stock upper intake manifold, porting it, then welding the pieces back together can pay off handsomely for a lot of work. Once popular on stock 5.0s due to the lack of any aftermarket intakes, the practice lives on only with the Saleen 351 engine. The two weld beads are visible where the plenum was enlarged to help feed this powerfully hungry engine.

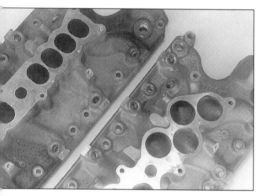

It's easy to see why the stock intake is called an "inline" design, while the GT-40 is a "staggered round." The stocker simply can't compete with the runner cross-sectional area of the GT-40 when it comes to making higher rpm power. A surprising number of aftermarket intakes are based on the GT-40 lower, which still scrunches runners 1 and 5 to clear the distributor.

(over 10-pound) blower cars and the like, but one in 24-pound trim would be useful for thousands of moderately modified 5.0s. This is potentially good news because this plastic meter is about half the price of SVO's aluminum meter.

The plastic housing is sourced from a Mazda application, making it quite inexpensive for SVO to produce. That's because Ford owns a controlling

interest in Mazda. So, this meter bolts right to a Mazda, but won't bolt to anything in a Mustang. That's okay, as the meter is so light it really doesn't need to be bolted to the fender; the air hoses pretty much hold it in place. Of course, you can fabricate your own bracket, or even tie-wrap it to whatever is handy.

The best thing about SVO air meters is that the electronics in them are calibrated, or trimmed, by Ford Electronics Division. SVO insists only the factory has the necessary machinery to properly calibrate air meters, citing the multimillion dollar cost of the calibration bench used. They're likely right, as the Ford meters work precisely as advertised, with excellent drivability and idle stability.

Pro-M

Pro-M is a well-respected name in air meters. Owned by ex-Ford electronics engineer Bob Attwood, Pro-M was first to offer seriously sized meters for the 5.0. Its cast-aluminum 77-millimeter meter is one of the oldest, most expensive, and best-respected meters on the market, and is often the meter selected by tuners when others won't work. It is a direct bolt-on to the 5.0

Mustang. The Pro-M 77-millimeter meter has been offered in various forms, from a stand-alone meter to part of a complete package of cast-aluminum air horns and piping. It was to have been released in a plastic version for considerably less money, but that version hasn't been seen. It is a direct bolt-on for the 5.0 Mustang.

Pro-M's less expensive offering is the 75-millimeter Bullet. Made from a section of plain pipe that's been chromed or injection-molded plastic, the Bullet uses the same electronics package as its 77-millimeter big brother.

The Pro-Ms are trimmed for 19-, 24-, 30-pound, and larger injectors, so you don't have to change the computer to use one.

In addition to their off-the-shelf meters mentioned above, Pro-M also builds huge Bullet-type air meters for Pro 5.0 racers. These range well, over 100 mm in diameter and support around 1,400 hp, so don't worry about being limited by an air meter.

C&L

C&L offers a very simple approach to air meters. All it sells is the aluminum housing. The stock electronics are unscrewed from the stock meter and placed in the new C&L housing, an easy three-minute job, provided you have the right Torx head tool. To give the C&L meter some flexibility when it comes to working with different-sized fuel injectors, the small pipe inside the main diameter can be exchanged. C&L offers these "sampling tubes" in various sizes to match 19-, 24-, 30-, and 36-pound injectors. To adapt the meter to another size injector, simply change the sampling tubes. It takes no longer than swapping over the electronics.

Besides its availability under the C&L name, the same meter is used by Vortech Engineering to work with its superchargers. Vortech calls it the Maxflow.

In some ways, the C&L meter is controversial. The meter always seems to run fine, once some rpm and load are on the engine, but small part-throttle operations have led to lightly hunting idles, lean spots, and reduced drivability around

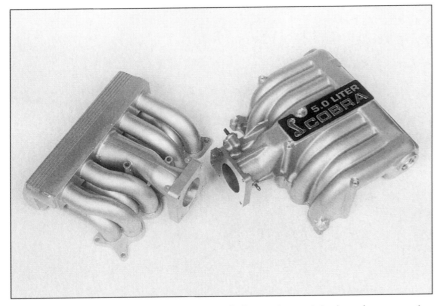

GT-40 uppers come in the more-expensive tubular version and the later, less-expensive cast version as debuted on the Mustang Cobra. For all casual bolt-on daily drivers, the much cheaper casting is the only logical choice. Big-power cars might do better with a tubular GT-40, but the latest crop of shorter, larger, and straighter runner intakes from Edelbrock make more power above 3,500 rpm, and less power below.

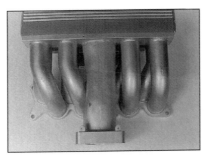

Ford crimped the intake tube to the GT-40 plenum for hold-down bolt access. Removing the bolt bosses and straightening the intake tube helps a little, but only at higher airflow, and it does make bolt (or stud and nut) access a pain. Such fabrication work is worth it only when searching for that last bit of power and is easier to get from a shorter-runner intake.

town. Results with positive-displacement blowers have been spotty, too, with detonation reported by some. There is a major difference between the low-rpm boost of the BBK and Kenne Bell blowers and the high-rpm-only boost of the centrifugals like the Vortech, of course, so it's entirely possible a meter might work better with one blower than the other. The bottom line is swapping meters with a friend will let you know if you are having a drivability problem from the meter. Thousands haven't, and appreciate the C&L's low cost and easy adaptability.

Bored Stock

You may run across a stock meter that has been bored oversize. This trick was more prevalent in the early days of 5.0 tuning, when no other air meters were available, and remains popular with drag racers looking for max performance from minimum money. These meters cause lean air/fuel ratios and add spark timing, so they occasionally work okay near WOT on lightly modified engines, but tend to have poor idle, low speed, and part-throttle

characteristics, and are a detonation problem with blowers. The bottom line is their airflow vs. metered airflow is out of whack, and today with so many good meters on the market, there's no need to run one.

Also, leave the air tubing alone several inches upstream and downstream of the meter, says SVO. Air straighteners and venturis will only foul the airflow through the meter, causing poor metering. You'll also note the stock meter has a wire screen protecting the internals. It's there to keep stones, bugs, etc. from damaging the metering wires, so you might as well leave it in there. It offers little airflow restriction on the stock meter.

Kenne Bell

Like SVO's combination of meter and computer, Kenne Bell offers his 80–millimeter meter only with an electronic chip. Together, the two have produced excellent power and drivability in bolt-on tests, but it's impossible to tell how much of the power increase is from improved airflow through the meter and how much is from whatever commands are in the chip. No matter, it makes sense to recalibrate the computer for the different air meter with a chip, and at 80 millimeters, the Kenne Bell is larger than Texas, so it will support all but seven-second drag racing 5.0s.

Kenne Bell's meter and chip combo are available for 19-, 24-, 30-, 35-, 40-, 45-, and 50-pound injectors. The chips are written using Autologic software.

Throttle Body and EGR Spacer

From the air meter, the intake air passes through the rubber inlet hose to the throttle body and EGR (Exhaust Gas Recirculation) spacer. Although the throttle body is more mechanically complex than the stone-simple air meter, the throttle body is much less troublesome because of its almost total lack of electronics. Only the TPS attached to the upper end of the throttle shaft is electronic, and it requires only occasional attention.

Hot rodding, however, means passing more air through the throttle body. The stock 58-millimeter (1986) and

Thanks to the Mustang Cobra, owners of 1994–1995 Mustangs have their own version of the cast GT-40 intake. Aside from having the extended inlet and EGR functions of the later upper intake, this manifold is identical to other GT-40s, and is a straight bolt-on, of course. This open element air filter is probably protected from fan wash by the radiator hose, but it still breathes hot underhood air.

60-millimeter (1987–1995) throttle bodies are probably less of a choke than the air meter, but still need attention relatively early in a hop-up program. The solution is simple—a larger throttle body. The GT-40 throttle body is 65 millimeters, and seems to work well on almost any street-driven car. Larger throttle bodies are available, of course, but like air meters, once past the 70-millimeter stage, you're just gilding the lily on a street driver.

Unlike carburetors, using a larger-than-necessary throttle body doesn't hurt too much, unless you really get carried away. That's why some companies offer only a 70-millimeter throttle body. They figure a 70-millimeter drives as well as a 65-millimeter, and has the bonus of supporting more horsepower, so why not step up to a 70-millimeter throttle body right away? That would save having to buy another throttle body should power be increased later. In practice, this has proven a good strategy; a 70-millimeter throttle body runs fine on a stone stock 5.0, yet will support

huge forced induction or naturally aspirated power gains.

The downside to going too large with the throttle body is twofold. If the rest of the intake tract is one size, and the throttle body is much larger, then it is like a bulge in a hose. The air will slow down through the throttle body, losing some of the energy that could go into ram effect in the intake manifold. Also, a huge throttle body has a correspondingly large throttle blade. This means large changes in area for a small movement of the throttle pedal just off idle, making drivability tough at small throttle openings without monkeying with the throttle linkage ratios, something you don't want to try at home. Also, as a practical concern, once the throttle body gets up to 75 millimeters or so, the rubber air inlet is difficult to fit over it.

There are 90-millimeter and even 100+-millimeter throttle bodies for 5.0s these days. It's doubtful if there are 50 Pro 5.0s in the country that need such large throttle bodies, so you certainly don't need them on a street driver.

As for the EGR spacer, from a performance standpoint it's just a hole that air passes through. It's there to provide an outlet for the EGR system into the incoming air stream, and has no moving parts other than the EGR valve. Under computer control, the EGR valve and spacer offer no obstacle to power production on street cars, and should be left intact to reduce emissions. On the garden variety 5.0 Mustang, Ford elected to make the EGR spacer separate from the upper intake manifold, while on the 1994–1995 5.0s it is cast as part of the upper intake.

All that's necessary is to ensure that the air path from the throttle body through the EGR spacer and into the upper intake manifold is smooth. All sharp edges should be ground or sanded off with a die grinder and sandpaper roll if you are combining mismatched parts. With the packaged parts from SVO and others, the EGR spacer and throttle body should be a straight bolt-on.

A quirk with the EGR spacer is that it is warmed with engine coolant to prevent throttle shaft icing in the throttle

body. Especially in the South and Southwest, this icing protection is not really necessary, and you see many 5.0s with the water hoses disconnected from the EGR spacer. The flip side is that the water warming hurts power output hardly at all, so disconnecting the hoses has no real performance benefit.

SVO

At SVO the story is really all about the 65-millimeter throttle body and matching 67-millimeter EGR spacer. Two such throttle bodies are offered, the M-9926-A302 for 1986–1993 Mustangs, and the M-9926-B50 for the 1994–1995 cars. The differences are in the location of the idle speed control and throttle linkage. Otherwise, they're both 65-millimeter throttle bodies and are bolt-on replacements.

The EGR spacer, M-94744-A50, is for the 1993 and earlier Mustangs only. It is not needed for the final two years of 5.0 Mustangs.

The SVO catalog also lists an 86-millimeter throttle body, but it requires extensive cutting of the intake manifold to blend the big throat to the intake. It's a race piece only, and has no place on the street.

BBK/Edelbrock

BBK started a line of throttle bodies for its own mail-order business, which Edelbrock picked up for its catalog as well. Now cast with both BBK and Edelbrock logos at the Edelbrock foundry and machined at BBK, the meters are available from either source. BBK lists 65-, 70-, 75-, and 80-millimeter throttle bodies for the 1986–1993 cars, with EGR spacers to match, except for the racing-only 80-millimeter part. All are sold with a TPS attached. BBK also has 65-, 70-, and 75-millimeter throttle bodies for the 1994–1995 cars.

Accufab

Accufab's claim to fame is billet construction. Billet just means the throttle body is whittled from a solid block of aluminum, not cast or extruded. Billet construction gives a seamless part that polishes nicely if

Edelbrock's Performer intake manifold's symmetrical lines are no false hope; this intake features straightened, more evenly spaced runners than any other replacement 5.0 manifold. In bolt-on tests, the Performer runs just the slightest hair ahead of the GT-40, but has more reserve potential as the rest of the engine is improved. The Performer's biggest assets, its straightened and raised lower runners, are pretty well hidden when installed. Put GT-40 and Edelbrock lowers next to each other on the bench and the extra height jumps right out. Still, there is just enough hood clearance.

Vortech picked up the original Saleen upper intake to round out its line of induction parts. Mated to a 5.0 truck lower, this intake is good at supporting top-end or blower horsepower. Here the owner has elected not to drill and tap the eight additional injector bosses, which are visible running down the right side in this view. Such secondary injectors have proven redundant. A single set of eight high-volume injectors is less expensive and easier to control with electronics.

When higher rpm horsepower is the goal, Edelbrock provides the only intakes that fit between the full-length GT-40 and the truncated box-type upper intakes. This is Edelbrock's Performer RPM, which puts the top end into a serious 320+ horsepower engine outfitted with good heads, gear, and cam. By killing low-end power below 3,500 rpm while supporting top-end muscle, this manifold should be controllable when launching at the drag strip. Now you can spin the tires at half-track instead of off the line!

you're into the shiny look, but otherwise it has no performance advantage for an unstresssed part like a throttle body, other than CNC-accuracy.

Accufab offers 65-, 70-, 75-, and 90-millimeter throttle bodies, all billet, all highly polished, and all for 1986–1995 5.0s. Matching EGR spacers are available up to 75 millimeters.

Intake Manifolds

Your choices are numerous when it comes to 5.0 intake manifolds. While there have been over 30 intakes offered for the 5.0, only a handful account for a huge percentage of those commonly used. To round up all the offerings into rough groupings, there are the (1) long-runner, stock-style intakes, (2) box-type uppers, and (3) cowl induction specialty pieces. You may also hear the term "inline" and "staggered round" runner. The stocker is an inline design, because when you look at the lower intake, the oval runners are all in a row, while the GT-40 uses round runners that are staggered left to right to fit in the allotted space.

Long Runner

The stock 5.0 HO intake is built in two pieces—upper and lower. Combined, and with the cylinder head ports included, they give the longest runner length available, which is where the 5.0 gets its excellent torque that's so handy on the street. Cut the runner length shorter and torque is lost while upper rpm horsepower is gained. Add runner length and the opposite happens.

Car 5.0 engines use an oval-runner intake, while truck 5.0 intakes make do with large rectangular ports. Ford got this one backward; the smaller, torquier oval runners work better on the trucks,

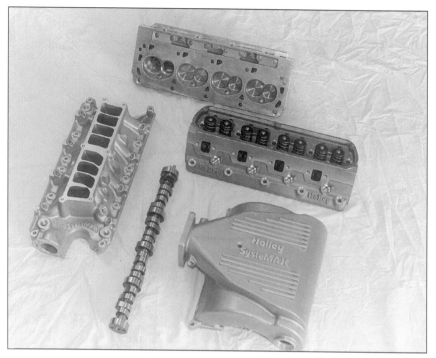

Holley's system II kit is a complete redo of the upper engine. The heads are unique to the kit, as is the camshaft; the lower intake is an improved version of the 5.0 truck lower, and the upper is an obvious continuation/improvement on the Saleen/Vortech part. Early reports on this kit said it sort of left low-rpm power wanting, but was big fun at high rpm. The kit is not emissions exempted; Holley offers the much tamer system I for street-legal duty.

This prototype BXR intake is very similar to the production part. A cross-ram intake with true line-of-sight runners, the BXR is designed for all-out, no compromises, naturally aspirated performance. A real animal at the race track, yet with plenty of torque for street operation, the BXR's drawback is its high initial cost. A great BXR feature is interchangeable plenum boxes at the ends of each bank of runners for tuning the powerband. The big intake requires relocating the distributor and the belt driving it, but it will just clear a stock Mustang hood.

where pulling power is the main goal, while the sporty Mustangs could use the higher rpm potential of the larger truck manifold. This is borne out by several aftermarket Mustang intakes that use the truck lower as a starting point.

Unfortunately for truck owners, the stock 5.0 intake won't work on the pickups, because the uppers point in the opposite directions, and unlike the GT-40 design, the manifold isn't symmetrical, so it won't reverse.

When it comes to making sporty intake manifolds for the 5.0 Mustang, the main variable is runner length, followed by runner shape and cross section. More 5.0 intake manifolds are coming from the aftermarket, but the general idea with bolt-on type intakes is to hold runner length near stock to preserve streetable manners. Racier intakes use shorter runners to promote top-end power. They also toy with runner diameter slightly for the same reason.

So, it's no accident the GT-40, Cobra, standard Edelbrock, Vortech, and Holley intakes all feature nearly the same intake runner lengths; it's a number set by the laws of physics. All these runners have been cut as short as their designers dared in the hopes of building high-rpm power, while hanging onto as much torque as possible.

Key to power in these street-ori-

ented intakes is attention to detail in the upper (especially in the 180 degree turn), somewhat larger cross-sectional area in the runners and straightening the runners in the lower intake as much as possible. The stock Ford lower intake pinches the No. 1 and No. 5 runners badly to provide plenty of clearance around the distributor, while the Edelbrock especially does its best to straighten them out. This helps equalize power among cylinders, which helps both power and smoothness.

Cut and Weld

In the first days of 5.0 hot rodding, there was only the stock cast intake manifold. To change runner and plenum shape, it was necessary to cut open the manifold, grind in the improvements, then weld the intake back together again. While such intakes won't win any beauty contests, they can run quite well, depending on how the inner manifold was modified and provided they're kept on hot street cars and not asked to uphold Ford honor in Comp Eliminator racing. Apparently the last remaining example is the welded intake used on the mega-dollar Saleen Mustang 351 engine. These engines make good power, to say the least, and while Steve Saleen would love to have his own cast intake manifold for cosmetic reasons, the cost of tooling up such a part means he's stuck with the just-as-effective welded part.

Extrude Honing

A better way of dealing with cast, long-runner intake manifolds is to Extrude Hone them. Extrude Honing is an aerospace process in which abrasive putty is pushed through a part to enlarge a passage or smooth its surface, plus it blends rough edges.

Extrude Honing is perfect for complex shapes, such as the 5.0's upper intake, because the abrasive putty can make tight turns. In the upper intake, this would be the 180 degree turn in the plenum (the big open area that hangs over the left rocker cover). Because the intake need not be cut and welded, the somewhat high price of the Extrude Hone process is

Box-type upper intake manifolds have one application—high-boost, high-volume blower and turbo engines. Many have tried to get these to work on naturally aspirated street engines without success, due to lack of low-end torque. Turbo engines, which build more mid-range power than even big centrifugals like this Vortech Mondo, do best with these low-restriction intakes.

thus offset, and the intake's eye-appeal or stealth qualities are not harmed.

What Extrude Honing can't do is appreciably change the shape of the runners (or cylinder head ports for that matter), especially in a localized spot. For that, you still have to cut and weld to get in there with a die grinder.

GT-40

Easily the most popular aftermarket 5.0 intake is the GT-40. Developed by Ford for the never released 25th anniversary Mustang, the GT-40 uses staggered round runners instead of the stocker's inline arrangement. The runners are larger and better shaped, and airflow is much improved. In fact, the GT-40 is the intake everyone else aims at, because it combines good top-end power with streetable torque.

Like any part, the GT-40 offers a compromise. As part of the GT-40 package, the GT-40 intake offers substantial mid-range and top-end power gains. It also costs about 18 lb-ft of torque way down low. As we've said, however, that's about the best of any 5.0 performance intake.

GT-40 intakes come in two major varieties, tubular and cast. The tubular

came first. It is an expensive manifold to produce, because the runners are individually bent tubes gathered together and welded into the plenum. It was designed to fit only the 1993 and earlier Mustangs, but SVO offers an adapter, M-9927-A50, to allow it to work on 1994–1995 Mustangs. You'll also need the later M-9926-B50 throttle body, of course, and you might have to trim the hood blanket for clearance—the tubular GT-40 is slightly taller than the later cast version. Furthermore, such a combination works only with the M-20201-A51 strut tower brace.

Cast GT-40 or, as they're called, Cobra intakes, are considerably cheaper to produce in volume, and thus cost about $200 less over the counter than the tubular variety. There are two cast GT-40 intakes, one built for the 1993 Mustang Cobra and another to fit the 1994–1995 Cobras, along with the 1995 Cobra R-model, which uses its own unique lower intake. It's wider to span the larger 351W valley. The later 5.0 upper intake is a bit lower to clear the late Mustang's lower hood, plus the air intake is curved forward to properly position the throttle body. Both versions share the same cast lower with the tubu-

lar GT-40 upper.

Somehow, to the performance eye, the cast Cobra intake seems lower performance than the tubular, but dyno testing has shown the casting runs with the tubular piece up to 400 horsepower. It can be Extrude Honed, too. Naturally, because it is cheaper, it is gaining popularity, and is a smart choice for a bolt-on project. Still, according to SVO, the tubular GT-40 remains the power king, good up to 425 horsepower worth of airflow, while the castings sign off at 400 horsepower of airflow. Also, the tubular weighs eight pounds less than the stock or cast GT-40. Of course, you can always Extrude Hone the casting, but not the tube-style. You make the call.

Tubular and cast GT-40s are both available from SVO. The tubular M-9424-A51 upper is SVO's standard GT-40 offering. If you want both the upper and lower tubular GT-40, ask for M-9933-A50. That nets you both manifold halves plus the EGR spacer and upper-to-lower gaskets.

Cobra intakes are available only with the lower intake, without gaskets. Alternately, you could buy them over the counter at a dealership as replacement parts.

Explorer, Thunderbird, and Others

Several other versions of the 5.0 intake are out there, all designed to offer good street power while clearing shock tower braces, low hoods, or to fit a special engine packaging challenge. The Explorer version of the 5.0 HO intake seems to do pretty well, while the Thunderbird version's main claim is its low height. You're best off with a Mustang-specific intake, either one of Ford's or aftermarket.

Edelbrock Performer

Edelbrock is the aftermarket leader in intake manifolds, and Edelbrock worked diligently in making its 5.0 offering everything it could be. Out of the box, the Edelbrock is indistinguishable from the tubular GT-40 in seat-of-the-pants performance feel, but it does seem to make a tad more top-end power on the dyno. It's also perfectly matched

Phenolic spacers, which fit between the upper and lower intake, have been sold on their heat insulation capabilities for years. While they can't hurt, it's unlikely they do any good that way. What phenolic spacers are good for is making enough clearance between the upper intake manifold and the valve covers. This area gets tight mainly due to taller-than-stock valve covers. Here the throttle linkage is bound between the throttle body and valve cover. Quickly slipping a spacer under the upper intake did the trick. Hood clearance is not affected enough to matter.

to the rest of the Edelbrock offerings, such as cylinder heads and throttle bodies. It's all the intake manifold most bolt-on 5.0s will ever need.

The Edelbrock has more performance potential as the engine's power level rises. The plenum has a removable cover, allowing easy access for porting, the attachment of the upper to the lower doesn't choke the main entrance as much, and, perhaps most importantly, the tall lower intake has some of the straightest runners available. The intake also meets Edelbrock's strict quality control and finish requirements.

One interesting characteristic of the Edelbrock manifolds is the removable side plate on the plenum. It's there mainly to access one of the hold-down bolts, which is something of a pain, but it does allow easy porting access (not really necessary) or plumbing stealthy nitrous lines.

Edelbrock Performer RPM

In Edelbrock hierarchy, parts start out as Performers, move up a notch to Performer RPM, then Victor Jr., and finally Victor. Considering that the Victor level is for professional

racing, Victor Jr. is more like amateur racing, and Performer RPM is for serious street/strip cars, it's easy to understand that the Performer RPM 5.0 intake is a hot number that's compromised toward high-rpm performance. Edelbrock says an engine should make 325 horsepower before a Performer RPM intake is used.

This is accomplished via a new upper casting featuring runners that are 1 1/4-inch shorter. This obviously cuts into low- and mid-range torque, but promotes top-end power. Bolted to a stock Mustang, the Performer RPM is a soggy ride that kills low end and can't build top end without more cylinder head, camshaft, and rpm. However, installed on a 325 horsepower 5.0L that already has good heads and 3.55 or steeper gears, the Performer RPM will certainly brighten up the top end with a racy feel that's fun to rev.

Edelbrock Victor 5.0

Take an even shorter runner upper and put a seriously tall and straightened lower, both unique parts, and you have the Victor intake manifold. Edelbrock characterizes this intake as a maximum effort part, and that means the racetrack. Considering Edelbrock offers the Performer and Performer RPM for any conceivable street duty, there is no need to put the Victor on the street. Edelbrock 400 horsepower and up engines will benefit from a Victor 5.0 intake.

Vortech/Saleen

You see fewer of them, but the Saleen/Vortech upper intake is another powerhouse manifold. Now offered by Vortech, the unit uses a stock 5.0 truck lower intake. These lowers feature rectangular runners that flow a reported 29 percent more air than the stock Mustang lower. To this, Vortech adds its custom upper with matching runners.

The current version of this intake is a bit lower than the earliest releases, to ensure hood clearance on the Mustang and save about five pounds of aluminum. A unique feature is eight additional injector bosses cast into the outside of the 180 degree turn. The owner has to drill and tap these bosses, which allow lawn sprinkler–like supplemental fueling in very high horsepower applications. With or without the extra injectors, the Vortech does best in boosted or high-horsepower applications where plenty of rpm or blower airflow can take advantage of its flow capacity. Pricing is a tad higher the tubular GT-40.

Holley SysteMAX I & II

A giant in aftermarket induction, Holley was one of the last to jump into the 5.0 intake ring. Holley offers two engine improvement kits, both of which feature an intake manifold. The SysteMAX I kit is relatively affordable and contains an upper intake manifold and a camshaft.

SysteMAX II is much more comprehensive, and expensive. It includes cylinder heads, upper and lower intakes, and a cam and associated parts. In short, SysteMAX II replaces the entire engine from the short block up. Information on the Holley kits was not widespread as this book went to print, but all indications are

Instead of a ram air kit, this smart SN-95 owner fabricated a cold air pipe. This arrangement looks like it might help, as air is being drawn from the cooler inner fender and not the hot engine compartment. Also, the inlet pipe is straighter than stock and free of air-disturbing corrugations.

that SysteMAX II is a superior top-end power builder. If its manifold looks similar to the rectangular runner 302 lower and Saleen upper combination, that is because Holley started with that combination when beginning its development. The Holley intakes are unique, however, with more hood clearance than the Saleen/Vortech offering.

BXR

Newest of the long-runner intakes is the dual-plenum Balanced Cross Ram (BXR). Developed by Bruce Gambradella, the BXR is aimed at excellent naturally aspirated performance via a one-piece intake, which replaces both the upper and lower stockers. The intake is cast with generous amounts of aluminum to allow port matching or full-on porting to meet any need. Out of the box, it mates with the stock intake port, so count on port matching the BXR to fit your cylinder heads. Replaceable plenum covers allow additional tuning as well.

To achieve its gun barrel line-of-sight runners, the BXR requires replacing the stock 5.0 distributor with a shortened unit, belt-driven off the crankshaft. All

this necessarily raises the price well past the casual bolt-on level, so the benefits of even cylinder filling and the best ram tuning available cost about as much as a blower. The BXR is an excellent piece, either by itself or with a centrifugal supercharger, but it is very pricey.

Box Intakes

There's little mystery how box intakes got their name. By using a standard lower intake, then placing a simple box plenum atop it, Cartech invented the box intake for its turbocharging system. Any semblance of normally aspirated low-end torque is lost, as the runner length is drastically shortened, but with a properly engineered turbo system, the lost torque is more than regained by the turbo. Then, as the tach climbs, the greatly reduced high-rpm restriction of the box intake allows excellent high-rpm power.

Box intakes aren't seen too often on the street and for good reason, but with their promise of high-rpm gain, box intakes surface regularly in 5.0 shootout racing. Outside of forced induction, however, the box intakes haven't done too well, probably because the lower intake they are used with is its own high-rpm restriction. Even on moderately

centrifugally supercharged engines (under 12–14 pounds of boost), the box intakes lose low-rpm torque they can't make up for with high-rpm power. The Roots and Lysholm screw (Kenne Bell) blowers that make tons of low-end power don't need the box upper intake, so they are no help there, either. Only on turbo engines, where a wastegate helps broaden the turbo powerband, do the box intakes seem to shine. Definitely not streetable nor street-legal.

Hartmann

Several box intakes have been made. Aside from two versions of the cast-aluminum Cartech, the plastic Hartmann is the only other to see relatively widespread use. Another source is Pro Mustang Performance, who offers the Cartech, Hurricane, and Outlaw uppers under the Powerbox moniker.

Ron Anderson Power Box

Yet another box intake is available from Ron Anderson Performance. Tweaked with a slightly lower but wider plenum than other box intakes, the piece is still a race- or turbo-only part.

Cowl Induction

Anyone who's followed motorsports knows Jack Roush and his teams come to the front of whatever competition they enter, and with years of racing technique boiled into a 5.0 specific induction package, you know it will be a good one.

Actually a variation of the long-runner intake, the cowl induction unit from Roush Racing is for the person seeking refined performance from a normally aspirated SN-95 5.0 Mustang. The intake package is very complete, essentially a reengineering of the upper engine and even the vehicle's bodywork where the new intake air path travels through the hood.

The intake combines long-runner design with generous plenum area (thanks to two plenums) for sparkling top-end power, along with cowl induction off the back lip of the special 1994–1995 hood it is sold with. The air pressure built up at the base of the windshield in the cowl area

Port matching involves carefully transferring the parting line of one part to another, then grinding the two parts until the openings are in perfect alignment. The machinist's bluing, scribe lines, and smoothed runner walls on this stock lower are all port matching evidence. Note also how the smoothing extends only a inch or so into the runners. Port matching is not a full porting job.

helps the intake air down the manifold, and the much shorter run from the air filter, mass air meter, and throttle body reduces restriction and gives the intake air less chance to heat up, as it spends less time in the hot engine compartment. Roush says the package adds 47 horsepower to a stock 5.0, 99 horsepower when combined with GT-40 cylinder heads and 120 horsepower with Roush Computer Numerically Controlled (CNC)-ported GT-40 cylinder heads. These are big claims, but the few driving trials I've had with the system yielded obvious power improvements.

The Roush Induction System is a very complete kit, as a quick listing of major parts illustrates. The UPS man will deliver a hood, fuel rail, valve covers, 65-millimeter throttle body, air filter, three-piece intake manifold and associated PCV, heater core and vacuum hoses, EGR tube, wiring jumpers, gaskets, and hardware. As expected with so much gear, not to mention from Roush, none of this is inexpensive. Furthermore, when bolting on this sort of upper-end breathing, you really won't be happy until the cylinder heads are

upgraded, so don't forget to price a pair of them, and painting the hood.

Installation Tips

There's not much rocket science to changing the 5.0 intake manifold. All small-block Ford V-8s require some skill in getting the lower manifold to seal along the block, and at the corners where the block and heads meet. Gasket sets include a pair of gaskets for the front and rear block areas, which need sealing, but experienced mechanics typically discard them because the gaskets always seem to squeeze out from between the block and manifold. The old hands prefer to rely on a bead of silicone sealer laid atop the block edge. It squishes out when the manifold is torqued down, of course, but not like a solid gasket, which pops completely out of position. An extra dab of silicone at the block-to-head intersection does the trick there.

Another problem is keeping the intake manifold gaskets lined up when setting the manifold in position, although the gasket makers supply a tab

and slot combination to hold the intake gaskets in place. Small tabs on the head gaskets hold slots in the intake gaskets, and normally that's enough. If not, install a couple of studs in the manifold bolt holes in the cylinder heads. They'll keep the gaskets from shifting.

If the cylinder heads are ported, expect to find the top of the port openings higher than stock to improve airflow. Many porters grind the ports to the gasket opening, but only after keeping the gasket as high as possible on the cylinder head. This is done by putting the intake gasket atop the tabs on the head gaskets, which doesn't hurt anything, but means you have to be a little more careful when installing the intake manifold.

Also be aware that the 5.0's lower manifold bolts thread straight down into the cylinder heads. This gives these small bolts stronger than expected leverage on the cylinder heads. It's said these bolts help pull the heads off the block, helping to cause blown head gaskets, which I find difficult to believe. However, it seems some sort of wedge action of the intake being pulled down between the cylinder heads upsets the cylinder head retention. No matter what, overtorquing the lower intake manifold does make the head gaskets easier to blow.

Ford engineers have also noted they can detect main-bearing bore distortion in the block when the lower intake is torqued—this should be all the clue you need to agree the 5.0 HO is lightly constructed. So, all said, it's obviously not a good idea to overtorque the intake manifold bolts. The specification is 18 lb-ft, and if it takes more than that to seal the intake, you have some other problem that needs attention first.

Fitting the upper intake to the lower is easier. A thin paper gasket goes between the two. Fit it dry, without liquid sealers. The joint is sealing only air, and you don't want beads of sealer squished into the air path—that could upset the airflow. If you are using a phenolic spacer, use a gasket on each side of it.

The upper intake is heavy and lopsided weight-wise, so having an assistant to help lift it over the fender and hold it level while the bolts go in is smart.

Phenolic Spacers

To help insulate the upper intake from engine heat passing up through the lower intake, phenolic spacers were developed. Available for stock, GT-40, and Edelbrock intakes, phenolic spacers certainly don't hurt power, but there's little proof they do any good, power-wise. Certainly, for the average bolt-on street car, they won't give any performance gain.

Still, spacers serve a useful purpose. Often the throttle linkage binds on the right rocker cover when non-stock covers are used. A phenolic spacer will lift the upper intake enough to clear the throttle linkage. Also, by stacking several phenolic spacers, the intake's runner length is increased and a little more torque made, a good trick for tuning around a problem at the track.

Remember, if you try to elevate the upper intake too high, you'll have to trim the hood's insulating pad to clear, especially with larger aftermarket intakes.

Trick Stuff

Like almost anything on 5.0 Mustangs, it seems nearly every idea has been tried on the induction system. Cold air, ram air, extra injectors, variable runner intakes, nitrous intercooling, and who knows what have been attempted. Many were simple tricks that don't work, some pan out at the track but don't matter on the street, and some need more development.

Cold/Ram Air

Picking up a light supercharging effect from the vehicle's speed is a time-honored speed trick. It works nicely on racing aircraft, Pro Stockers, Bonneville racers, and some road racing cars where 200+-miles per hour speeds mean there's enough energy in the windstream to matter, but considering it takes 100 miles per hour of breeze to really measure this effect, it's not much help on Mustangs except for Pro 5.0 racing.

The side benefit from so-called ram air systems is cooler air. But since the 5.0 Mustang already breathes from inside the inner fender, there's nothing to be gained from the ram air kits on the market, at least, not on a street car.

Wet Manifolding

The 5.0 intake manifold is called a dry intake because it flows only air, and not an air/fuel mixture. Because fuel is so much heavier than air, it has much more inertia and cannot make the sharp bends in the upper 5.0 intake without separating from the air stream. This is why attempts at extra fueling around the throttle body are unsuccessful.

Don't confuse "around the throttle body" to mean the additional injectors possible on the Vortech intake. They point down the relatively straight passages past the 180 degree bend in the upper intake, and pose no fuel puddling problems, especially at high rpm.

Wet nitrous manifolds add their own unique trick of blowing apart from time to time, thanks to nitrous/fuel puddling.

Port Matching

Not all tricks are a waste. Port matching means to carefully blend the metal where intake manifold halves, cylinder heads, and EGR spacers mate. The term also covers the exhaust port to header interface. With matched induction kits, the port matching is typically pretty close, but on mass production stock parts, and when putting together different aftermarket parts, the ports are often misaligned. A machine shop can port match the parts for a smooth joint. This is worth it when searching for that extra edge on an engine that sees track use.

Dyno Testing

Should you have an engine dyno tested, the shop may want to run it carbureted on the engine dyno. Unfortunately, this is pretty standard, and for breaking in the rings and camshaft, checking for leaks and a general idea of the power potential, it works fine. You need the injection and its manifolding to get an accurate power test, of course, but to run injection on the dyno requires a bit of support equipment on the dyno (return fuel system, computer, wiring harness), so many shops just slap on an Edelbrock/Holley. It's much better than no dyno at all.

CONTENTS

The Stock Exhaust 46

Street or Race? 48

Short-Tube Headers 48

Long-Tube Headers 55

H-Pipes 56

X-Pipes 56

Cat-Back 57

Cat-Back Installation 57

Although a big step up from traditional cast-iron manifolds, factory tube headers could be better. As seen here, not only are 1986–1993 Mustang header tubes pinched at the flange, they are also squeezed at each curve, thanks to a lack of mandrel bends. Each constriction costs a bit of power. Note also the position of the number-three stud and nut header hardware; it's there for accessory mounting. The small holes in each primary pipe are to accept pyrometer probes on an engine dynamometer.

EXHAUST

Nothing in high performance is ever easy, and when hot rodding the 5.0 for maximum performance the exhaust system is one of the most compromised systems in the car. Even for pure track duty, running the headers inside the inner fender, then finding enough room under the car for collectors and exhaust pipes is challenging. At least from a practical, bolt-on street-driven standpoint, the exhaust poses few headaches, but only because there is just so much you can do, given the limitations of short tube headers, catalytic converters, and mufflers.

The Stock Exhaust

The stock 5.0 exhaust system is pretty simple. Bolted to the cylinder head are the headers. Ford used low-grade 1 1/2-inch stainless-steel tubing to form the primary pipes (sometimes called head pipes, hence headers). Their nonmandrel bends are full of sharp kinks, and the tubes are crushed flat near the mounting bolt flanges to allow the assembly robots enough clearance at the factory. Where the primary pipes join is called the collector, and on the stock 5.0 headers, this area is extremely short, to the point where the pipes simply join together so the remainder of the exhaust system can be bolted on. The 5.0 exhaust uses a semispherical joint at this point because it allows considerable misalignment with the H-pipe while still providing a gas-tight seal. Ford uses studs on their headers at the header-to-H-pipe flange.

The H-pipe is the next section. It is formed by the 2 1/4-inch diameter left- and right-side exhaust pipes, along with a crossover tube that joins the two. Welded into a single piece, the H-pipe also contains the stock 5.0's four catalytic converters. Technically, the first two cats are precats, while the larger, rear-most units are simply catalytic converters. The precats are designed to heat rapidly upon engine start-up, an

For the 1994–1995 Mustangs, Ford stepped up to mandrel bends, which helps. Still, the flanges are tightly pinched, which hurts flow near the critical port exit. This was necessary to ensure the bulky factory assembly tools fit easily around the pipes. Obviously, Ford used individual flanges on its headers.

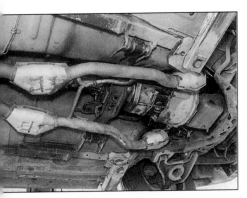

As evidenced by the scrapes in this one, even at 2 1/4 inch and with compact cats, the factory H-pipe still sees its share of bottoming on lowered 5.0s. Note how far forward the precats are; this is for quick cold-start emissions reduction. The air injection tubing and crossover pipe are also visible aft of the transmission cross-member.

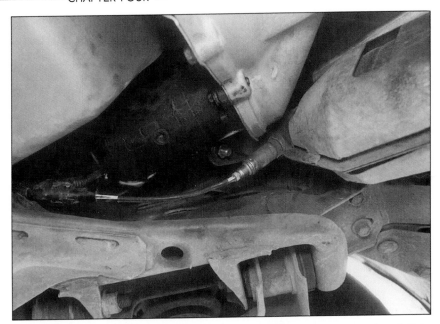

The oxygen sensors are located close to the header flange on the H-pipe. There is little to do with these except avoid breaking them and leaded gasoline. They should remain close to their stock location for proper calibration. Long-tube headers force the oxygen sensors too far downstream to work as the factory intended.

Stock mufflers are one of the first things to go on street-driven Mustangs, but your performance dollars can be better spent elsewhere. Until gas flow increases significantly, such as from a power adder, a cat-back system adds but a couple of horsepower, and that only at the peak. As power grows, better mufflers and 2 1/2-inch tubing definitely help.

especially dirty period of the federal certification test.

The crossover allows the exhaust system pulses to communicate between the two sides. This reduces the annoying booming and droning of separate, non-crossover V-8 exhausts, but has no dramatic power-producing effect, at least not on street cars.

Aftermarket H-pipes are available without catalytic converters for race use. These are called "off-road pipes" or an "off-road H-pipe." They are illegal on the street anywhere in the United States under federal law, and should anyone start enforcing this law vigorously (occasionally done during EPA shop inspections), the fine is $2,500 per occurrence. As the owner you can be cited, and so can the shop that installs them, which is why you won't find too many muffler shops willing to bolt in a set on the 5.0 you drove to their shop. They might consider it if you trailer the car in and out, but if they're smart they won't touch it.

Behind the H-pipe are the two mufflers and their associated 2 1/4-inch tubing. Stock mufflers are not identical left to right; the left is smaller. This is a deliberate noise-tuning tactic, and especially helpful in reducing the droning that V-8 exhausts are prone to at 1,700 and 3,400 rpm. Behind the mufflers, the

Stuffing all the tubing required to make equal-length primaries in a short-tube header means one crowded header, with plenty of power-robbing bends. The cost, installation, and maintenance hassles of equal lengths are maybe worth their modest power benefits.

Warping is a problem with too-thin header flanges. Single-piece, 3/8-inch thick flanges like this will withstand many heat cycles while retaining their shape and avoiding leaks.

2 1/4-inch tailpipes snake over the rear axle and exit under the rear valence.

Street or Race?

The major question to answer when deciding what to do with your exhaust is whether your 5.0 is a street car or a race car. If the car is driven on the street, it's a street car and that's that. Sure, thousands of guys are running 11-second race cars that are streetable enough to make it through three stoplights in a row without boiling over, but as emission laws tighten, these are becoming rarer.

The point is, if you have a street car, run catalytic converters; if you have a race car, take the cats off. It's undeniable that catalytic converters cost power, but there are other ways of gaining that 10–20 horsepower when running on the street. The emissions scrubbed by the cats is incredible, and the damage done to the atmosphere from a noncat 5.0 is just as incredible. Besides, the more the hobby polices itself, the less government intrusion we are inviting upon ourselves. Don't run off-roads on the street. Use high-flows instead.

Short-Tube Headers

Thanks to having to package the H-pipe, the 5.0 Mustang was the major player in introducing the short-tube header to the performance world. Very compact, with no appreciable collector, short-tube headers are a necessary item, but a definite power loss compared to a long-tube header. Long tubes extend all the way under the car and have a distinct, well-developed collector. Just the same, short tubes are the only choice on a street car.

Aftermarket short-tube headers for the 5.0 are numerous and highly beneficial. On an otherwise stock car, a set of unequal length, 1 1/2-inch short tubes release about 7 extra horsepower, and gain much more as the engine is tuned up. When a blower or nitrous goes on, headers are a must.

Two basic short-tube header styles have been typically offered by each manufacturer. Low cost, "replacement" headers are 1 1/2-inch, unequal length designs, which mimic the factory parts, but with mandrel bends. Then a more performance-oriented 1 5/8-inch unequal length follows. Some manufacturers also sell an "ultimate" short-tube header, which is also 1 5/8 inch, but with equal length pipes.

When scouting for short-tube headers, consider the following criteria.

Pipe Diameter

The larger a header pipe, the greater its volume and the slower the gas velocity. In other words, in theory the larger 1 5/8-inch pipes support horsepower and cost torque. On stock engines, 1 1/2-inch headers provide better

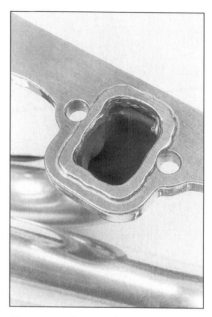

Some manufacturers leave some of the weld bead protruding around the pipe-to-flange joint. This concentrates the clamping force around the exhaust port to ensure a tight seal, and is not something that needs to be ground off!

power and especially torque. Once past the mildest of bolt-ons, however, the 1 5/8-inch headers definitely provide a more useful boost in horsepower. Numerous dyno tests have shown the 1 5/8-inch unequal-length short tubes are worth 11 horsepower over the stock headers, a gain of 4 horsepower over the same headers in 1 1/2 inch. Considering the price is typically the same, the 1 5/8-inch unequal-length short tube has become the de facto 5.0 Mustang header; many companies don't even offer the 1 1/2-inch version any more.

That said, stock convertibles, especially with automatic transmissions, are better off with 1 1/2-inch headers. These heavy cars need all the torque they can get, and the automatic's low-rpm shift points (often well below 5,000 rpm) don't allow the use of high-rpm power.

Supercharged and nitrous cars place heavy demands on the exhaust system because both assist the intake part of engine breathing, but do nothing to aid the exhaust. Thus, forced induction cars need 1 5/8-inch headers. It's also better to go with the larger header if you are on a power-building

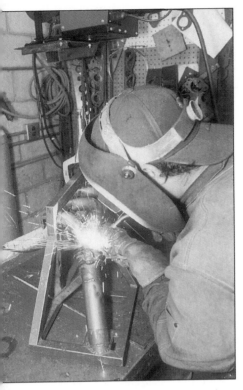

Quality is important with 5.0 headers, because there are so many outfits building them and the pressure to keep costs low are strong. Look for heavy gauge construction (14- is better than 16- or 18-gauge) in both the flanges and pipes. Tube headers are a wear item, and the less expensive versions will wear faster than you'd like.

Low-ball exhaust parts are a complete pain, fighting you during installation and offering sometimes persistent leaks and finally, not lasting very long. This set needed some attention from a Ford tool (two-pound ball peen) to get on and off, and the dipstick tube required "adjustment."

program, adding parts as you can pay for them. You'll quickly build into the larger header's power range.

An old industry rule of thumb is to use 1 1/2-inch headers up to 275 horsepower, 1 5/8-inch units starting at 300 horsepower, and either one in between. Chances are excellent you'll end up with 1 5/8-inch headers.

Finally, a few special short-tube applications are worth noting. Will Burt Street Heat (the old TFS high-port) cylinder heads have a noticeably raised exhaust port. It's possible to use a standard short-tube header on these, but it typically pulls the H-pipe too close to the floorboards. It's better to use the headers specifically built for these heads by JBA and MAC. Also, MAC has offered a 1 3/4-inch header. It's aimed at SVO's J302 cylinder head, which is now out of production.

Equal vs. Unequal Primaries

Because the idea behind a header is to introduce the exhaust gas pulses to the exhaust pipe in evenly spaced intervals to build an extraction effect, it stands that equal length primary pipes work better. The short answer is they do, but the full answer is not as much as expected with short-tube designs. It seems what is gained by the equal length is somewhat negated by the tight turns required to package all the tubing into such a small area. Plus, short-tube headers are so short the tuning frequencies of the pipes fall far above the rpm range of the engine. In other words, short-tube headers make power from gentle bends and pipe diameter, not tuning length.

Various dyno tests have alternately shown small gains and no gains for equal-length designs, and in the end, the expense and hassle of equal-length headers are only worthwhile, if at all, on hard-running blower and bigger nitrous cars. Typically horsepower remains the

same between equal and nonequal length short tubes, but the equal lengths muster up to five more lb-ft of torque.

Spark Plug Access

Mainly a continuation of the equal- vs. unequal-length debate, spark plug access is something to consider, especially as you plan to spend more time at the track tuning (reading spark plugs). The big culprits are the tumbling, curving pipes of equal-length headers, which cover up the spark plugs. At best they make a plug change a pain, and when hot, you really need a pair of gloves. Unequal headers even make spark plug wire routing troublesome. It can be tough to keep the wires from burning on a pipe, and high-temp plug wire boots are thus desirable.

Even on 1 5/8-inch unequal-length headers, bolt and spark plug access is reduced, compared to the smashed-up stockers, so be prepared to exercise some patience. It well may be the case that by the time you can use an equal-length short header, you are already at the point to move on to a full-length header.

Flange Style

Headers are offered with either a single- piece flange at the cylinder head mating area, or four individual flanges. It seems the single-piece flanges—the ones made from a single length of 1/4- or 3/8-inch thick steel—fit better. They definitely stay straighter after repeated heat cycling. So, if you have to remove the headers, perhaps to replace a head gasket, then the single-piece flange is the better choice.

Makers of individual flange headers say they allow the various pipes to adjust a bit as they go on. True, but that means you have to do the adjusting with a long bar in your third hand while putting the headers on. The advantage is individual flanges are less expensive, so it comes down to whether you'll be taking your headers on and off for head changes and so on. If so, spring for the one-piece flanges; if not, save a few bucks with the individual flanges.

Another flange variation is the use of a weld bead around the runner

Continued on page 54

Short-Tube Install

This 1 1/2-inch header installation demonstrates what it takes to get short tubes on a stock 5.0. This job was on a 190 Mustang at JBA in San Diego, California. A Vortech supercharger was being installed at the same time, so you may notice some of the front engine dress and air plumbing are missing. That helped clear the way for photos, but isn't necessary for the header installation.

The passenger side is the slightly more difficult, because the air injection plumbing is located there, and the engine is actually offset a little bit to the right for steering column clearance.

Start under the car by removing the passenger-side oxygen sensor, to keep from banging it into the floorboard, and the two nuts from each flange where the stock headers meet the H-pipe. Then pry the H-pipe to the rear. You'll only move it about an inch, as the exhaust hangers limit play. All you need is some clearance between the headers and H-pipe to clear the header studs and H-pipe flanges.

Now go topside and remove the driver-side spark plug wires from the plugs. There is no need to remove the spark plugs. However, if a plug change is needed, now is a good time, because of the increased clearance. Next off are the header nuts, bolts, and studs. Also remove the engine lift bracket and dipstick assembly. The dipstick tube needs to be unbolted from the header, then it simply pulls out of the block. Where the brackets attach, there'll be studs and nuts. Otherwise, expect bolts in the header flange.

With all the hardware off, you can lift the stock headers out from the top. The driver-side header is especially easy to extract, but neither side offers any real resistance. Remove the gasket, and scrape off any remaining gasket material from the cylinder head. This shouldn't be much of a chore, as the Ford gaskets aren't bad about sticking to the heads. A heavy-bladed scraper with a longish handle will keep your knuckles from getting banged up.

The JBA headers shown here are sold with bolts; JBA tack welds the H-pipe flange bolts to the header on all in-house installations. That keeps the installation a one-man job. If you don't have a welder at home, go ahead and drop the bolts into the header flange now. They'll stay put during header installation, and save you from having to fish the bolts into the holes deep inside the engine compartment. It'll still take a friend to hold the bolts while you tighten the nuts, though. Guide the header into place on the H-pipe ball-joint and cylinder head, and start the outer two bolts. Use anti-seize lubricant with aluminum heads.

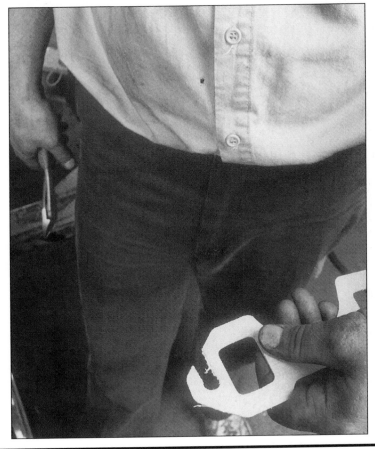

Cutting a path to the two outer head bolt holes in the gasket allows slipping the gasket between the head and header until it is captured by the front and rear bolts. This is the easy way to get the header in place. A light bead of high-temperature silicone around both sides of the port openings is also desirable.

Once the sealer is spread on, the gasket can be slipped into position. This is much easier than attempting to install a goopy, sealer-coated gasket along with the headers. If nothing else, it keeps from accidentally smearing silicone all over the top of the engine.

To install the dipstick tube, the forward leg of the mounting tab must be relieved to about half its width to clear the thicker header tube. This is easily done on a bench grinder. At the other end of the tube, a bead of silicone should be run right where the tube expands. This seals the potential oil leak where the tube runs through the engine block. Install the tube, giving it a good push down to seat it, tighten the tab under the fourth header bolt, and reinstall the spark plug wires. That finishes the driver-side upper installation.

On the passenger side, there are two large air injection hoses and associated hardware. Unplug the two vacuum lines to the vacuum motors and unclamp the two large hoses where they join the metal piping. Then the assembly can be bent forward out of the way. There's no need to disassemble the air injection valves and hoses. They are long enough to bend forward and wrap out of the way.

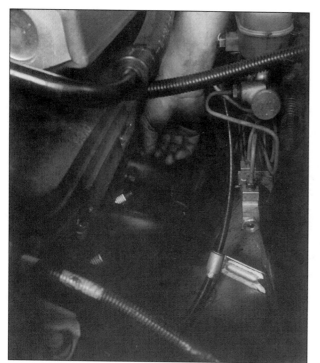

Now all the header bolts should be installed and all but the fourth one back tightened. JBA leaves off the engine lifting bracket. If engine removal becomes necessary, JBA says its mechanics reinstall the bracket or use the power steering bracket bolt, upper-to-lower intake manifold bolt holes or holes in the rear of cylinder head.

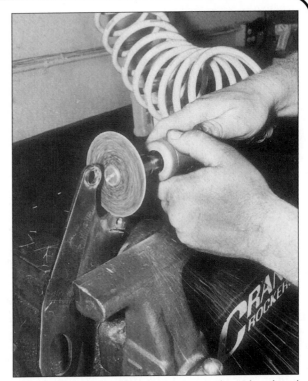

The upper air injection pipe sits too close to the engine for use with aftermarket headers. Using a large bar, gently bend the pipe outward—toward the fender—about 3/4 inch. This gives more hand and tool clearance, and will provide needed hose clearance with the new headers. Now the header and gasket can be removed, and the gasket surface scraped. Then install the new header, using the slotted bolt hole trick on the gasket, and being sure to line the ball and socket joint up on the H-pipe end.

The engine lift bracket cuts most easily with a band saw, but a die grinder fitted with an abrasive wheel also does the trick. You can do the same, a bit more slowly, with a hacksaw.

Now install the bracket leg under the rearmost header bolt and tighten it. Then install the small bolt through the air pipe and to the bracket leg. That gives a factory-like secure mounting. The entire lifting bracket cannot be reused because it doesn't fit over the header's larger primary pipe. The rest is buttoning up the plug wires, air plumbing, and under-car connections with the H-pipe and oxygen sensor. If the H-pipe is a nonstock, multipiece affair, you must support it while tightening the header connections, or it will twist out of shape and thump against the floor. Having a helper support the H-pipe while tightening is best.

The engine lifting bracket found at the rear of the right head, seen being removed here, includes a threaded bolt hole for bracing the lower air injection pipe to. JBA cuts that leg off the bracket, then refits only the amputated piece. Many people simply let the air pipe dangle, but it rattles noisily and eventually breaks unless it's tied down.

Several aftermarket headers use some sort of taper inside the collector, like this "fire-cone" in a JBA header. They might help a bit, and they certainly don't hurt anything.

Continued from page 49

opening. This bead faces the cylinder head, and is there to provide a stress concentration to help seal the flange gasket. Don't grind it off thinking it's a production left-over!

Coatings

Mild steel headers eventually rust through, from water naturally formed by gasoline combustion on the inside and from road splash on the outside. Stainless steel is therefore a much superior header material, but stainless steel costs more than the market is willing to bear. Thus header coatings over mild steel tubing have become very popular.

Coatings are more than window dressing, and significantly increase header life spans. Coatings vary from the common industrial nickel finish found on many regular 5.0 short-tube offerings to premium ceramic protectants offered by many header manufacturers and coating specialists. The industrial nickel jobs are an improvement over high-temp paint on mild steel, while ceramic coatings are that much better. Get the best you can afford. Low-buck coatings will still allow minor cosmetic rusting; ceramic coatings pretty well avoid this. Ceramic coatings are less porous than the nickel variety and don't stain as easily. If you keep a show-like engine compartment, ceramic coatings are for you.

Don't spend money on exotic coatings on short-tube headers for a street car hoping for a power improvement. You aren't stressing the engine enough to see any. Coatings for durability and looks are worth the investment, though.

Stock 5.0 headers use studs at the H-pipe flange, while many aftermarket headers employ less-expensive nuts and bolts. Both seal well, but the studs are easier to install because one person can quickly wrench down the nuts from underneath. One trick is to tack-weld the bolts to the flange before installation, effectively making studs out of them, although it's not that big a deal to have a friend hold them from the top.

Build Quality

Selling 5.0 parts is big business, and plenty of people have jumped on the bandwagon. Not all of these folks are primarily motivated by your desire to own top-rate parts at bargain prices. They offer the bargain prices, sometimes, but they don't offer the last word in quality.

When it comes to short-tube headers, there are distinct variations in fit and material quality, and the cheapest headers are typically not the ones that fit

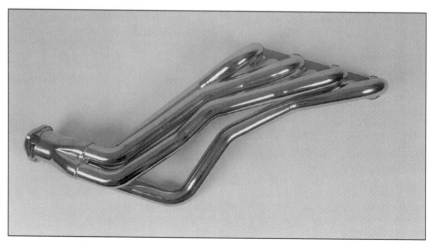

Long-tube headers are a must on a race car. Because they are more sensitive to tuning, and more capable of assisting horsepower production, more care is necessary in their selection. Length; tube diameter; stepped primary construction; and collector diameter, length, and taper all need consideration. Your best bet is to consult a respected engine tuner or header manufacturer about your specific package. Be ready to spend money, and ignore the low-ball advertised specials. Expect to use 1 5/8-inch, 32-inch-long primary tubes for most applications; big-power engines (400-plus horsepower) can use 1 3/4-inch primaries.

the best. Some headers are built from 16-gauge material, some from 14-gauge. If you won't be keeping your 5.0 for long, or plan on changing headers soon, then a 16-gauge header will give a couple years service. If any sort of longevity is desired, get 14-gauge parts. Fit is best determined by asking others how they've fared, and don't expect the best from the least.

Don't forget you'll need some form of coating, too. All aftermarket short-tube headers are built using mild steel, which rusts when left bare. The only exception are the 1986–1993 and 1994–1995 stainless-steel offerings from Ford SVO.

Bolt vs. Stud

Some headers use studs at the H-pipe end; these are easier to work with than bolts. Both fasteners seal fine, but the bolts require someone hold the bolt

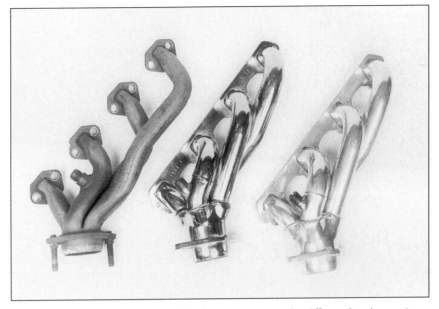

These three right-hand 1994–1995 headers demonstrate the different header coatings. At left, a stock part demonstrates its characteristic light surface rust, possible from low-grade stainless steel; at center is the aftermarket standard industrial nickel finish; while a ceramic-coated set is at right. Both nickel and ceramic coatings are applied inside and outside the header. The nickel is dipped, the ceramic sprayed.

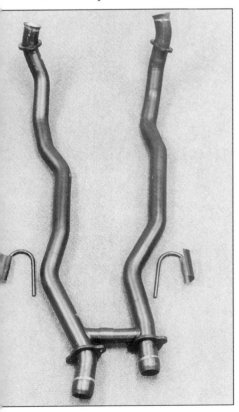

An off-road H-pipe is a sure power gain, especially when getting into the mid-300 horsepower range, and is an absolute requirement at the track. Their lack of catalytic converters transforms a 5.0 into a mobile ecological disaster, so they are justifiably illegal on the street. Don't even think of running them there.

from the top with a ratchet and long extension, while someone else handles the nuts from the bottom. The stud style is easily worked by one person, plus it gives the H-pipe something to hang onto while working with it.

If you have bolts, you can tack weld them to the flange to aid installation.

Long-Tube Headers

When you're headed for the track, long-tube headers are the way to go. They're more work to install and they're much more expensive than short tubes, but they unlock the path to power.

Long tubes make more power because it takes well more than 30 inches of primary tube to realize the optimum scavenging effect from headers on a typical V-8 engine. The shorter the primaries, the higher the rpm where the header will have maximum effect; unfortunately 5.0 short-tube headers are much too short to have a strong scavenging effect. Their benefit is smooth bends, which reduce flow losses. Long-tube headers also have room for a better collector, which is where the scavenging effect is formed.

Compared to short tubes, long-tube headers help across the powerband,

Nickel-coated headers (left) are a big jump over high-temperature paint. The finish is pretty durable, but not bulletproof against rust. Small imperfections are not filled by nickel coating, nor is the finish even across the header. Those concerns are met by the more-expensive ceramic coatings (right), which leave a smooth, even satin finish that is much more durable. Blower and nitrous cars should definitely opt for ceramic coatings, as their higher exhaust temperatures are tough on the metal, especially in the collector area, where extensive welding weakens the metal. Any application in which looks are important or top durability is desired are definitely best with ceramic.

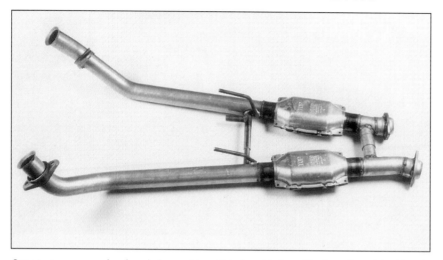

Street cars can run hard and clean with a high-flow H-pipe. The benefits of 2 1/2-inch, mandrel-bent pipes and premium, low backpressure converters provide the necessary flow improvement in street-driven 5.0s.

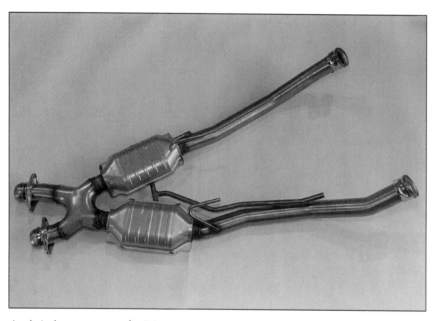

A relatively new concept for 5.0s, X-pipes are gaining popularity. Available with or without cats, X-pipes definitely improve the acoustic signature of the small-block Ford for street use by greatly reducing the throbbing boom at low rpm. The idea is to provide the engine with bank-to-bank balancing of the exhaust pulses, and while an X-pipe is not as effective as a 180 crankshaft or headers in this regard, it's still an improvement.

from torque to high-rpm horsepower. Near stock engines dramatically improve with long tubes, where they wake up the mid-range. On such mild engines the benefit is mainly in torque, as engine breathing is strangled at the top anyway, typically by the cylinder head or intake parts. That's not to forget that the move to long tubes is typically made with the elimination of the catalytic converters, so the improvement is dramatic.

For all of you wondering why Ford doesn't use long tubes, it's because the oxygen sensors need to sense all the cylinders on that bank. By the time long tubes collect in a long-tube design, the exhaust gas is too far from the engine for the computer to work with the information in time. Also, the exhaust cools as it travels away from the engine, and with long tubes, the gases are too cool to keep the catalytic converters working. The hotter the cats get, and the quicker they get hot, the better for the all-important cold-start test. It is even possible for the catalytic converters on long-tube installations to cool down and stop functioning at light throttle cruising on the freeway. So, short tubes are with us to stay.

H-Pipes

Like headers, there are plenty of 5.0 H-pipes on the market. Some are 2 1/4-inch replacements, most step up to 2 1/2-inch, which is always preferable for all applications.

We've already discussed cats vs. off-road pipes, but there is a third choice, high-flow cats. Legally cats may not be changed unless damaged or after 50,000 miles, and when it's time for replacement, high-flows are a definite power improvement. With so many high-mileage 5.0s on the market, high-flow cats are an excellent choice.

Still, even a high-capacity H-pipe offers more back pressure than an off-road pipe, and when reaching upward from the mid-300 horsepower level, that back pressure costs power. If you are wondering why your buddy's blown 5.0 is a tick faster than yours, and you have stock cats to his off-road pipes, then, unfortunately, you've probably found the answer. You'll have to look elsewhere for that power.

X-Pipes

A variation of the H-pipe is the X-pipe. Instead of using a cross-over tube, an X-pipe crosses the two main exhaust pipes in an X-shaped junction. This offers a much larger, easier path for merging of the exhaust gases. Like 99 percent of the all V-8 engines, the 5.0 HO ends up with firing impulses that are not evenly spaced along either bank of cylinders. This means the headers are not as efficient at bringing together the exhaust pulses in the right order as they could be. The X-pipe helps with this situation more than the cross-over tube in an H-pipe can.

The jury is still out on just how much power, if any, an X-pipe makes over an H-pipe on a street car. However, X-pipes do seem to really help reduce the booming

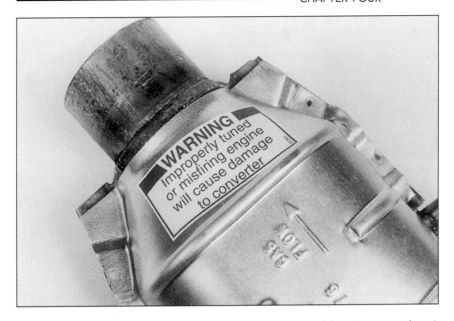

Rich mixtures can easily overheat a cat, causing it to burn out and clog. Transient rich periods, like those commonly found on typical 5.0 supercharger installations during mid-range rpm operation, don't seem to bother the cats too badly. Still, you want to keep your 5.0 tuned (avoid misfiring cylinders, which pump raw fuel down the exhaust) to keep your high-flow cats flowing freely. Conversely, new, right-out-of-the-box catalytic converters can apparently clean up anything for 500 miles, which is beneficial when trying to pass emission testing with a difficult car.

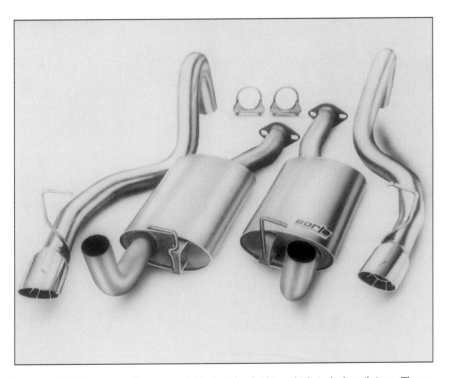

Late-model Mustang mufflers are sold in "cat-back" kits which include tailpipes. These bolt-on kits can be installed in the driveway by a determined owner, although exhaust work is always a pain. A whiz-wheel cutter is a godsend for removing the stock system, and hanging the new parts should be done with care to avoid annoying knocking noises. The Borla system is top of the line for looks, quietness at cruise, longevity, power support, and price.

exhaust note that can be so annoying in a street car. They tend to give a higher-pitched, higher-revving sound, but one that still sounds like a powerful V-8.

Cat-Back

Ford built the 5.0 with mufflers and tailpipes welded into a single unit. When changing mufflers you have to cut off the tailpipes, so the aftermarket sells muffler and tailpipe combinations for the 5.0. These are known as cat-back systems, and vary all over the map in price and quality, but mainly in sound production.

On mild cars, you can't beat the stock mufflers. For one, they're free, seeing they're already on the car. Secondly, designed to work with the cats that have a muffling effect, the stock mufflers are particularly efficient. On a stock engine with cats, the power difference between stock and completely open pipes (no mufflers or cats) is not even 10 horsepower; the best you can hope for with any muffler is half that, call it 4 horsepower. Add big nitrous or a blower and that number goes up, of course. The stock cat-back is stainless steel, so until it's at least five years old, there's no servicing excuse for replacing it. Finally, you can't beat the stock mufflers for quiet. No other muffler is as quiet, period.

Nearly every 5.0 muffler is sold for its sound, so if you like the boom of Flowmasters, the smoother baritone of Walkers, or the quiet idle and sporting WOT signature of Borlas, suit yourself. This is especially true on street cars. There is no power difference worth mentioning.

Strip warriors, slalom toys, and A-sedan contestants have ruggedness considerations with which street cars aren't as concerned. The heavy, aluminized, mild steel box construction of Flowmasters seems to get the nod for most of these applications. Flowmasters come in one-, two-, and three-chamber varieties. The two chambers are louder . . . a bit much for the street. They are especially outspoken when combined with an off-road pipe. The three-chambers are better street mufflers, and shouldn't hurt power much compared with two-chambers.

Standard bypass mufflers are called turbo mufflers from their original application on Chevy's Corvair turbo in the 1960s. They package well, sound fairly mellow, and are pretty good on power. This Pacesetter and the Walker are popular examples of the breed.

Fans of late-summer weather enjoy the rolling thunder of Flowmasters. Built strictly from welded steel, without any internal fiberglass insulation, Flowmasters have a distinct sound that's synonymous with 5.0 Mustangs. Flowmasters are durable in a heavy-metal sort of way, and come in one-, two-, and three-chamber varieties. Single chambers are for meeting "quiet roar" noise requirements at racetracks, two chambers are bearable by some on the street, while three chambers are nearly socially acceptable. Street cars should run the three chambers.

So-called turbo mufflers tend to be a bit quieter than the baffled can designs like the Flowmasters and their imitators. Many such two-pass mufflers are available, with Walker and Pacesetter being two of the better known names. Both have tested well when it comes to supporting power. At the top of the price scale is Borla, a premium design built of quality stainless steel. The Borlas give a mellower, quieter note, and support power well. Borla also makes premium racing-only mufflers.

Cat-Back Installation

Exhaust work is one step removed from blacksmithery, and considering it must be done under the car, requires more than hand tools (a torch, welder, and whiz wheel are all nice), and typically makes you work with rusted-shut hardware, it is less than the ultimate in driveway how-to projects. If you want to do the work, or need to save the money, make sure you can get the car high enough in the air with good jackstands. The stock cat-back system must be cut apart just aft of the mufflers (or the rear axle removed!) to get it out of the car, and even after cutting, considerable room between the floor of the car and ground is necessary to fish out the pipes. This part can be really tough when the car is on jackstands, as the jackstands are seemingly never tall enough. Taking the rear wheels and tires off helps.

Cutting the stainless pipe takes a sharp hacksaw blade and all day. If you have a whiz wheel or cutting torch, now is the time to use them.

Getting the new pipes in isn't as bad because the mufflers and tailpipes are separate pieces, joined by clamps. Whether installing just cat-backs or the entire system, it's vital to install all parts with the clamps loose before cinching anything down. Tightening the clamp crushes the pipes together to form a seal, and once tightened, they won't adjust. You'll need to support the entire system with stands until it is at the proper height, get all the hanger hardware correct, make final, small adjustments, then tighten the entire system.

If you want to avoid crushing the pipe with standard muffler clamps, use DynoMax Easy Seal stainless-steel strap bands. They wrap around the pipe in a wider swath so they don't crush the pipe, yet provide an effective seal, which can be taken apart and remade.

C
O
N
T
E
N
T
S

Inductive vs.
Capacitor 59

Maintenance 60

Forced Induction
Requirements 63

Aftermarket
Ignitions 63

Installation Tips 65

Distributors 65

Drive Gear 66

Battery 66

Timing the arrival of the spark in the cylinder is probably the most important power-making tool in the 5.0 tuner's toolchest. Unfortunately, many inexpensive timing lights are not that accurate or repeatable, so use a quality tool. MSD brought its timing light to market for just this reason; other name manufacturers also offer quality lights.

IGNITION

For all its computerized glory, the ignition system on a fuel-injected 5.0 Mustang isn't far removed from those found on its carbureted predecessors. Like them, it features a distributor and an inductive coil. Its timing curve, however, is controlled by the EEC-IV computer, which takes rpm, engine temperature, mass airflow, and throttle position into consideration to determine an engine load figure, then consults the spark tables to come up with the ignition timing based on that load figure.

Another way of saying it is the 5.0 HO distributor distributes the sparks and sets initial timing, but nothing else. From a tuning aspect, this eliminates recurving the distributor for a hotter ignition curve. However, simply twisting the distributor allows you to advance whatever curve the computer comes up with. This is crude ignition tuning, but it is usually quite beneficial, which is why everyone seems to run

around with 12 or 14 degrees of initial timing instead of the stock 10 degrees. The price is right, too.

Inductive vs. Capacitor

Ford gave the 5.0 engine a good ignition system, one easily powerful enough to handle stock duty, plus a relatively generous reserve for light bolt-on modifications. Ultimately, however, the system is limited by its "inductive" nature.

To explain, a conventional ignition coil, as on the 5.0, consists of a central iron "core" surrounded by two separate windings of copper wire. The "primary" winding consists of a few hundred turns of comparatively thick wire; the "secondary" winding has thousands of turns of much finer wire. When electric current from the battery flows through the primary, a magnetic field is created in the core, and maintained as long as current is flowing. But if this flow then suddenly stops, the magnetic field in the core collapses, and the stored magnetic energy "induces" a burst of electricity of several thousand volts in the secondary—thus the name "induction coil."

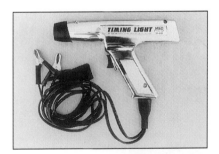

Even with all the electronic diagnostic tools in the world, the spark plug is still the only eyewitness to what's going on in the combustion chamber. While daily drivers with the usual bolt-on modifications don't really require it, anyone playing with supercharger pulleys or nitrous jets needs to learn how to read spark plugs on the insulator surrounding the center electrode. The No. 1 danger sign is small, glassed-over balls stuck to the porcelain. They are pieces of melted piston. More experience with the colors that show deeper, up inside the steel shell, can help with richening or leaning the mixture, but with unleaded fuels there is typically little color to see today. This plug looks basically okay, but is missing a small piece of the center electrode insulator.

Spark plug wires eventually wear out. Check their resistance with an ohm meter; it should not exceed 10 ohms. Also, the resistance should not change while the wire is handled. Such intermittent or variable resistance indicates a wire with a broken core. Replacement is the cure.

Basic ignition system maintenance is all that stands in the way of better performance on many real-world 5.0s. Wiping the distributor cap and internals with a clean, dry rag to remove carbon tracking is occasionally beneficial. More often, it may be necessary to dry this area with a rag to remove moisture accumulated from car washes and excessive humidity.

Ford uses aluminum contacts on the inside of its standard distributor cap, which leads to rapid corrosion. However, there is another Ford cap, and several aftermarket caps, with brass contacts. These resist corrosion better than aluminum, and are worth getting in humid climates.

The timed interruption of the current flow is accomplished by the distributor. After each discharge of the coil, the distributor restores the flow of current through the primary, and so reestablishes the magnetic field in the core, ready for another cycle.

The problem is that it takes a certain amount of time for the magnetic field to build to full strength again—for the core to become "saturated." Spinning the engine faster leaves less time for the coil to saturate, and above some high rpm, the coil simply can't keep up with the engine's appetite for sparks.

This high-rpm problem is not encountered on the street, because the ignition is designed to operate up to the stock 6,250-rpm rev limit and does a good job of it. Apart from poor maintenance, the practical problem under the rev limit is forced induction. When blowers, turbos, or nitrous increase cylinder pressure, the spark can actually be blown out. The solution is a high-output, capacitor-discharge (CD) ignition.

In a CD system, battery voltage is stepped up to a few hundred volts by a separate device called a DC-to-DC

converter, and this medium-high voltage is stored in a capacitor, or condenser. When triggered by the distributor, an electrical switch dumps the contents of the capacitor into the primary side of the coil and the sudden surge in current works very much the same way as a sudden interruption does in an inductive system—a brief burst of very high voltage from the secondary. Because the coil does not have to become saturated first, though, means that a CD system can operate at higher revs.

Another issue is changing the curve. By curve, I mean the amount of timing applied by EEC-IV for a given rpm and load. There is no way to do this directly with stock EEC-IV, but many aftermarket ignition retards are offered to tune the spark curve for use with

nitrous, blowers, and other sources of high cylinder pressure, and these are necessary tools. The practical concern is maintaining advanced ignition timing as supplied by the stock system when running at part throttle (light load) for good throttle response and fuel economy, then retarding the spark at high cylinder pressures (full throttle, under boost, with the nitrous on) to avoid detonation.

Maintenance

Whether you are running a blown street 5.0 or a naturally aspirated track car, the best ignition module is not going to make up for a poorly maintained ignition. A worn cap and rotor, leaky plug wires, or fouled plugs all lead to a miss, which is a problem on naturally aspirated 5.0s and death on forced-induction 5.0s.

Poor maintenance of the stock system is a major complaint of professional tuners when speaking of their customers. The stock system wears out, just like aftermarket ignitions, so periodic parts replacement is necessary, especially when cylinder pressure is increased.

A well-maintained 5.0 ignition can hang in there longer than you might think. There are plenty of 5.0s making 10 pounds of boost and running fastidiously maintained stock ignitions, so don't think a shiny new ignition box is automatically going to cure your troubles. Make sure the stock system is running perfectly first.

Spark Plugs

Gap erosion and fouling are the foremost spark plug enemies. All spark plugs burn open their gaps, and frequent plug changing is the best solution. Your 5.0 is always going to run its best with fresh plugs, no matter what the brand or style. For pure street cars, platinum plugs extend tune-up intervals considerably, but for max power on every track night, plan on buying plenty of plain-old plugs and changing them often. Even the slight residue left on a plug in a correctly running cylinder is conductive, and bleeds away plug effectiveness. Don't waste money on gimmicky plugs like Splitfires, either. Stick

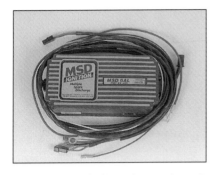

Granddaddy of all modern multispark CD ignitions is the MSD 6A. While the MSD ignition and control system is not integrated into just one box, as others are, the diversity of the MSD line-up allows a custom ignition and electronic control system at a reasonable price. MSD's line-up is full of 5.0 specific parts, too, so installation is pretty much a plug-in affair.

As long as you have places to mount them, MSD has control boxes to add. This "window switch" does not automatically raise your door windows at 120 miles per hour, it provides an rpm window where an accessory can be turned on or off. By quickly changing the two white "pills" at the bottom of the box, you decide what rpm band to build the window at. MSD offers the pills in 100-rpm increments and uses them on all sorts of devices.

with major manufacturers, with either platinum or conventional massive ground electrode designs. The supercharger manufacturers prefer massive ground plugs to help prevent detonation. If you are into indexing the spark plugs, some say the gap should lean to the right, toward the exhaust valve.

While the widest plug gap nets maximum horsepower, don't get carried away, especially with forced induction. The ignition current is looking for the path of least resistance to ground, and if the plug gap is too wide to jump, it will find another ground. This could be

down a dirty spark plug exterior which leads to the engine, or a faulty plug wire to a header. Such arcing and resultant "missing" can cause a big problem if a mixture preignites out of sync with the combustion cycle.

Use the chart below as a starting point when tuning:

Power Adder	Spark Plug Gap (in.)	Heat Range
stock	.054	stock
6-lb blower	.054	stock
10-lb blower	.045	1 colder
up to 150 hp nitrous	.054	stock
approaching 200 hp nitrous	.030–.035	1–2 colder

Closing the spark plug gap helps under high cylinder pressures, so if the ignition breaks down with a six-pound blower kit, don't be afraid to close gaps to 0.045 inch. Knowing when the ignition is breaking down is easy, once it happens to you. Suddenly the engine misses in a big way, stumbling and surging. This will only happen under high load and high rpm. If the engine suddenly starts bucking or missing near redline, suspect too wide a plug gap or other source of high resistance such as a bad plug wire.

Most tuners want a colder plug, even on mild 5.0s, for detonation protection. Forced induction 5.0s should run as cold a plug as possible for the same reason, the limit being plug fouling at light throttle. Running colder plugs makes the seemingly voodoo ritual of spark plug reading even more important. Tuners often remark that owners don't know a thing about plug reading, but should.

Examine each plug at the base of its insulator, the point where the white insulator meets the metal shell up inside the threads. This is usually a light brown, somewhere between the sooty black of dead rich and the white of piston-burning lean. Tell-tale purple coloring on the "cone" (the center porcelain insulator) means detonation occurred, and little balls of material stuck to the

insulator sides are a sure warning to back off the boost, nitrous, compression, or timing. Unfortunately, those shiny little balls are melted, departing pieces of piston, so get serious.

Consider all cylinders. Don't just check one plug, as cylinders don't all run evenly. Variations in coolant temperature—the back runs hotter than the front because it's farther from the coolant inlet at the water pump—and cylinder filling due to port and runner variations make a difference.

Spark Plug Wires

For stock and light bolt-on 5.0s, the factory spark plug wires are perfect. As you squeeze more power and the wires age from underhood heat, it's time to consider low-resistance wire.

Even if you increase ignition power, you don't want it restricted by stock wires. They use a cost-effective carbon core to reduce electromagnetic interference that causes "buzz" in radio reception, among other more serious problems, but are relatively high resistance. Quality replacement wires allow more spark energy to reach the plugs while maintaining adequate noise suppression.

In reducing resistance, you don't want to sacrifice suppression of electromagnetic interference, also called RFI for Radio Frequency Interference. It can foul the ignition and even the EEC, and is why unsuppressed wires are to be avoided at all costs. Durability is another critical factor. Heat is the major large influence on plug wire life, short of abusive handling by ham-fisted owners. Take boot configuration and construction into consideration. If you have equal-length, short-tube headers, do the boots clear? If you have a turbo, are the boots sufficiently shielded? In either case consider adding a thermal barrier (heat wrap or fire sleeve) over the boots, or purchasing wires with ceramic boots, like those sold by Jacobs Electronics. The latter is a good but pricey choice for severe-duty applications.

Setting Ignition Timing

For the home mechanic, there's one great thing about the 5.0 Mustang's ignition system—it uses a distributor. Because the 5.0's distributor times the ignition, making coarse ignition timing adjustments is as easy as rotating the distributor. That's an easy trick no newer car will ever have again, as distributors are phased out in favor of locked-in computer timing and multiple-coil ignitions.

To set a 5.0's timing, you want a reliable, accurate timing light and a 1/2-inch wrench for the distributor hold-down bolt. After hooking up the light, poke around just under the distributor until you locate the spout connector. This is a short pigtail of wires with a dead-end connector on it. In the connector is a small, removable module. Take it out.

What you have done is remove the spout connector, which, once out, takes out all ignition advance and sets the distributor to its base timing curve. If you set the timing with the spout connector in place, the timing will be off by some varying amount, so you must remove the spout connector. If you forget to remove the spout connector and set the timing, you can't be lazy; you must go back and set the timing properly.

With the connector out, start the engine and set the timing in the normal fashion, using the strobe light and the timing marks on the harmonic damper against the pointer on the front cover. When finished, replace the spout connector and you're done. Typical problems are not being able to see the timing marks and not remembering to deal with the spout connector. Taking the time to clean the timing marks is well worth the effort, and always removing and replacing the spout connector at the same point in your timing routine will help you to remember that step.

The $25 question is where to set the timing. Stock timing is 10 degrees before top dead center (BTDC), but everyone advances the stock timing when they first start hot rodding their 5.0s. Experimentation will zero in what works best for you, considering the variables of fuel quality, driving style, computer calibration, temperature, terrain, altitude, and so on. That said, 13 or 14 degrees initial timing gives peak power 99 percent of the time with average stock and bolt-on type cars. For a street-driven car, when you don't want to worry much about hot days or who's driving the thing, 12 degrees of advance is a good place to be. On the other hand, you'll hear stories about 18 or more degrees of initial timing, and while some people have undoubtedly used that much lead with some success, the dyno inevitably shows 14 degrees as the power peak.

Forced induction is a different story. Do not advance the timing from the stock 10 degrees if the engine is supercharged, nitrous-assisted, or so on. The risk of engine-damaging detonation is very real with forced induction, and the higher cylinder pressures from forced induction typically respond better to less aggressive timing anyway. When running lots of blower boost or nitrous, an ignition retard is necessary. With such a retard, it is possible to tune the initial ignition timing up to 12 or 14 degrees for better response, fuel mileage, and power when running naturally aspirated, then retard the spark when the boost comes on, using the ignition retard. Sneak up on this and always beware of detonation in force-inducted cars!

When moving up to computer chip tuning, the timing should be set to 10 degrees unless the chip supplier specifies otherwise. The interaction between the various engine sensors and the way the computer establishes ignition timing after consulting those sensors and factoring a load figure means the engine management works best and will have fewer drivability problems when working from the stock initial ignition timing point. Remember, when moving the distributor, you are adjusting the initial ignition timing and shifting the entire ignition curve, not changing the shape of the ignition curve. That can only be done electronically via chips or retard boxes.

Plug wire quality, even more than most aftermarket parts, ranges from world class to abysmal. Buying brand-name hardware is always smart, and be sure to avoid parts store bargain wires at any cost. They're junk.

Cap and Rotor

There's little wrong with the stock cap and rotor. Cleanups with sandpaper or a nail file and occasional replacement keep all but the slightest contact wear and carbon buildup at bay. To increase cap and rotor durability, you can buy replacement units from ACCEL, Ford, Jacobs, and Performance Parts, Inc., which feature more durable brass inserts.

In case you're wondering about the small knob on the outside of the distributor

To get the most out of CD ignitions, a CD-specific coil is necessary. Obviously, sticking with the same brand as the spark box and coil is smart, as the pair are designed to work together. The compact Crane PS92 that goes with the HI-6 allows easy mounting near the distributor, although the stock coil location works, too.

As cylinder pressure increases, the need for ignition advance decreases in the thick "atmosphere" provided by superchargers, turbos, and nitrous. As boost rises into the 8–10-pound range, the need to reduce ignition advance becomes mandatory to prevent detonation. Tuners now have an almost bewildering array of timing retard controls, from simple add-ons like this Crane that senses only rpm, through sophisticated stand-alone engine management systems that use laptop computer tuning to precisely control the spark. Typically such timing retards are cockpit mounted, but underhood works about as well and looks better.

cap, it's commonly called the ion port, and is actually a vent. It allows charged, or ionized, air inside the cap to escape. There's also the numeral one cast-in nearby; it denotes the terminal for the number one cylinder's plug lead.

Forced Induction Requirements

For naturally aspirated 5.0s, a tuned-up stock system augmented by low-resistance wires is plenty, but when applying forced induction, spark timing

and energy become much more critical. This is not only for power production, but for detonation prevention.

Spark energy is a tough concept for many enthusiasts, who often get sidetracked by advertised system voltage; voltage is not a measure of electrical energy. Technically, electrical energy is measured in joules. But rather than get bogged down in electrical engineering, here's an analogy: Let's say you want to light a huge log on fire. A match won't do the job, but a flame thrower will, even if no (equally sized) part of its flame is any hotter than the match. The difference is that the flame thrower puts out a much larger quantity of flame. That's what you want from an aftermarket ignition—a large quantity of electrical energy.

Furthermore, that large amount of ignition energy absolutely must arrive at the correct time. Too much spark advance (timing) will destroy your engine and insufficient advance will leave you lumbering down-track as your opponent whisks by. Short of computerized electronics, the primary choices for 5.0 timing management are piggyback ignitions with adjustable boost timing retards.

Like all tuning advice, dialing in ignition timing on blown and nitrous engines sounds deceptively simple in theory: advance timing at the distributor for good off-boost power, then back it out under boost as necessary with a retard. Regardless of the retard strategy, a high-output ignition is also mandated by forced induction and attendant high cylinder pressures. If you have an ignition retard already, a quick spin on a Dynojet can tell you wonders about how much retard vs. power is necessary. Just don't get too close to the edge. That is, back off a degree from maximum power on the dyno, unless you're tuning for that particular day. Otherwise, when the weather gets hotter, you risk detonation from too much timing advance.

Aftermarket Ignitions

Numerous aftermarket ignitions have been developed since the mid-1970s, and in recent years ignition manufacturers have built dedicated 5.0 Mustang ignition systems because of the

Stock 5.0 distributors are more than enough for bolt-on performance, but when they wear out, the aftermarket offers high-quality alternatives. MSD got things going with its line of billet distributors, one of which is a dedicated 5.0 part. Its main claim is accuracy, as production tolerances are held closely.

huge 5.0 market. Thus, you can buy several systems that plug right into the Ford wiring, a good deal because they avoid troublesome homemade wire splices and connectors.

Most aftermarket ignitions offer much more than increased spark energy. Timing retards, multistage rev limiters, rpm-controlled switches, and controllers are all found in ignition catalogs. The proper strategy is to plan out your 5.0's ultimate ignition and electronic control needs and then find the system that best integrates your needs.

MSD

The most time-tested name in aftermarket ignitions is MSD. It stands for Multiple Spark Discharge and offers multiple sparks for 20 degrees of crankshaft duration up to 3,000 rpm. While MSD offers a host of ignitions using this technology, those most applicable to 5.0 Mustangs are the 6A family. The MSD 6A simply offers capacitor discharge, while the 6AL and 6 BTM add a soft-touch rev limiter and boost timing retard. MSD also offers plug-in adapters, which allow fitting their ignitions to the factory system without cutting wires. The 6A family is plenty for any street car.

Racers running big boost, nitrous, or compression may need MSD's higher-output 7 or 8 Series ignitions, but never on the street. They also offer a host of ignition add-ons, like timing retards, shift lights, rev limiters, rpm switches, and spark plug wires.

When two cylinders are adjacent to each other both physically and in the firing order, there is a real danger of crossfiring. This happens when the two spark plug wires lie parallel with each other for several inches or more, thus transferring energy to each other via induction. The resulting crossfire costs power, and can be destructive at high cylinder pressures. On 5.0s, cylinders 5 and 6 are at risk; therefore their plug wires should be separated as far as is practical, using plug wire guides.

Crane

Crane Cams purchased Allison electronics to enter the ignition business. As with its camshafts, Crane's ignition products have been well received, especially its Hi-6 family, which is most applicable to the 5.0. The basic Hi-6 provides capacitor discharge and multiple sparks, for the first 20 degrees to 2,999 rpm, and the HI-6TR adds a boost timing retard. A Hi-7 is available for hard-core racers running plenty of boost, and Crane offers PS91 and PS92 coils. PS91s are fine for up to 10 pounds of boost, if you plan to run beyond that in the future, you might as well step up to the PS92, which can only be run with a CD ignition. Crane also offers a stand-alone boost retard and low-resistance spark plug wires.

ACCEL

ACCEL's "plus" line of ignitions packs capacitor discharge power in a compact, expandable package. ACCEL's 300+ ignition is ideal for most 5.0 Mustangs. It offers multiple sparks up to 3,500 rpm and a computer-controlled rev limiter, which alternates the limiter through the firing order to avoid fuel buildup in the cylinders. This system comes as a bolt-on kit (PN 49326), which includes a coil and a plug-in harness, for 5.0s. Also available from ACCEL are a trio of adjustable controls: timing computer, three-stage rev limiter,

and multistep timing retard. Like most of the other companies discussed here, ACCEL also offers shift lights, high-performance spark-plug wires and the like.

Holley

Like Crane, Holley is another old-school hot rodding company that jumped into the ignition market. Also like ACCEL and Crane, Holley's capacitor discharge Annihilator line-up features microprocessor-controlled functions, unlike the analog MSD.

Annihilators start with the HP Annihilator, which simply offers capacitor discharge and one rev limiter. The Strip Annihilator has three rev limiters, two rpm switches, a start-up retard of 0–20 degrees, and a QuickShot Programmer. The ProStrip Annihilator serves up four rev limiters, four rpm switches, four timing retards, a boost retard, a built-in timing computer, and a QuickShot Programmer—not for the guy who can't operate a VCR.

Aside from Holley's all-in-one packaging, the slickest aspect of the Annihilator systems is the QuickShot Programmer. This two-button, two-LED hand-held controller allows you to write all your timing settings to a rewriteable EPROM, so even if the battery goes dead, your settings remain and can be infinitely adjusted. Initially, Holley did not offer a plug-in 5.0 harness for its Annihilator ignitions. It does offer matching wires and coils.

Mallory

Mallory rejects the popular multiple-spark philosophy in its ignition offerings, preferring to light the mixture with one powerful spark. Its systems do use capacitor discharge to increase the spark energy.

Mallory ignitions, sold under the HyFire brand, include the HyFire CD/IS, HyFire IVa, and HyFire IVc. The HyFire CD/IS combines a capacitor discharge and inductive storage ignition in one box. It includes two rev limiters and exemplifies Mallory's single-spark mentality. HyFire IVa simply offers capacitor discharge and uniform output, while the IVc adds two

Installing Crane's HI-6

Installing Crane's HI-6 is roughly similar to fitting other aftermarket 5.0 ignitions. A spot for the spark box must be located, then mounting holes drilled and wires connected. The following photos give an idea of what's involved in this home garage job.

Step one in installing an aftermarket ignition on a 5.0 is finding a place for it. This car has a K&N FIPK filter, which dispenses with the stock airbox. Thus, there was extra room on the passenger-side inner fender. For the top holes, the self-tapping screws provided by Crane were used. On the lower holes longer screws and a stack of washers were required to achieve a level installation.

We trimmed back the wires not needed for our application, per Crane's instructions. That left power, ground, and another four wires which coincidentally match those on the plug-in harness. The ground is piggybacked with a nearby factory ground and the other five wires were bundled and routed across the engine. After installing the inconspicuous PS-91 on the factory coil bracket, we plugged the adapter harness in series between the factory harness and the new coil, as shown here. The PS-91 can easily be added by itself as a first step.

After crimping on female spade connectors, the HI-6 wires are plugged in with the corresponding wires on the adapter harness. Color coding makes this easy. The power wire was the only wire needing extension after routing the loomed set across the engine. It took its own crimp-on connector and was attached to the battery terminal. Plug in the coil wire, reattach the battery cable, and you're done. The loose wires can also be neated up with a few zip ties or plastic sleeving.

Here is the HI-6 with the air filter reinstalled. Extra clearance for the ignition module was gained by tweaking the filter's front support bracket. If your Mustang has its stock airbox, this mounting location won't work; a popular solution is to trunk-mount the battery and install the ignition on the driver-side inner fender.

adjustable rev limiters. Also available from Mallory and BBK is Mallory's Boost Timing Control. This pricey inductive ignition delivers a wealth of trick features.

Jacobs Electronics

Another inductive ignition is Jacobs Electronics. Jacobs markets all-in-one OmniPak and OmniMagnum systems, as well as more serious Energy Pak Mileage Master, Pro Street, Pro 10, and Marine Master setups. The Pro Street system offers one rev limiter, while the Pro 10 is equipped with two. Jacobs also markets a series of coils, plug wires, timing retards, rpm switches and anti-theft devices. Their ceramic-booted severe-duty wires are a favorite of turbo owners because they handle extreme heat well.

Installation Tips

Where to mount your aftermarket ignition is regulated by mounting room. As such, where you mount it plays a part in how you mount it. If your 5.0 is stock, you'll find it difficult to find an empty space underhood, depending, of course, on the size of the box. Small units like the BBK/Mallory BTC and the ACCEL 300+ can go behind the driver-side shock tower. Those opting for MSD's 6a or Crane's HI-6 ignitions could use the trick Ignition Box Bracket, marketed by Verdich Engineering. It mounts the spark box beneath the factory battery tray. Relocating the battery to the trunk not only aids handling, but opens an expanse on the driver-side inner fender.

When selecting a mounting site, cooling air is important, but not at the expense of water splash. Also, in high vibration applications (race cars or bumpy terrain), use rubber isolators between the ignition and the mounting spot. The easy way to avoid all these challenges is to extend the wiring and mount the box inside the cockpit, preferably hidden under a seat. This protects it from the elements and makes the applicable rev limiters accessible for use as valet limiters.

Distributors

The stock Duraspark distributor is good for almost anything when augmented by a high-output ignition box and a set of low-resistance plug wires. All it does is distribute the spark, so as long as all its connections are clean and the bearings relatively tight to prevent spark wander from a wobbly distributor shaft, it should be fine. For high-rpm racing, ACCEL, MSD, and Mallory all offer billet distributors, and these make fine replacements for worn high mileage stockers.

Some superchargers and intake manifolds encroach on the stock distributor location. Kuntz and Company offers an offset version of MSD's billet distributor in that case. A distributorless ignition is a lighter, cleaner, more accurate alternative, but the electronic hookups are much more difficult.

Drive Gear

When swapping in an aftermarket distributor, it is important to remember hydraulic roller camshafts found in 5.0s demand the use of a 0.498-inch (inside diameter) steel distributor gear. Use of a cast-iron gear will result in rapid wear and metal shavings throughout the engine. Bronze gears are available, but wear out in about 10,000 miles and lead to timing scatter. There's a bit more on this in Chapter 1, under the Camshaft heading.

Many times you are better off with a wrecking yard, or new distributor if all you need is a fresh distributor gear, as the gear is already set up on the shaft. If you do replace the gear, you'll have to redrill the dowel pin hole through the gear and distributor shaft, as Ford does not center the holes. Alternately, SVO offers the proper replacement steel gears.

Battery

There's no rocket science in a 5.0's battery, but it is critical to producing horsepower. Keep the battery clean, charged, and well grounded and you'll save yourself many tuning goose-chases. This is because modern ignition systems draw around seven amps and the fuel pumps are electrically hungry as well; a so-so battery costs ignition energy and fuel flow. That's why even drag cars should run a charging system. The Pro 5.0 crowd uses so much electrical power that managing the electrical load is

something they work at, and they're already running stout alternators.

Despite pit-rail experts, there is nothing gained by draining the EEC-IV memory by momentarily disconnecting the battery. The EEC-IV relearns very quickly, the newer the Ford the faster, and in mere seconds of operation it will adapt to conditions. By far the best thing you can do with the battery is relocate it over the right rear tire.

Underdrive pulleys are popular, but they should not be overdone. Unless truly racing, stick with street-ratio underdrive pulleys or you'll have trouble keeping the battery charged. As battery voltage drops, ignition system and fuel pump efficiency drop, hurting performance.

Mustang Electrical Specifications
Ignition

Type	Inductive
Timing	Universal-Hall Effect (in distributor)
Firing Order	1, 3, 7, 2, 6, 5, 4, 8
Cylinder Numbering System	
Right bank	1, 2, 3, 4
Left bank	5, 6, 7, 8
Knock Sensor	None
Spark Plug	Motorcraft ASF-42C (ASF-32 is one step colder)
Spark Plug Gap	.054 inch

Electrical System

Battery	12 volt
Cold Cranking Amps	540
Reserve Capacity	100 minutes
Amp/hr, 20-hr rate	58 (since 1988)
Alternator Rating:	
1986–1993	75 amp/hr
1996–1995	130 amp/hr
Regulator	Electronic, w/integral regulator

Starting System

Motor	Motorcraft
Current Draw	290–315 amps
Power Rating	1.7 horsepower

CONTENTS

The 5.0 Fuel System 67

Definition of Terms 68

FUEL

Designing an adequate fuel delivery system is one of the most frequently overlooked modifications by the average hot rodder. Lack of familiarity with engine requirements and the confusing array of technologies found in electronic fuel injection can make for migraine headaches.

Also, with the advent of high-performance engines from Detroit in the 1950s and 1960s, very few so called "super cars" came with even a close approximation of a fuel system that could properly supply the engines they were feeding. Two four-barrel Holleys and 427 cubic inches will not work with 5/16 fuel line and a six-pound mechanical fuel pump, but because the car was delivered that way, most people never questioned the installation. They tended to spend their money on other go-fast parts, and ended up wondering why their vehicles were not going much faster. Upgrading the fuel system from the fuel tank forward never caught on with enthusiasts. It is not unreasonable to expect a factory fuel system to meet all the needs of an unmodified car, but it is unreasonable to expect a stock fuel system to keep up with a modified engine.

With that in mind, the first thing to understand is an engine needs a certain amount of fuel to make a certain amount of horsepower. This simplistic statement sounds stupid at first, but is the key to lost performance in many modified and racing vehicles. Many of us have had a vehicle that ran very well for the setup we were using, and then with just one further tweak that was "really going to make a difference," like a hotter camshaft or new cylinder heads from your ex-NASCAR mechanic neighbor, the blasted thing ran the same, or worse yet, slowed down. Many times such engines never exhibit any fuel starvation symptoms, such as popping or stuttering, white spark plugs, bog, or whatever, but can stubbornly refuse to pull through the gears or run the expected miles per hour.

The 5.0 Fuel System

Before discussing how to augment the 5.0 Mustang fuel system (5.0 truck fuel systems are essentially the same), a review of the stock system is necessary. Fuel is kept in the tank, which is mounted behind the rear axle and retained by a pair of steel straps. Inside the tank, accessible through a hole in the top of the tank once the tank has been lowered, is the electric 88-liter per hour vane-type fuel pump. The pump is submerged in the tank, so the gasoline can muffle the pump's high pitched whine. (Yes, the electric pump runs while bathed in gasoline.) Attached to the pump and its sheet metal bracket are a short-metal pickup tube with a sock-like filter fitted over it, and a return line tube. Also accessible from atop the tank is the fuel level sender.

Inside the fuel tank, gasoline is sucked up by the pump via a fuel pump pickup and sent through a 5/16-inch diameter metal fuel line running under the car to the engine compartment. There the fuel passes through a relatively short section of

With the exception of some of SVO's pumps, replacement in-tank fuel pumps are sold by themselves, or with just a new sock filter. This means swapping the pump into the in-tank assembly, which is no big deal other than having to drop the fuel tank. When advancing past the bolt-on stage of power building, the in-tank pump is typically eliminated by a large diameter fuel pump pickup, and all pumping is done by pumps external to the fuel tank. This results in less restriction to the large capacity inline pumps.

Inline fuel pumps are available in nearly any size or capacity. For bolt-on applications a single inline boosts fuel delivery nicely; racier applications may run larger or dual pumps, like this twin installation. Inline pumps can be quite noisy, so street cars should use isolation mountings, and hard-launching drag cars do best with a fuel sump built into the fuel tank or cell. It is important to ensure the pump never draws air, or you risk pump failure as well as leaning the engine. A fuel sump traps enough fuel to avoid such momentary dry-outs.

rubber fuel line, which passes up from low under the right fender to the right front corner of the engine. A Schraeder valve, the type of valve used on a tire, is provided in this area for bleeding air out of the system after servicing and for hooking up a fuel pressure gauge. The fuel rail is a chromed metal pipe that runs atop the lower intake manifold, directly above the four fuel injectors on the right side. The 19-pound injectors have O-rings at both their tops and bottoms. This allows their bottoms to simply slide into the lower intake manifold, and their tops into the fuel rail, without the bother of hoses and clamps. The fuel rail is bolted to the

Ford uses spring lock connections to join the fuel lines at several key points on the 5.0 Mustang. These connectors require special tools to disconnect; reassembly is a simple push together operation. Shown here is the very inexpensive disconnect tool available in any auto parts store. A bit awkward to use, they'll get you through the occasional use. Pro mechanics use slightly more expensive plastic collar tools that wrap around the fitting. These may be more difficult to find, but any tool truck should have them. Typically they are color coded for size; you want the red and green tools.

lower intake manifold so that, once assembled, the injectors are captured between the rail and intake.

At the end of the fuel rail, a length of rubber hose leads the fuel to the left side of the engine, where another fuel rail and four injectors await. At the end of this fuel rail, the gasoline is routed back under the car in a second 5/16-inch line paralleling the supply line. The return line returns unused fuel to the fuel tank.

Thus, the system is designed to constantly circulate fuel from the tank to the engine, with any unused fuel returning to the tank. This keeps the fuel from sitting in any one spot too long and soaking up enough engine heat to boil in the fuel line (vapor lock). On long drives the fuel in the tank will absorb a surprising amount of heat from its trips across the top of the engine, but vapor lock is still not a 5.0 problem.

Because the injectors need a constant 38–42 psi of fuel pressure to correctly meter fuel, a nonadjustable diaphragm regulator is fitted at the beginning of the return fuel line, next to the right fuel rail. In this position it controls the amount of fuel returning to the tank, and thus the fuel pressure upstream of it, between the pump and the fuel rails.

The injectors are electrically opened and closed by command of the EEC-IV computer. The amount of time the injector is open is called the pulse width, or occasionally dwell time, of the injector. It's smart to note that the injectors open and close, or "fire," in engine firing order. This is called sequential firing. It times the injector's squirt of fuel with the opening of the intake valve, so each electrical connector to the injectors must be hooked up to the appropriate injector. If the injector wiring is hooked up randomly, the engine will still run and drive fairly normally, but you'll know something isn't quite right as power will be low and the engine rough.

Truck 5.0 engines with speed/density EEC-IV are bank (sometimes called "batch") fire designs. That is, all the injectors on one side (bank) of the engine open and close at once, then the other bank opens and closes. This system is older and simpler, and delivers slightly poorer fuel economy.

Definition of Terms

First, we need to define some fuel system terminology, such as pounds per hour, BSFC, liters per hour, specific gravity, and gallons per hour. If you find these terms difficult to understand, you are not alone. Many of the different fuel system rating methods and terms are based on scientific convention, while others are arbitrary. To get a handle on these terms, all you really need to understand is how to mathematically convert from one to another, so in the end you know what you have to work with.

BSFC is the abbreviation for Brake Specific Fuel Consumption, a scientific term for rating the efficiency of an engine. It helps to understand that the term "brake" refers to the engine dyno, which is scientifically referred to as a brake, as in brake horsepower—"bhp." Anyway, BSFC is not a measurement of air/fuel mixture, as many believe, but simply a value or number that describes how efficiently a particular engine converts fuel into horsepower. The result is fuel used (measured in pounds of fuel per hour) divided by horsepower.

Just behind and to the left of the distributor is the fuel system test port. It's a simple Schraeder valve, which can be used to relieve fuel pressure before working on the fuel system, or purge air after the system has been opened. Put a rag over the valve when releasing pressure to avoid spraying fuel into your eyes or onto hot surfaces. Always beware of fire when working with gasoline; it's powerfully dangerous stuff.

on capacity, engine No. 2 will be down on power in the car compared to engine No. 1. Because the average enthusiast has no way of determining the BSFC for the engine without testing on a dyno, you must design a fuel system with some rule of thumb assumptions and add in a safety factor.

Liters per hour is the new way to measure fuel pumps for fuel injection systems. In our government's and the manufacturers' effort to bring our industry into compliance with the rest of the world, we now measure soda pop and fuel in liters. The conversion is 1 liter = 0.264 gallons, or 1 gallon = 3.785 liters. Thus, the popular Ford "High Volume" 110-liter per hour fuel pump will deliver 29.08 gallons per hour and the 190-liter per hour pump will yield 50.16 gallons per hour.

Gallons per hour has been the common way of rating fuel pumps, and is self-explanatory. It should be noted that until recently, most of these ratings

For example, a particular engine is tested on a dynamometer and found to make 400 horsepower and consume fuel at a rate of 220 pounds per hour. This is a BSFC of 220/400 or 0.55. The lower the BSFC number, the more efficiently the engine converts fuel into power. Typically BSFC numbers range from the low 0.40s on extremely efficient engines, up to 0.60 for a real fuel hog. Supercharged, turbo, and nitrous engines run toward the rich side when under boost and should be expected to return a brake specific of 0.6 under boost. This is because extra fuel is used to cool combustion and avoid detonation.

When an engine is evaluated, the BSFC number can show if one combination is more efficient than another. For example, two engines the same size and built with different combinations both make 500 horsepower. Engine No. 1 has a BSFC of 0.45 and engine No. 2 has a BSFC of 0.52, which means that engine No. 1 is using 250 pounds per hour of fuel and engine No. 2 is using 260 pounds of fuel per hour. Both engines run the same in the vehicle, but if the fuel system in the vehicle is short

The stock fuel pressure regulator is not adjustable, but is sensitive to manifold vacuum. You can manipulate the vacuum the regulator sees by hooking up a hand-held vacuum pump to it. More vacuum leans the mixture, less richens it. This occasionally comes in handy when tuning, provided you have a way of measuring the engine's fuel mixture or are willing to do some trial and error testing. Just remember to err in the rich direction first. The regulator is at the rear portion of the passenger side fuel rail.

Pro 5.0 racers have been quite inventive in managing fuel volume and pressure with mechanical regulators and FMUs. Compared to the control offered by electronics, such systems are fairly primitive and are responsive to relatively few conditions. Thus, they are successful at the drag strip, where idle and WOT are the only operating parameters that matter, but are not seen elsewhere. This older sort of fuel management is increasingly yielding to electronic control, thanks to the growing number of add-on electronics and custom-tuned chips. Adjustable fuel pressure regulators, like the squared-off guy shown here, are much better than fiddling with the stock regulator, and offer true adjustability rather than test-only manipulation.

represent the "free flow" of fuel, not flow at five to eight pounds through a regulator and 12 feet of fuel line and fittings. For example, the popular Holley "Blue" pump in carbureted applications is rated at 110 gallons per hour free flow, but reduces to 70 gallons per hour at nine psi.

Specific gravity is the weight of something—in this case fuel—compared to the weight of the same volume of water. The specific gravity is published by the fuel refiner, which allows you to calculate the precise weight of your fuel via simple multiplication. If your fuel has a rated specific gravity of 0.75, then multiply 0.75 X 8.31 (the weight of water per gallon at 74 degrees Fahrenheit) to determine that your fuel weighs 6.23 pounds per gallon.

Okay, what does this all mean? Well, say we have an engine that hopefully will make an honest 500 horsepower, and we want to know its minimum fuel requirements. First, we assume that even though this may be a killer combination and may have excellent BSFC characteristics, we will use the somewhat inefficient figure of 0.6 as a design number. (It gives a useful safety

margin to use an inefficient, or "rich" BSFC value.) This means 0.6 X 500 horsepower = 300 pounds per hour of fuel at maximum power. If we assume the gas we are using has a specific gravity of 0.75, we will need to have fuel delivery at the injector fuel rail of 48 gallons per hour (300/(.75 X 8.31)), or 182 liters per hour (48 X 3.785).

Doesn't sound like much fuel flow, does it? Just slap in a 190-liter per hour pump and forget about it. But here is the final fly in the ointment: Engines that accelerate at high rates of speed need a fuel system with nearly double their steady-state fuel consumption when accelerating. This is because the airflow is increasing very rapidly, and moving ever-increasing amounts of fuel to match the airflow is not easy. Fuel is much heavier than air and requires much more energy to accelerate. Thus, when the throttle snaps open, the air rushes into the engine in relatively little time, while the fuel system struggles to heave a matching amount of fuel out of the tank and to the injectors.

On top of this, empirical evidence from the drag racing world shows that fast accelerating engines want even

more fuel when winding up quickly than that calculated to match the airflow. As an example, super gas race cars free-flow a gallon of fuel in 30 seconds through all of the filters, lines, fittings, and regulators, as measured by the carburetor. In other words, the fuel capacity is 120 gallons per hour to satisfy this requirement. That's 2.5 times the fuel flow required to make 500 steady-state horsepower. Again, for our rule-of-thumb engineering, what is necessary is building a fuel system with approximately twice the capacity of the engine's highest steady-state fuel requirement.

Free flow is not what is happening in the car! A factor frequently overlooked is the sudden acceleration generated on the starting line from a hard launch at the drag strip. A good launch will yield over 1.0 *g* and the fuel in the line from the pump to the carburetor will suddenly "weigh" several pounds opposing the fuel pump output. This can lead to the fuel slowing down or actually stopping in the lines for a short period. When this happens, the engine continues to consume fuel, and the system has to play catch-up to keep from leaning out. When the fuel system can't maintain the required fuel flow, the mixture leans out, leading to loss of power. This won't always result in a obvious miss, especially with the good ignitions available today.

A common rule of thumb for a fuel system in a super gas-type race car is one that can free-flow a gallon of fuel in 30 seconds through all of the filters, lines, fittings, and regulators, measured at the carburetor. Well, this means that our system capacity needs to be 120 gallons per hour to satisfy this requirement, 2.5 times the actual fuel flow required to make 500 horsepower.

So, for general purposes, figure your maximum power level, calculate the fuel requirement, and multiply by 2.5 to arrive at a free-flow value. This is easily measured by timing how long it takes to fill a gallon can of fuel at the fuel rail, but obviously you must be extremely careful of fire when handling fuel in this manner. If you've never seen a fuel-fed fire, it is difficult to imagine

Pro 5.0 racers have found increasing parts of the electrical system voltage to 14, 16, and sometimes even 18 volts useful, as it spins fuel pumps faster and makes a hotter spark. Accuvolt systems are popular with the racers. On the street, Kenne Bell offers the Boost-a-Pump, a simple cockpit-mounted control unit that raises fuel pump voltage, thus increasing fuel volume via higher pump speed. The maximum increase is 50 percent more voltage, for a total of 18 volts. This should give an approximately 50 percent increase in fuel volume. Kenne Bell uses the BAP to run the ignition timing, boost, and fuel grade on "safe" during the week, then turn up the boost with a pulley change for track duty on the weekends. Simply turning up the Boost-a-Pump on Saturday night brings in the extra fuel demanded by the extra supercharger boost. The trick is knowing how much air and fuel you're fiddling with—a good job for a Dynojet tuning session.

Mechanical FMUs are at least sturdy, reliable, and the one sure way to avoid burning down power adder engines from too lean a fuel mixture. All FMUs sense boost via a vacuum hose, moving a diaphragm inside. This closes the return fuel line to the gas tank, thus raising fuel pressure and volume available at the fuel rail. By varying the aggressiveness of the diaphragm, a coarse control of the enrichment is achieved. The trouble with FMUs is that they are mechanical devices inserted into an electronically controlled fuel system. This is especially evident when combined with centrifugal superchargers, where they typically deliver a very rich 9-to-1 air/fuel mixture in the mid-range, then progressively lean with rpm until at the horsepower peak, the air/fuel ratio is in the very high 11-to-1 or low 12-to-1 range. More power can be made in the mid-range if the mixture is leaned with electronics

just how fast it can spread, or how seemingly impossible it is to put out.

Now that we have defined some terminology, and have a closer handle on fuel system flow requirements, let us examine the issues around electronic fuel injection. There seem to be a few "black magic" theories circulating regarding secret calibrations, and fuel pressure tricks that will somehow make a stock fuel system support mega horsepower. There is also some severe misunderstandings of the relationship of fuel injector size, and the power and rpm ranges that are possible.

The 5.0's fuel system has several design advantages: The fuel is at a relatively high pressure and is not overly sensitive to the "surge" effect of acceleration, mentioned above; the fuel is constantly being circulated from the tank to the engine and back to the tank, avoiding heat saturation of the fuel and resulting vapor lock; and

Complete fuel systems are the latest addition to the long list of 5.0-specific parts and systems. This one is from Vortech and includes dual T-Rex pumps and all necessary hardware and fittings. The advantages of a fuel kit are that the owner knows he's getting a matched set of components, and there's no need to run wild digging up the numerous fittings. Vortech's system will easily handle 450 horsepower with reserve capability, and could go much higher on an efficient engine. It certainly will handle the typical 10 pounds of boost, stock cam, and mild cylinder heads with ease. Other outfits offer nearly complete fuel system coverage, with Paxton having a line-up more complete than most, including very high capacity pumps for the pure race market.

because the fuel is being regulated by returning excess fuel to the tank rather than restricting the amount of fuel being fed forward, the entire capacity of the fuel system can be put to use without restriction by the regulator. At idle, almost all the fuel is returned to the tank, while at WOT, only enough fuel is bled off to maintain the pressure set by the regulator.

A stock 5.O HO engine is equipped with an 88-liter per hour fuel pump (about 144 pounds per hour) and injectors rated for 19 pounds per hour fuel delivery at 40-psi fuel pressure. Using the formulas to convert to horsepower, we see that with 0.6 BSFC, the injectors can only support 253 horsepower and the pump only 240 horsepower.

"Wait a minute," you say. "We all know that you can make over 300 horsepower with a stock 5.0!" Yes, this is true under the right conditions. But the combination of cam, heads, manifold, and mixture has to be a good match, because to support that much power, the engine must be very efficient in converting fuel to horsepower. The BSFC would have to be 0.50 to make that power. Fortunately, with the good distribution inherent in fuel injection, these efficiency numbers are attainable.

To make more power with these 19-pound injectors, we need to increase the efficiency of the engine (difficult) or somehow get more fuel into the engine. If the injector is rated for 19 pounds per hour at 40 psi, it will flow more fuel

with higher pressure. So, to squeeze the most out of a particular injector, the fuel pressure can be manually set higher with an adjustable regulator for small mixture adjustments, or if a larger amount of extra fuel is required, double the pressure. This is a common technique with many nitrous oxide and supercharger kits. A special auxiliary fuel control regulator (FMU, or Fuel Management Unit) is spliced into the return line of the fuel system, and when conditions require extra fuel (during boost), the FMU restricts or shuts off the fuel return to the tank and all of the output of the fuel pump is directed into the fuel rail.

This is great until the pump can't keep up and the engine needs more fuel than the system can supply. For one thing, it is a characteristic of the pump that the fuel flow volume decreases as the pressure required from the engine increases, so fuel volume is decreasing many times just when it is needed most.

Also, the increase in fuel flow with an increase in pressure is not linear, meaning that doubling the fuel pressure does not double the fuel flow through the injector; the increase is more on the order of 15 to 20 percent, so this technique has its limits. Knowing all this, we can calculate that, under ideal conditions, we might squeeze 22 pounds per hour out of the injector, and assuming 0.5 BSFC, we can make 352 horsepower.

Okay, what's wrong with this picture? Consider that we are dealing in maximum ratings, and the whole idea behind electronically controlling the injector is to have control of the mixture. If the engine power level requires 100 percent of the injector, and we cheat it upward even more by playing with the fuel pressure, we have bypassed any control we may need and have effectively converted from EFI to mechanical fuel injection. To properly select an injector size we must first look at how the injector works, and the electronic signal that comes from the ECU.

The mixture is varied electronically by use of "pulse width modulation" of the injector. The principle is simple. Like a light switch, the injector has only two states: on or off. The ECU turns the injector on, then off, the complete action being a single pulse. By varying the on time versus off time during an individual pulse, the amount of fuel delivered is varied. When the injector is on all of the time

(100 percent duty cycle), the injector is wide open and no more fuel can flow. To understand how this works in an engine, consider that we have the element of time to contend with, and this is where most of the complications and misunderstandings occur. This is very important to realize when programming aftermarket fuel injection ECUs, when the rev control is bypassed on the stock EEC and mixture control is needed at higher rpm. If your 19-pound injectors are already locked open by 6,000 rpm, the fuel flow will not increase from that point on no matter how much pulse width the tuner types into the program. Tuners report seeing vehicles programmed with pulse widths twice as long as the time available to fire the injector. Larger injectors will solve this problem, but a new factor comes into play when larger and larger injectors are used—trying to get a smooth idle and low speed control.

Let's say we want to make 400 horsepower at 7,000 rpm. Furthermore, we want a larger injector that is not maxed out, to be able to adjust the pulse width and thus control the mixture. To keep control of the injector, we do not want to exceed about an 80 percent duty cycle, so we calculate that using an efficient BSFC factor of 0.5, we need 200 pounds per hour total, or 25 pounds per hour per injector. But if that is at 80 percent duty cycle, then the injector needs to supply 31.2 pounds per hour at 100 percent duty cycle—and we thought 30-pound injectors were pretty radical. Okay, so we run out and buy 38-pound injectors just to be safe, and guess what? Now it runs like a banshee on top end but fouls the plugs and is hard to start.

The fuel requirement is so small at idle, compared to maximum power, that the pulse width required is smaller than the injector can respond to when turning on and off again completely. This is called hysteresis, or just call it the delay in reaction of the injector to the control pulse. If we feed a pulse to the injector long enough to get any fuel at all, we get too much.

Once an individual injector requirement is so large the engine loses control for low-speed operation, computer chips are mandatory for regaining control of the fuel system. This works very well. For example, 38-pound injectors on a nearly stock engine can work well if a chip is used. With superchargers, it is possible to gain some flexibility with the careful sizing of the injectors and use of the auxiliary fuel control valve bypass regulator (FMU) to extend the operating range of a smaller injector by boosting pressure, as discussed earlier.

It is imperative that some form of pressure regulation be used when using a supercharger with a larger mass air meter and large injectors. If the manifold has 8 psi of boost, and the regulator was set for 40 psi and has no connection to the manifold, the net pressure on the injector is 32 pounds At a minimum, we need to have 1 pound increase of fuel pressure for each pound of boost, even if the injector is large enough to handle the horsepower without an FMU, simply to overcome the pressure working against the injector inside the manifold. While other fuel systems are certainly possible, we have covered most of the requirements of a high-volume performance fuel system for popular 5.0 racing and high-performance street applications.

CONTENTS

Power Adding as a
Kit 74

Street, Strip, or
Track? 75

Convenience 76

Future Increases 76

Cost 76

You must have a plan when building up your 5.0, or you'll waste money impulse-buying parts you don't need and miss parts you should have bought. Monitoring the Ford magazines is smart, and working with a pro engine builder is also important. A good one should help you plan your engine build and keep you on track. The experience such guys offer is golden, so listen carefully.

POWER ADDERS

The term "power adder" is relatively new. It means an add-on system that fundamentally increases engine power. Power adders include supercharging, turbocharging, nitrous oxide, and in the 5.0 world, I'm including increased displacement because of the popularity of stroker kits for the 302. You could say an engine swap to the 351W is a power adder to the 5.0 Mustang, but is a different engine, after all, so we'll stop with the stroker kits.

Another power adder in reality, but not in common thought or most rule books, is the head and intake package. Starting with a stock 5.0, then adding a GT-40, Edelbrock, Roush, or Holley package, certainly has a power adder effect, although some would say it isn't an add-on engine accessory, but rather engine tuning. Because they are sold as matched systems in kits, and roughly approximate the blowers and turbos in price, they're best thought of as power adders. They certainly compete with the blowers and nitrous in your mind when

laying out an engine-building strategy, and because this chapter is devoted to helping you select a power adder, if any, I'll refer to the induction packages here.

Power Adding as a Kit

There have always been superchargers, nitrous oxide kits, and the like, but it wasn't until the mid-1980s that these powerful engine add-ons came into wide use. It was a systems approach that made these viable alternatives to conventional, normally aspirated hot rodding. The modern power adders have been packaged as bolt-on systems by their manufacturers. Before the mid-1980s, the Paxton had been packaged for use on early Mustangs, but nitrous oxide was something mysterious you bought in a bottle and you had to do the plumbing yourself; turbos were bought the same way and the only other superchargers available were roots designs. Those too were barely packaged, and were just for generic, carbureted, small-block Ford use.

Today, power adders are hugely popular and for several good reasons. Now that they have been assembled into add-on systems, they can be easily joined to the basic engine in a neat, bolt-on package. Besides hardware, that package includes a tremendous amount of engineering development to make the system work smoothly on a 5.0. It's one thing to bolt on a blower, it's another thing to engineer the necessary pulleys, belts, fuel mixture, ignition timing, and the rest. That work has already been done with the modern power adder kits.

All the power adders work with EFI, specifically the 6,250-rpm EEC-IV rev limiter. In fact, power adders tend to augment the existing mid- and top-end

Central to the power adder concept is that they are kits. Besides buying the hardware in a convenient package, you're buying the engineering it takes to spark and fuel something like a supercharger, After all, hanging a blower on an engine is only the first step.

power of the 5.0 engine, and don't try to raise the powerband. This is vital, as in the early days of the 5.0 movement, there was no way of raising the rev limit, and even now when it can be done via electronic controls, you don't want to. Raising the powerband means a loss of low-rpm torque, which kills streetability. High rpm is also plenty expensive. The 5.0's puny connecting rod bolts and light crankshaft would not prove so durable at high rpm as they have at the moderate engine speeds the 5.0 runs at. This means the basic engine, in other words the short block, can be left stock, saving time and money.

Such compatibility is likely the power adder's best ally. The manufacturers have learned to package their gear precisely to the 5.0, making it easy to bolt on. Since nothing ever happens unless it's easy, this user-friendliness shouldn't be underestimated.

Street, Strip, or Track?

Not all power adders are suitable for every use, so when considering a power adder, the first thing to decide is what you want from your car. Most 5.0s are street cars and ought to stick with streetable power adders. Many, however, also see drag strip duty, and a few are

pure drag race or road race/slalom cars. In the pure race cars, the rule book is the controlling factor, so consult it first if you're going racing.

On the street and Saturday night strip scene, you have plenty of choices. Do you want long- or short-duration power from your power adder? Turbos, superchargers, and stroker kits all give long-term "extra" power. Nitrous oxide is limited to the capacity of the bottle, and that puts a serious crimp on duration. Furthermore, if very long-term power is the need, such as in road racing, then more displacement is often best, because superchargers and turbochargers cause intake charge heating.

Do you want an instant power hit, or is throttle control more important? In drag racing an instant hit of power is often useful. Nitrous leads as the "on-demand" power adder. A roots or Kenne Bell supercharger would also seem a good choice, as both of these units blast off the instant the throttle opens, but then traction becomes the overriding concern. Furthermore, the BBK kit with its M90 roots blower is too small for racing and has no reserve capacity. Kenne Bell offers blowers large enough to keep charging at the strip. That brings us to the common centrifugal supercharger kits. They don't

do a thing below 3,200 rpm, so they have a softer power delivery that allows getting out of the hole at the strip. Their building rush of power also feels powerful and racy to most enthusiasts, and is a big reason such blowers have proven so popular.

There is power flexibility to consider, too. That is, is the power adder's characteristic oomph delivered all over the powerband, or is it peaky or suffering from throttle lag? For all-around street driving a broad powerband is a must. Stroker kits do extremely well here, as they are natural torque builders, and so are the Kenne Bell and BBK superchargers. The centrifugal blowers are all slight mid-range to big top-end power builders, while turbos typically spool up impressive mid-range and top-end power after a touch of throttle lag at lower engine speeds.

Can you live with an all or nothing power adder? Nitrous is on or it's off; there is no such thing as a part-throttle power boost when running bottle fed. Thinking the other way, the GT-40, Edelbrock, Holley, and home-brewed head and intake kits give excellent throttle modulation. The centrifugal blowers are next most responsive, followed by turbos, which tend to be nonlinear in their power delivery. As the power builds, it usually keeps swelling upward, although this is tunable by substituting turbos, and the power curve from low to high rpm can be made flatter.

The on-off aspect of nitrous is one of its strongest characteristics, and one normally not discussed much in magazines or bench racing sessions. If you're drag racing, it's no problem, but on the street, it's kind of a pain. Often you want more passing power in top gear on the freeway, or more grunt off the corners. This doesn't mean full throttle every time, and that leaves nitrous out of the picture. With the nitrous off, your 5.0 is just another 5.0; digging into its special talents means arming the system and standing on the gas. Then you get full 5.0 power, plus whatever you've pilled the nitrous system for. If you're running 150 horsepower worth of squeeze because that's what you enjoy at the drag strip, then you're going to get all that

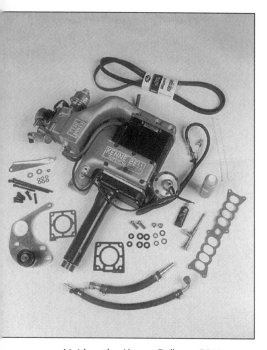

Neither the Kenne Bell nor BBK supercharger packages are considered hairy knuckle-draggers at the strip, but they do have a 460-like torque hit that is easy to live with on the street. A relaxed but fast daily driver can be built around these superchargers.

power right there on Main Street, too. That's different from giving a stroked or blown 5.0 three-quarter throttle and being able to short shift it smoothly.

Then, of course, how much power do you need? All power adders can ultimately be tuned for real muscle, but some are better suited to big power than others. From a bolt-on perspective, nitrous is the heaviest hitter for street and many drag race 5.0s. When racing seriously, however, the efficiency of reclaiming waste heat from the exhaust makes turbocharging the ultimate; more fast 5.0s should explore this option. The available 5.0 superchargers span quite a range, from a good bump in street performance with a Powerdyne to mind-bending speed from a Mondo or Novi.

Then there is the stealth factor. If you don't want anyone to know you're packing a power adder, the easiest thing to hide is a stroker kit, with nitrous a close second. All the rest are out in the open for everyone to inspect. The only possible exception would be some turbo installations. These are often so low in

the engine compartment that a casual underhood glance, especially at night, won't show the turbo. Naturally, if they're looking at all they'll find it.

Convenience

Casual street power adders should be convenient. As much fun as any power adder is at first, filling bottles or tending a high-strung blower with canned octane boosters gets old fast.

Cubic inches are easy to take care of—you simply feed their appetite at the gas pump. Blowers are next. All of them require the engine oil be changed around 3,000 miles maximum, and spark plug life is shortened as well. Sometimes the belt tension needs attention, and the ball-drive SN-93/Novi GSS Paxtons require oil changes of their own when the engine oil is changed, plus an expensive overhaul if you overspeed it. The turbo systems are like the blowers when it comes to spark plugs and oil. The tough guy is nitrous. The bottle needs filling from a supplier, and there can be a surprising amount of system maintenance when it comes to opening, warming, and changing the bottle.

If you want to count the cylinder head and intake packages, they're pretty convenient, but you will pay a very slight price in low-rpm torque when dogging around town. This is often covered up by 3.55 or steeper rear axle gears, so count that cost in your calculations.

Future Increases

While even more power may seem completely over the moon when putting down the money for a supercharger, combining power adders is done more frequently than you think, and it's something you may want to consider.

If you are counting the GT-40 package and its ilk, then the most accepted power adder grouping has been the GT-40 and a centrifugal blower. Of course, any nicely modified 5.0 with a centrifugal supercharger pretty much falls into this camp. The Roush intake is so specialized for cowl induction that packaging a blower to it is wildly impractical, even if the Roush stuff makes fabulous power.

Then there are cubic inches (stroker kit) and a supercharger or nitrous. If you want to go this route, build the cubic inches first. This allows you to get the basic engine running well, then come back and tune it up with nitrous, blower, or turbo. You'll also save working around the external power adder when installing the stroker kit if you build the engine first.

The other combination tried occasionally is a blower and nitrous. In this case, install the blower first, then use the nitrous to augment the blower in the mid-range, plus cool the intake air charge at the top end. Trying to augment a nitrous system with blower boost is dumb. You can simply add more nitrous and get the same results. Either way you look at it, mixing nitrous and a blower looks good on paper, but is extremely difficult to control.

Cost

In the end, it's interesting how all the power adders come out to around the same price—expensive! Of course, for the absolute cheapest in speed, take a stock 5.0 and put a nitrous kit on it. For plain old fun and drag strip duty, the nitrous option beats the rest by a factor of two.

Don't forget, when figuring the cost of a power adder, to consider installation and operating costs as well as the initial purchase price. The initial price on most power adders is pretty well fixed, but if you want to start with a GT-40 or equivalent package, you can at least buy the parts as you go. This spreads the costs from paycheck to paycheck and avoids the financial ruin of credit card payments.

Ranking power adders' initial cost will likely put nitrous at the top of your list, then the less-expensive centrifugal superchargers such as the Powerdyne/SVO piece, then a clump of huffers like the ball-drive Paxtons, Kenne Bell, BBK, and V-1 Vortech units. The turbo kits and high-output centrifugals such as the Vortech Mondo and Paxton Novi 2000 tend to be the most-expensive power adders—at least initially.

If your 5.0 is a daily driver, keep it that way. It's possible to put well over 400 horsepower to the rear tires, like this supercharged S-351 Saleen is doing, but it takes plenty of money to do it right. In the long run, going with a proven power-adder and some electronic tuning, along with the few necessary supporting mechanical parts, will put way over 300 horsepower to the pavement, and that's plenty. If you want to go faster, get a second chassis and build a 5.0 race car. Then you can let it all hang out while keeping your street car fun to drive on the street. Maxing the boost or playing with big cams on your driver is fun at first, but gets old fast unless extra effort is made to keep the drivability near stock.

Installation costs really don't vary much from one kit to the other, and typically you can do this work yourself anyway. We'll outline the variations in supercharger installation in Chapter 9, but for now, we'll note that the centrifugals go on pretty easily. Nitrous is easy enough to install, but thanks to plenty of wiring and some plumbing, it's more complicated and time-consuming than you'd first think. The turbo kits are pretty much bolt-ons but extensive, while a custom turbo installation requires the services of an all-out fabrication shop and is definitely not a job for the beginner.

Operating costs are negligible for all but the nitrous cars. Even then, on the street you won't go through enough nitrous to break the bank, at least not after running through your first two bottles in four days because you just have to play with your new toy. At the drag strip, however, a nitrous car can require a nitrous budget to run. I'm not talking about the casual Saturday night bracket racer, but the more involved 5.0 racer who goes through the squeeze two runs to the bottle. Then there are spare bottles to lug around, the driving to the speed shop for bottle fillings, the occasional bum solenoid or dirt in the jet, and in the muggy Midwest and East, the running of the tow truck's AC system all day to chill the bottles. But then, we all know speed costs money.

Power Adder Comparison

Power Adder	Install	Power Boost	Power Duration	Instant/ Gradual	Flexibility	Stealthy
Head/Int	moderate	small	long	gradual	moderate	no
Stroker	difficult	moderate	long	instant	extremely	yes
Centrfgl	easy/mod	large/xl	moderate	gradual	moderate	no
Roots/Lsh	easy/mod	large	moderate	instant	extremely	no
Turbo	mod/diff	large/xl	moderate/long	gradual	moderate	no
Nitrous	moderate	large/xl	short	instant	rigid	yes

CONTENTS

Theory of Operation 79

System Description 79

Wet vs. Dry 80

Nitrous Accessories 81

Fuel and Driveline
Requirements 82

NITROUS OXIDE

When it comes to making big power, especially for relatively little money, nitrous oxide is king. Nitrous is also something of a mystery to many enthusiasts. Like some magic genie, it comes in a bottle and has a fearsome reputation for both power building and blowing up engines. Because it makes so much power, nitrous is also commonly thought of as cheating, as too easy a way to build power.

The truth is, nitrous oxide is a well-thought-out, highly tunable, and powerful way of boosting power in the 5.0 Mustang. Installed and operated according to the instructions, nitrous will not harm the engine. Of course, it does cause higher cylinder pressures, so normal engine wear is accelerated during the short periods the nitrous is engaged, but it is not some engine-killing drug as you may have heard. Thousands of 5.0 owners enjoy the excitement of a good 65-to-75-horsepower nitrous shot with absolutely no engine concerns.

More than anything else, what has given nitrous its occasionally difficult reputation is its ease of making power.

Because it is so simple to add 140 horsepower or so to a 5.0 with squeeze, many people make the mistake of thinking they can add even more. This is not true.

Approaching the 150 horsepower level, adding more nitrous yields diminishing results on stock and lightly modified 5.0s. This is because the engine breathing is restrictive at these power levels—the cylinder heads must breath the nitrous as well as the base engine air, after all. So, to safely make more than 150 "extra" horsepower with nitrous will take all the usual normally aspirated breathing modifications such as cylinder heads, intake manifolds, headers, and so on.

Such power levels also demand improved engine durability. Forged pistons and improved blocks, such as the Motorsport A4, are needed for complete engine durability. I know you've heard of people who run 11s with tons of nitrous and stock blocks, but I assure you they won't do it for long. Plus, when the stock block, piston, or connecting rod lets go under boost, it often

Nitrous oxide is known by many nicknames, but whether you call it spray, juice, or squeeze, the kick is still the same. Nitrous is probably the most explosive, and fun, of the power adders, and for a low-dollar street/strip car it is likely ideal. Commuting to work can be done with absolute stock drivability and fuel mileage, then at the strip you can easily enjoy up to 150 extra horsepower, and typically a bit more than a second off your ET. Many a 5.0 runs in the 12s with 150 horsepower worth of "spray" and little else.

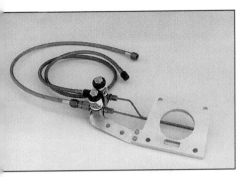

Nearly every 5.0 nitrous installation uses a "10-pound" bottle, which refers to the weight of the nitrous in the bottle. All up, a 10-pound bottle weighs 25 pounds and should be installed over or near the right rear tire for traction and chassis balance. The larger bottle is a 20-pound unit, which allows twice as much fun between refills, but at a cost in overall weight and trunk space. Note that both installations include bottle heaters and gauges, and both are in 1994–1995 Mustang trunks.

Wet manifold systems get fuel and nitrous into a 5.0 with a simple plate, or sometimes just a nozzle, at the throttle body. Such systems work okay at regular mixtures, but mean keeping on your toes when it comes to leaning the mixture. Otherwise an explosive backfire will occur. Also, because of the 5.0's folded air path in the upper intake manifold, good fuel distribution is unlikely with a wet system, especially with big nitrous loads. When looking for 150 horsepower or more of nitrous, a plate between the upper and lower intake manifolds is the way to do it. Definitely an advantage of the simple throttle body plate system shown here is its low cost.

takes all but the intake manifold with it. With the light late-model blocks, which insiders say were lightened even more after 1987, huge nitrous loads can separate the block right through the main bearing saddles or through the core plugs. To build really big nitrous power, you need the high dollar engine to match, just as you would with a turbo or blower.

Even at lower power levels, there are a few considerations. Owners of 1993 and later 5.0s should keep in mind their hypereutectic pistons are not as durable as the earlier forged variety. Keep the nitrous load to 100 horsepower or less, preferably 75–80. Another caution is the AOD automatic transmission. It doesn't like power adders much, so either get it beefed with an aftermarket kit or stick with a basic 65-to-75-horsepower kit.

The bottom line is that nitrous is just like any other power adder. It will give you more of what you already have, but it is not a magic potion that will turn a tractor-like stock 5.0 engine into a high-revving race motor. Always remember to build the basic engine first, then add nitrous to it. The nice part is, for the first 140 to 150 horsepower, you don't have to do much to a stock 5.0.

Theory of Operation

Nitrous oxide is a gas containing 36 percent oxygen by weight, with the rest nitrogen. It is stored under pressure as a liquid. When fed into an engine, the N_2O expands rapidly as it is released from the bottle pressure, and changes state from a liquid into a gas. This change of state has a powerful cooling effect, as nitrous sprays out of the nozzle at approximately -120 degrees Fahrenheit. Thus, nitrous oxide absorbs heat from the charge air and surrounding engine parts. This cooling effect increases charge air density, which by itself helps raise power.

While the nitrogen in the N_2O is inert and does not promote combustion, the extra oxygen does increase the rate of combustion, and provides more "air" for extra fuel to burn with. Injecting just nitrous oxide into an engine would increase combustion tremendously, just like a blower on a forge. It would be exactly like running the engine super lean, with the same result of burned or holed pistons and cracked blocks from detonation. Therefore, to take advantage of the extra oxygen atoms in N_2O, it is necessary to inject both the nitrous and some extra gasoline for it to combust with. Think of a nitrous system as having two sides, one for nitrous, the other for fuel.

The speeding or heating up of combustion can get you in trouble. You absolutely do not want to run a nitrous system too lean, because the extra oxygen in nitrous acts like a cutting torch on the pistons and head gasket. Stick strictly to the manufacturer's recommendations until you really know what you are doing. It is far better to be a little bit safe with nitrous than just a tad over the line.

It's worth noting a nitrous system requires essentially no energy from the engine to run. This helps make its power gains substantial. Also, while nitrous is commonly referred to in terms of horsepower, such as a "150 horsepower system," it is effective over a wide range of engine rpm, and raises torque tremendously. This is another reason why nitrous cars run so hard. Thus, unlike a common eight-pound centrifugal supercharger, a 75-horsepower nitrous kit also puts plenty of kick in the mid-range. However, it is vital not to operate the nitrous at too low an rpm, or detonation will occur. This means no less than 2,500 rpm, and preferably starting at 3,000 to 3,500 rpm.

System Description

A 5.0 nitrous system runs all over the car. We can start our description at the bottle. Typically mounted in the right rear of the trunk or hatch to aid traction, the typical 10-pound bottle actually weighs 25 pounds when full of liquid nitrous. A manual valve is fitted to the bottle to isolate the system from the 850 to 950 psi bottle pressure; otherwise the nitrous would seep out over several days. A steel braided hose leads from the bottle

Nitrous systems require an arming switch in the cockpit. This allows running with the bottle valve open, but the system turned off. Then, when nitrous use is anticipated, the arming switch can be thrown and the nitrous activated by the full-throttle switch. Most arming switches in nitrous kits are cheesy junk you don't want in your car, and adapting a factory switch is better. This SN-95 uses a second fog light switch on the center console; the other popular spot is a horn button, although this could be a safety issue.

Stealth is a nitrous strong point, but it takes some doing to hide the solenoids and plumbing. The giveaway solenoids can also be dressed up with sleeves, if desired, for a cleaner underhood appearance. This 5.0 uses chromed solenoid covers and fender solenoid mounting for dress-up purposes. Unless stealth or looks demand otherwise, mount the solenoids as close as possible to the intake tract for better response.

forward to the engine, where an electrical solenoid is fitted to control nitrous admission to the intake manifold.

On the most widely used 5.0 nitrous system, the so-called "dry manifold" kit from Nitrous Oxide Systems (NOS), the extra gasoline is provided by increasing the fuel pressure in the 5.0's regular fuel system. Thus the extra fuel simply passes through the stock fuel injectors. To raise the fuel pressure, NOS employs a second nitrous solenoid. It meters a slight amount of nitrous on the fuel regulator to jack up the fuel pressure. It meters a slight amount of nitrous onto the fuel regulator to jack up the fuel pressure. The extra fuel pressure is needed to increase the injector's fuel flow when the engine is nitrous-assisted, otherwise larger or extra injectors would be needed. Like the main nitrous flow itself into the engine, the very small volume of nitrous working on the fuel pressure regulator is adjustable via a changeable jet. Therefore, when more nitrous assist is desired with a dry manifold system, both the main nitrous jet and the fuel pressure regulator jet are changed.

Once the fuel pressure is raised, the extra fuel pressure is sensed by the fuel safety switch NOS provides to replace the Schraeder valve on the one fuel rail. Therefore, only when the fuel safety

switch closes will the nitrous solenoid trigger, allowing the nitrous to flow into the intake manifold.

Occasionally, the fuel safety switch is deleted by the owners as an unnecessary complication, but it does safeguard against a weakened or malfunctioning fuel system.

In the 5.0 world, nitrous systems are either "dry manifold" or "plate" systems. Dry manifold means the extra gasoline is admitted via the fuel injectors. Plate systems use an aluminum plate at the throttle body or between the upper and lower intake manifolds. The plates hold the nitrous and gasoline spray bars. Such systems are also called "wet manifolds" because the intake manifold is wetted with fuel. With the plate nitrous system, as offered by Compucar, Nitrous Works, 10,000 RPM, and several others, including NOS' own between-the-intakes plate, a separate fuel system is used. Then a fuel solenoid and hoses are necessary to bring the fuel to the plate. In this case, there is a nitrous solenoid, a fuel solenoid, and either spray bars for each or a nozzle that squirts both fuel and nitrous. Both solenoids are energized at the same time.

Much of the complexity of nitrous installation is in the various control circuits. The solenoids need to be switched on and off, so a relay and wiring need to be rigged for them, that is, the relay needs a solenoid. This is the arming circuit. A WOT switch or other engagement switch needs to be wired, as does the fuel pressure safety switch on the NOS dry manifold system. An essential part of any nitrous system is a bottle warmer, which requires some simple wiring to the bottle, and if a remote bottle opener (an electrically operated valve on the nitrous bottle) is desired, that needs to be wired too. So, while drilling the holes for the bottle mounting and running the high-pressure hose under the car takes a while, all the wiring typically takes longer. With the well-thought-out kits dedicated to the 5.0 available today, installation is no big deal, but be prepared to spend a good long day at it, plus drill a few holes and do a bit of wiring.

Wet vs. Dry

The battle rages constantly over wet vs. dry manifold nitrous systems. Both styles make horsepower, with at least a theoretical advantage going to the dry

A Nitrous Favorite

I'm often asked to name some of my favorite 5.0s. It's an impossible question, of course, as 5.0 performance ranges from the street to drag strip to road course. Still, several cars stand out as especially fast, efficient, or practical.

One that was definitely fast, and could probably take honors in financial efficiency, was a simple white LX coupe with a good amount of road grime outside and a low sea of candy wrappers, baby gear, and plain old stuff inside. This five-speed car had only two modifications worth mentioning, a full Griggs Racing GR-40 suspension system and an NOS 150 nitrous kit. Otherwise the car was stock, and rode, drove, and looked the plain-Jane role perfectly when simply motoring around. But turn on the juice and hammer the throttle and the rear axle bit hard and the engine bellowed with authority. The street tires could barely hang onto the 375 horsepower, but the vastly improved suspension made sure the coupe was stable and controllable even while the Traction Loc hazed both rear tires out of a bumpy turn. I always thought this machine was a great testament to making plenty of power for one-fifth the price of a supercharger. It went like stink, hung onto the pavement, was quite stealthy and safe handling, and puttered around town on chore duty like a minivan. It even had a child's car seat belted in during my test.

system for best fuel distribution. After all, the upper intake manifold on a 5.0 was never designed to flow an air-fuel mixture, and squirting fuel down it will result in puddles and uneven distribution. But in practice, wet manifold nitrous systems do flow fuel through the upper intake and make plenty of power doing it.

The major difference is that the dry system is more sophisticated, and is more forgiving of mistuning. Nitrous doesn't burn by itself, so you can't explode an upper intake full of nitrous. But a wet manifold full of nitrous and fuel can definitely blow up, and wet manifold systems do have nasty backfires when the mixture is leaned out too far by an eager tuner. When that happens, the throttle blade can be bent back like a taco from the explosion, or the upper intake cracked or blown apart. More typically, however, a backfire blows like a dragon, starting a fire in the airbox and surrounding area, requiring action from a fire extinguisher. If you do get a backfire, keeping the throttle open may suck the fire back into the engine.

Casual street nitrous users are best off with the dry manifold system. The cost advantage of a wet manifold system isn't so great that the safety factor should be dismissed.

Nitrous Accessories

Getting right to the point, every nitrous system needs two accessories: a gauge and a bottle warmer. Some drivers may benefit from an rpm switch, ignition retards are necessary on the larger systems, and after that, it's mostly convenience or fluff.

Bottle Gauge

The gauge indicates the bottle pressure, which is vital to tuning the nitrous system. When the bottle gets warm on hot summer days, the nitrous pressure rises and the system runs leaner. On cold nights the bottle pressure drops and the engine runs rich. Without a gauge you have no idea of exactly what the bottle pressure is, and thus cannot fine-tune the system; a requirement because the fixed nitrous jet is optimum for only one bottle pressure. Without a gauge, you're tuning in the dark, and typically run richer and slower than you should.

Bottle Warmer

The bottle warmer is necessary to raise the bottle pressure whenever the bottle is below the optimum temperature. The optimum temperature varies with manufacturers. Because it is more practical to warm the bottle with a heater than cool a hot bottle with wet rags or ice, the nitrous system should be tuned to run at the high end of the bottle pressure scale, usually around 900 psi, but sometimes a bit higher. Then your only concern will be the hottest days, when the bottle pressure can exceed the 1,100-psi limit.

The bottle warmer is a simple device, nothing more than a small electric blanket that wraps around the bottle and is retained by spring straps. It requires a 12-volt power source to splice into, and a switching circuit. Typically these devices don't fit snugly, and may fail to warm the bottle because their thermostats weren't in contact with the bottle. Anything you can use to belt or wrap the thermostats to the bottle will help this.

RPM Switch

Depending on who is operating the car, an rpm-activated switch is an excellent idea. This switch does not allow nitrous application below a preset rpm to avoid engine damage. The experienced nitrous user probably doesn't need this, but if a variety of drivers are in the car, or the owner is new to nitrous, then it can save the engine from excessive low-rpm loads. Furthermore, with an rpm switch, the driver need not worry about when to hit the juice, but can simply drive the car and let the switch supply the nitrous when the engine can take it. It's a smart gizmo to have.

Numerous other nitrous accessories are available, but none are mandatory. One that is mighty convenient is a remote bottle opener. This saves having to run back to the trunk and turn on the bottle each time you want to use it. If all you are doing with nitrous is running it at the drag strip, then a remote opener is simply extra weight, but on the street it means you can turn on the system quickly. You'll hear people say a remote opener hurts nitrous flow, and technically, they're correct. However, unless you're running 1,500 horsepower worth of nitrous in your Pro Mod car, it's not

Nitrous bottles are filled by weight. The typical 10-pound bottle should be refilled when it drops to 17 pounds total weight. Your local nitrous vendor will refill it to 25 pounds. Often cited as a downside of nitrous, bottle management is pretty easy if you have a spare bottle. Each 10-pound bottle provides 1 1/2 to 2 minutes of nitrous operation at around 65–75 horsepower. That doesn't sound like much, but after the first couple of bottles of goofing around, you'll find two minutes of nitrous power can be stretched over quite a few bursts. Serious drag racers may wish for up to four bottles for a busy racing weekend. That way, a nearly full bottle is always available; they always seem to run just that much better.

Changing the horsepower increase with nitrous is as easy as changing small slip-in jets. The popular NOS 5115 kit uses a single nitrous jet at the inlet air pipe, just upstream of the throttle. It's almost too quick and easy to change at the track.

a factor, so get a remote opener if you want. Billet aluminum mounting brackets, bottle blankets, and the like are all more fluff than stuff, so suit your own taste in dress-up gear.

Nitrous Retard

Hotter combustion is faster combustion, so with large nitrous kits, say 150 horsepower and larger, a boost retard is necessary for the ignition timing just as it is with a supercharger. The standard 80-horsepower kits get by without an ignition retard because they have you dial back the initial timing to 8 degrees. Plus, unlike a supercharger, the charge air is cooled, not heated, which suppresses detonation.

This brings up one drawback to the popular nitrous kits. By having you drive around with less than stock ignition timing, normally aspirated performance and fuel mileage are slightly affected. Leaving the initial ignition timing stock and retarding it with a nitrous retard, nitrous controller (Jacobs), PMS, or even an EPEC/DFI or chip is preferable, but obviously more expensive.

Nitrous Controller

For standard street kits, a dedicated nitrous controller is not needed. A standard kit is either on or off; that is, a progressive application is not necessary. The slight initial ignition retard doesn't hurt normally aspirated performance enough to worry about, or most of the time, even notice. Once the 150-horsepower level of nitrous assist is reached, however, more sophisticated nitrous tuning is desirable, especially more aggressive ignition retardation. This can be handled with a dedicated nitrous controller, along with multistage nitrous applications, multistage ignition retardation, or progressive nitrous application.

On the other hand, many stand-alone engine management systems, and many of the newer piggyback-style engine management aids have nitrous functions, eliminating a need for a dedicated nitrous controller to adjust the ignition timing in response to the nitrous system.

Progressive Timer

Depending on the engine, amount of nitrous, tire size, chassis, and other factors, there comes a point when bringing the nitrous in progressively, as opposed to a single big event, is necessary to avoid

massive wheelspin. Electronic timers are available to bring the nitrous on at a controllable rate. These are easily adjustable, and can be the answer on a street-driven car employing a big load of nitrous. In practice, it seems that a progressive timer is most useful when at or above 150 horsepower, especially at the strip. Honest-to-treaded street tires can lower that number, however, and it is a help when running between corners.

Fuel and Driveline Requirements

More power requires more fuel—that means fuel system upgrades when squeezing a 5.0 past 80 horsepower or so. Thus, basic nitrous systems get along with the stock pump, pressures, and injectors, then starting around 65–80 horsepower worth of boost, an additional inline pump, typically a T-Rex pump, is used to increase volume and mainly pressure. NOS aims for 80 psi of fuel pressure with the stock 19-pound injectors when fitting its 5115-II kit, which takes its standard 5115 kit from around 75 horsepower to something like 140 horsepower of nitrous. Trying more than the 65–75-horsepower nitrous level with just the stock fuel pump is begging for a blown head gasket.

An exception to this could be a wet manifold system, in which all extra fuel is handled through the nitrous system, leaving the stock injectors with just their stock job. Thus some tuners say that with a wet manifold system they've been able to run mid-11s with the stock 88-liter per hour fuel pump and stock injectors. Still, the smart tuner should go for a larger in-tank pump as soon as possible. It doesn't hurt anything, and can help with those tough transient fuel requirements.

Dry manifold tuners need to step up to 24-pound fuel injectors pretty quickly, once the engine is hot rodded. Aluminum heads or a cam, along with all the other usual breathing mods, mean you should have 24-pound injectors. If you clip the rev limiter with a chip, PMS, or the like, and are running over 6,000 rpm, then 30 pound injectors are called for.

With the upper intake manifold removed, access to the jets on a plate system is easy. Just don't drop anything down the intake runners. Another plate advantage, whether it be between in the manifold halves or at the throttle body, is that there is no need to change the stock injectors. Some people try jacking the dry manifold system past 150 horsepower by using larger injectors, but this leads to off-nitrous drivability problems. If you want big nitrous on an EFI Mustang, a plate is the way to get it.

Reading spark plugs is how nitrous is tuned. The system should be set to run rich, then can be leaned until the plugs begin to show small balls of molten aluminum—your piston crowns starting to melt. Then the system can be rejetted a step rich for the optimum power on that day. This is fine for the racer who is tuning often, can read spark plugs with some accuracy, and won't forget to retune when the weather changes. For the street, the manufacturer's recommendation is what to jet to. It will be a bit rich, but safe.

Large nitrous hits on street tires can be controlled with a progressive nitrous controller. On this NOS unit, one knob controls how long the nitrous is ramped up (by pulsing the solenoids). The delay can be set from 0 to 10 seconds. The second knob controls how much power is initially supplied, from 0 to 100 percent of maximum power. As an example of the possibilities, 75 percent of the nitrous could be allowed initially, followed by the last 25 percent being gradually fed in over a couple of seconds.

When reaching into the serious squeeze territory above 150 horsepower of nitrous, fuel rails, tank-to-engine compartment lines, and so on need enlarging. This is especially true because the instant hit of nitrous requires an almost equally strong hit of gasoline, so the fuel system has to be up to handling high volumes, quickly, under high-*g* conditions. This is especially true of the dry manifold NOS system, which has really done its all by 150 horsepower. At that point, it's time to move to a plate system, where the extra fuel is handled by the plate and its own fuel lines. You still need big enough fuel pump and lines to handle the total fuel flow, of course.

Like any form of forced induction, nitrous strains the rest of the drivetrain and chassis, so a full regime of clutch, axle, suspension, and chassis reinforcement is required. The instant hit from nitrous asks more than the corresponding amount of power from the gradual spooling up from a centrifugal blower or turbo, so don't forget to budget for these parts. You'll also discover money spent on a good suspension kit from someone like Griggs, Hotchkiss, HP Motorsport, or others is many a racer's secret weapon. The power, after all, has to hook to the ground to do any good.

Centrifugal vs. Positive
Displacement 84

Centrifugals 87

Positive Displacement . .89

Accessories 91

Fuel 91

Air Filters 92

Low Restriction
Air Inlet 93

Cat-Back Exhaust 93

Boost Retards 93

Octane Boosters 93

Bypass Kits 93

Drive Belts and
Pulleys 94

Blower Braces 95

Intercoolers 95

SUPERCHARGERS

While Mustangs and superchargers have been associated since the Paxton-supercharged 1966 Shelby GT-350, it was electronic fuel injection that linked the two so thoroughly. The centralized intake packaging of fuel injection makes it simple to route boost from a centrifugal blower into the engine.

On a carbureted engine, a "suck-through" supercharging system is generally regarded as superior to a "blow-through" arrangement. Fuel injection's advantage is simply in packaging. The EFI Ford intake manifold mates easily with a centrifugal blower. Besides packaging ease, the centrifugals allow simple emission exemptions because they do nothing to little at low rpm. The soft low-end boost is something of a blessing at the racetrack, too, where a lack of tire-shocking boost at low- and mid-range rpm allows the typical poorly suspended Mustang to get moving before the big power ramps up. So, with street legality, easy packaging, and usable power, the centrifugals have dominated the 5.0 market. Today a 5.0 seems almost incomplete without a centrifugal blower, and that widespread acceptance has paved the way for all forms of forced induction, including roots and screw superchargers. Today, 5.0 supercharging is well developed and easy to purchase, install, and use. All said, it's probably the most convenient power adder, which is why it is so popular.

Before plunging into the belts and impellers, it's important to understand 5.0 superchargers come in a wide variety. Some are strictly for the street, others are pure race, and many fall in between. Prices vary and so do boost characteristics. So first decide on what you want from your blower, then get on with selecting the one that's right for your combination of needs.

Centrifugal vs. Positive Displacement

Popular 5.0 superchargers come in two basic varieties, centrifugal and positive displacement. The fundamental difference between these two blower families affects the type of power made, and the tuning necessary.

Both roots (BBK) and screw designs (Kenne Bell) are positive displacement blowers, that is, their air output is linear. Except for pumping losses, if these blowers are turned twice as fast,

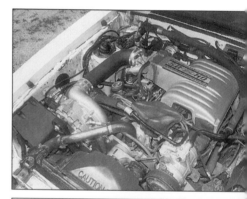

Centrifugal blowers, such as the Vortech, and positive displacement superchargers, such as the Kenne Bell, make two very different types of power. The high-rpm rush of the centrifugal feels racey and does work great at the drag strip because it is easy on the tires. The Kenne Bell muscles up from off idle and has a big-block feel that's more explosive.

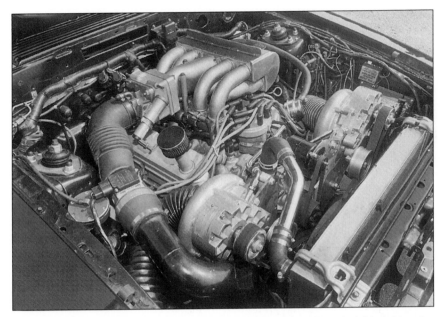

Before Mondos and Novis, there was experimentation. Craig Radovich fielded this twin-blown, intercooled package in the early 1990s, but abandoned it pretty quickly. The difficulties of getting everything working in unison, overcoming drive losses, and small airflow hardware downstream of the blowers doomed this valiant effort. Modern racers should really appreciate the big bolt-on blowers that deliver more boost than a small-block can take.

they put out twice as much air. (Pretty much the case with the Kenne Bell, especially.) This is the same as a piston engine's air consumption, so they are well matched to a 5.0's air needs. It is also why they deliver big boost right off idle as soon as the throttle is opened.

The traditional roots blower uses paddle-like rotors to fan air through its case, pumping that air into the intake manifold in a series of discharges. With the roots blower sized larger than the engine, the air in the intake manifold piles up, compressing it to greater than atmospheric pressure.

The Kenne Bell screw design, casually known as a Whipple after the Chevy version of the same supercharger (and less casually, as the Lysholm screw, after its inventor), uses tightly meshed male and female screw-shaped rotors to more smoothly move air through its case. The air is compressed directly inside the case and is discharged in a constant stream of compressed air. This eliminates the high energy pulses of the roots blower, which can bounce around the intake manifold and cause reversion problems.

Because they are positive displacement units, the Kenne Bell and Eaton-built roots blower, as used by BBK,

Paxton started the 5.0 blower boom with its quiet ball-drive supercharger. These blowers are suited for low-boost applications in which quiet operation is paramount. They are intolerant of overspeeding, and should be limited to about six pounds of boost to ensure blower longevity. In early 1998, Paxton revised its ball-drive blower with better bearings and two shafts instead of three for reduced cost, greater precision, and reliability. The new blower goes by both the Novi GSS and SN 2000 names. The two small black hoses attached to this one indicate it is using the highly recommended blower cooler.

achieve maximum boost by 1,700 rpm or so. Thus, they deliver big-block style torque down low. They feel big and muscular in a street-driven 5.0, which is their natural habitat, because both are airflow-limited by the size of their cases.

BBK is dedicated to the street supercharger concept, while Kenne Bell offers three blower sizes to allow developing from 5 1/2 pounds of boost up to 20 pounds or more.

The BBK/Eaton combination is an eventual dead end for those needing to continually step up boost for racing. Swapping pulleys for more boost usually run the BBK roots blower into less and less efficient operational zones. Thus it won't outrun a developed centrifugal blower on the track, and it wasn't designed to. It will, however, run right with a centrifugal on the street at 7 to 10 pounds of boost. To move up with a positive displacement blower, you need a larger supercharger, which BBK doesn't offer.

Kenne Bell starts with a 1.5-liter supercharger, which can be replaced as a direct bolt-on in a 5.0 Mustang with a 2.2-liter. This larger blower should provide all the block-straining, tire-spinning boost a 5.0 can take across its powerband, but for those pressing on, there is a 2.6-liter. This requires custom mounting, and is really a bit much except for the over-the-moon crowd.

Centrifugal blowers are more open-ended. Like the BBK and the Kenne Bell, centrifugal blowers are driven by a belt pulleyed to the crankshaft. They, however, are much like belt-driven turbochargers (see Chapter 10) using an impeller to blade air into the engine. Thus, unlike the positive-displacement blowers' nearly linear airflow delivery, centrifugals are dependent on rpm to increase their airflow output. Because of this dependency, you might not even know a centrifugal 5.0 is supercharged until you reach nearly 3,500 engine rpm. Then, as a result of the increase in output relative to rpm, the centrifugal blowers expel all sorts of volume as rpm rises.

Centrifugal blowers are also geared to run at high rpm. This gearing is done

In the heavy-hitter class, Paxton offers the Novi 2000, generally referred to simply as the "Novi." An extremely versatile supercharger, with different impellers and pulleys, it works great from 8 to 27 pounds of boost and boasts bombproof reliability. The Novi is in the upper price bracket for a blower, but has the gear-drive beef for track duty. The cowl induction is smart, too, as the inlet side of the supercharger is naturally aspirated and benefits from the high pressure air at the base of the windshield. This early Novi installation uses a custom mounting; Paxton's Novi kit features a beautiful double-plate mount on the passenger side that's far better than this.

with the crankshaft and blower pulleys and also inside the blower drive. Centrifugal impeller speeds reach up to 50,000 rpm and well beyond in racing applications, so you can see how a relatively small change in engine rpm results in much larger changes in impeller rpm.

Because of this relationship with rpm, you can spin the blower faster with smaller pulleys and make more boost, although at the outer limit there is a cost in diminishing boost, as inefficiencies show up as heat or less boost increase. Eventually, as is the case for positive displacement types as well, the blower's mechanical design speed limit is reached and that's that.

Nevertheless, centrifugals do respond well to various pulley sizes and are quite adaptable to different impeller rpm and boost outputs. This characteristic has helped make centrifugals a popular choice for 5.0 racers. Once you hit a performance wall, a pulley change will often allow more power. Also, centrifugals almost always have a higher adiabatic (heat) efficiency than the roots. That is, they don't heat the air charge nearly as much, because of their efficiency.

Choosing a supercharger for your 5.0, like choosing most other speed parts, requires you to be honest with yourself. If you plan on driving your car on the street 99 percent of the time, don't plan to continually modify it, and like a hit of low-end torque, a positive-displacement supercharger is a good

5.0 Blower Hints

Supercharger combos require some attention and tuning to pump out maximum horsepower while remaining streetable. Here's a list of tips:

• The common mistake is underfueling. Just more air is not going to make an engine produce power. You've got to get fuel in the engine and light it. Just air doesn't work.

• Pick the largest reasonable throttle body. You want to make sure the throttle body flows as much as your mass air meter, which lacks a restrictive butterfly like the throttle body. Most cars do well with a 70-millimeter, but big engines might want a 75-millimeter.

• Beware restrictions upstream of the supercharger. The blower must draw in air like a normally aspirated engine, and recent experience has shown large air inlets help.

• Ported heads still help. Don't think the supercharger will "push" the intake air into the engine. It can somewhat, but intake air heat goes up, as do the drive loads on the blower. You'll be much happier with a blower and head combination than just the blower.

• You don't need to go crazy with ported aftermarket cylinder heads. Most out-of-the-box heads, such as Twisted Wedges and Edelbrocks, flow plenty for a street power-

plant. If anything, smoothing the exhaust side helps. On the other hand, stock E7TE heads are still a choke on blower engines. A good street aluminum head is the smart choice for blower street engine.

• Run a good quality head gasket and fasteners, but remember a blown head gasket is easier to change than a burnt piston.

• Run the largest, best exhaust you can, but street cars should stick to short-tube headers and high-flow catalytic converters.

• A Ford Motorsport E303 camshaft is a good default cam for street-going centrifugal 5.0s, though you can likely beat it with a custom or tuner-specified grind on the track. Still, the stock cam is best for maintaining drivability and fuel mileage, and should be the choice of the vast majority of 5.0 blower cars.

• Electronic tuning (EPEC, PMS, or custom chip) is the best way to squeeze maximum power from typically rich supercharger setups. If that's out of reach, changing diaphragms in the FMU can help match the oversized injectors and the blower's fuel system. There's nothing like custom electronic tuning to get the most out of a blower car. It's money well spent.

• Unless experimentation is your game, stick with standard combinations. Hot rodding is expensive enough without tempting fate.

choice. However, if you plan to regularly visit the drag strip, and want to keep adding parts until you run out of money, and you know you won't be satisfied with the initial boost level for long, a centrifugal blower is the better choice. It's more complicated than that, of course, as there are centrifugal superchargers designed just for the street and others for racing, but the important first point is to decide on what you want the supercharger to do for you.

Except for the torque freaks, most people who get the boost bug want to keep stepping up. If you want the best of both worlds, a stroker (see Chapter 7) and a centrifugal will let you have torque and horsepower. All it takes is money. Furthermore, as this book went to press, several enlarged and improved superchargers were being developed, and I expect the torque and horsepower conundrum to be answered better and better as more development takes place.

If your 5.0 is a street driver, you can't get too carried away because your supercharger must remain emissions legal, as determined by the California Air Resources Board. Most superchargers offering moderate boost levels of 5 to 10 pounds of boost are CARB-exempted. Look for an EO number or "50-state" legal wording to determine street legality.

Centrifugals

Paxton

Because Paxton superchargers were the first to be associated with the Mustang, it was only fitting Paxton developed the first street-legal supercharger for the fuel-injected 5.0 Mustang. Paxton offers two types of centrifugal drive mechanisms to serve different needs. The SN-93 and VR4 superchargers are both belt driven via a gearless planetary ball drive that smoothly and quietly steps up the speed of the impeller relative to the input shaft. The Novi 2000 supercharger utilizes a helical-cut gear drive to step up input shaft speed.

SN-93

The SN-93 is an improved version of the venerable ball-driven supercharger

found on the Shelby GT-350s. The quiet unit is easily installed because of its self-contained lubrication and, compared to the other blowers in the Paxton line-up, is relatively inexpensive. However, the SN-93 requires frequent fluid changes (every 3,000 miles) and will not live at high impeller speeds, and thus boost is limited. The basic SN-93 is said to be good for 850 cubic feet per minute, while high-output impeller delivers 1,200 cubic feet per minute. That's 8–10 pounds maximum.

The ball drive has not proven durable, either. Kept within its limits, the SN-93 will live, given regular fluid changes, but high boost, lackadaisical maintenance, and age eventually require its ball-drive mechanism to be rebuilt, a costly eventuality. The basic SN-93 kits lack a larger fuel pump or a bypass valve, too, so count them in your calculations. These simple, vacuum-driven parts route unused boost back to the blower inlet. The optional oil cooler is also a very smart idea. All said, there are better ways to produce six pounds of reliable boost on a 5.0, and gunning for more with the ball-drive Paxton is asking for expensive trouble.

VR4

Paxton's initial race-oriented blower was the VR4. It is an upgraded version of the SN-93. It retains the quiet ball-drive mechanism, but is good for 1,500 cubic feet per minute and 12 to 15 pounds of boost. This blower demands the use of Paxton's optional Paxta-Trac fluid, which improves the traction of the ball drive, and Paxton's optional oil cooler to reduce its self-contained lubricant temperatures. Naturally, it is more expensive than the SN-93. This blower also goes by the Novi GSS name, but when the guy in the pits says "Novi," he means a Novi 2000.

Novi 2000

At the top of the Paxton mountain, and a huge step up in durability and output, is the Novi 2000. This supercharger is reputed to be capable of producing 1,700 cubic feet per minute and 27–30 pounds of boost. These are figures far

Say "5.0 blower" and Vortech's V-1 blower comes instantly to mind. A bit noisy, but it's powerful, durable, adaptable, and easy enough to install. Being first to market when these qualities were lacking made it *the* 5.0 supercharger. The tight air inlet to the blower is a limiter on SN-95 installations, but is forced by the chassis packaging.

beyond a bolt-on engine's capabilities, but pulleyed for less boost, the Novi 2000 makes quick boost at relatively low engine rpm. Also, the temperature of the output air is low because the unit has high adiabatic efficiency. Unlike other Paxtons, the Novi can utilize self-contained lubrication or use engine oil like Vortechs and turbochargers. The robust helical-gear drive makes the Novi a natural for racing applications, but, according to Paxton, it is CARB-exempted for street 5.0s. On street cars, it is often spun slowly, producing relatively cool boost. Reports from owners of street Novis say the big blower also kicks boost in far earlier than most centrifugals.

Not an inexpensive blower, the Novi has blown away all the SN-93 weak points, and has reasserted the Paxton name in the blower market. It got off to a relatively slow start in the street market due to a lack of a dedicated mounting kit, but now features an excellent, extremely rigid mount. Paxton or long-time Paxton dealer Central Coast Mustang can now get a Novi mounted, however.

Vortech

A group of former Paxton employees formed Vortech Engineering. They replaced the Paxton's ball drive with a straight-cut gear mechanism. This is a durable, but noisy, method of stepping up the rpm of the input shaft. These stout blowers immediately ate into Paxton's market share, as power-hungry 5.0 owners tried to squeeze more and more power from their small-blocks.

Installing a Vortech is just slightly more complicated than a basic SN-93 Paxton kit, because the straight-cut gear drive must be bathed in a constant supply of engine oil to keep it lubricated. This requires picking up pressurized oil by teeing into the oil pressure sensor fitting and punching a hole in the oil pan for a return line. Still, experienced shops slap these blowers on in four hours. The straight-cut gears also emit a rhythmic whine, which exhibitionist gearheads seem to love and stealth proponents can't take. Over the years, Vortech has quieted its gear drive with ever-better gear sets; modern Vortechs are thus heard mainly at idle and are nearly inaudible inside the car when cruising.

Noise or not, Vortechs have proven the most popular superchargers for 5.0 Mustangs to date, because they are durable, produce good power, are relatively easy to install, and are cost-effective. Thus there are a variety of aftermarket parts designed to augment them, and most tuners know how to work with them.

V1

Little has changed with the two-gear V1 supercharger housing since its introduction. What has changed is its impeller. The V1 was originally equipped strictly with an A-Trim impeller, which was good for airflow up to 450 horsepower. Eventually, Vortech released the more aggressive B-Trim, which flowed 20 percent more, for up to 540 horses. Vortech also released the race-oriented R-Trim configuration, said to support 900 horsepower. Eventually, all but the R-Trim were supplanted by the highly efficient S-Trim impeller, then the T-trim. In typical S-trim condition, this blower produces around 10 pounds of boost on a stock 5.0.

The S-Trim impeller was set to be standard in the mysterious V2 supercharger. The V2 was to include various detail improvements; a quiet, helical-cut gear drive; and the aforementioned S-Trim. To date, the V2 has not been seen. Instead, V1 S-Trim blowers are simply sold in standard and High-Output kits, which are determined by pulley size and accessories. Vortech doesn't like to talk in terms of pounds of boost, as it does get misleading after a while and we should all be talking in terms of air mass. Figure on about six pounds with the standard kit and eight pounds with the more popular High Output version. Besides the pulley differences, the High Output kit includes the somewhat noisy but necessary T-Rex inline auxiliary fuel pump and a bypass valve.

Mondo

Vortech's V3, popularly known as the Mondo, was designed as a marine supercharger. In its J-Trim configuration, the Mondo is capable of supporting 1,200 horsepower. Of course, this supercharger quickly found a home under the hoods of many all-out drag race 5.0s, especially those with stroked 351s. After the success of the big blower, Vortech released the V4 supercharger, which uses the same case as a V3. It, however, contains upgraded bearings and more aggressive X-Trim impeller. Neither blower is CARB-exempted, and both require a prepped engine to withstand their 20-plus pounds of boost.

Powerdyne

Jim Wheeler, a former employee of Paxton and Vortech, formed Powerdyne, delivering yet another spin on the centrifugal supercharger. Concentrating on a pure street blower that would be inexpensive, easy to install, and quiet, the Powerdyne was designed with high-temperature ceramic bearings and a Kevlar cog belt impeller drive. The resulting blowers deliver extremely quiet operation and low cost. Also, Powerdynes are by far the easiest centrifugals

Vortech's bad boy is the Mondo, a max-effort blower that's fine for Pro 5.0 work, but a bit much for the street. Still, Vortech offers a mounting kit, cog drive, blower strut brace, and a Mondo cooler specifically for the 5.0 Mustang, which makes things easier for racers. This is the Keen brother's 1,200 horsepower, Mondo-cooled racer, which is a custom installation.

to install, as they have no lubrication requirements. They are available in six- and nine-pound configurations, but both kits, particularly the nine-pounder, lack a larger fuel pump, boost retard, and bypass valve. Powerdyne says the bypass valve is nice, but not mandatory, on a six-pound blower. You really do need it on the nine-pounder. The valve bypasses the blower discharge air when the throttle is closed at high engine rpm, which lessens charge air heating.

Working as advertised most of the time, the Powerdynes suffered a rash of internal belt failures, which sullied the name. In 1997, Powerdyne upgraded, expanded, and renamed its blower line-up. The standard blower, which had used an idler pulley on its internal belt, was christened the BD-11. The idler gear, whose bearing turned out to be the

Powerdyne's BD-11 is the ticket when low-cost, super-easy installation and moderate street boost are the goals. Not a race winner, the basic Powerdyne is a quiet street blower that puts a nice six-pound urge into a 5.0. If stepping up to the nine-pound pulley, be sure to get a larger fuel pump, bypass, and ignition retard.

source of the "belt failure" problem, was eliminated. To hold the belt tight against the sprockets, the belt specification was changed to a more robust Gates part number, and all internal rotating parts lightened to work without need of an idler (tensioner). Remember, the less weight, the less belt tensioning is required. Powerdyne also released the smaller BD-550 for the 4.6 2V Mustangs at the same time.

Furthermore, Powerdyne joined the geardrive brigade in 1997 with its XB-9000 supercharger. At press time for this book, early tests showed the XB-9000 was good for around 17 pounds of boost. Using the same housing as the BD-11 and BD-550 so it would interchange into existing applications, the XB-9000 promises to be a good street/strip supercharger.

For a pure street application where a bit more top-end power is desired, it's tough to beat the BD-11's price and ease of installation, something even the factory is impressed by. That's why Powerdynes are sold by Ford SVO.

Accessible Technologies

Something of a wild card in the centrifugal market is the ProCharger sold by Accessible Technologies, Inc. The only centrifugal manufacturer without any historical ties to Paxton, ATI is also the only centrifugal maker to offer a standard air-to-air intercooler with all but its basic 6- and 9-pound kits. Intercooled ProChargers are available in 9-, 11-, 14-, and 17-pound P600 configurations, and have proven popular in hot climates because of their standard intercooling.

These blowers are likely the most involved of the centrifugals to install, thanks to their driver-side mounting and intercooler routing, but it is a routing that makes sense as the air goes from the blower, through the intercooler, and into the engine. ProChargers come with larger fuel pumps and bypass valves, but lack ignition boost retards. ATI claims the intercooler alleviates the need for a retard.

ProChargers work well enough, but don't perform up to the earth-rotating expectations set by advertising hyperbole (just like 90 percent of aftermarket parts). This is probably most likely due to their primitive, but mechanically strong, billet impeller designs. This may account for why they haven't caught on like some other blowers, even though they are competitively priced, especially when the intercooler is considered. As another consideration, the ProCharger's belt drives and other items of hardware have been a bit crude over the years, but they have noticeably improved lately.

A nice thing about ATI's blower line-up is that you can buy the bare-bones seven-pound, nonintercooled kit, then upgrade all the way to the P1200 race blower by adding the intercooler and changing impellers. At press time, ATI was working on a completely new blower, the huge, 8-inch impellered Dominator. A contemporary of the Mondo and Novi, the Dominator is said to make 30 pounds of boost and support 1,400 horsepower.

Positive Displacement
Kenne Bell

Although it looks like a roots blower, the Autorotor compressor packaged for Fords by Kenne Bell is a more sophisticated and expensive design. Internally, the blower uses meshing rotors, one male, the other female. They scroll air from one end of the housing to the other in an ever-tightening space, providing a smooth, nonpulsing flow of compressed air to the intake manifold.

Installation is also unique and easy. The blower simply bolts in place of a stock or GT-40 upper intake manifold and shares the serpentine accessory belt. Additionally, the "Whipplecharger" features self-contained lubrication, so there are no oil feed or return lines to run. A few bracket modifications and fuel line connections keep the installation from being totally brainless.

While still not as heat-efficient as the best centrifugals, the Kenne Bell is close, and has the advantage of being a positive displacement blower. It keeps its air discharge temperature within reason (under 200 degrees) unless idled for extended periods or subjected to extended rpm with the throttle closed. This typically happens at the drag strip after powering through the lights and then coasting down to the turn-off road. Another Kenne Bell heat oddity is that it heats the air even at cruise loads and rpm. This is because the Kenne Bell is a compressor, so even if small amounts of air are fed through the unit, that air is compressed and thus heated. This quirk doesn't seem to make a practical difference.

Another interesting aspect of the Kenne Bell is that its heat efficiency is not only pretty good, but varies negligibly with blower rpm. The smaller 1.5-liter Kenne Bell is good up to about 12 pounds of boost on a 302, then the 2.2-liter compressor is required for higher boost pressures. However, using the bigger 2.2 to make 8 pounds of boost does not realize any efficiency advantages over the 1.5 pulleyed for 8 pounds of boost, so either blower makes the same power at the same boost.

Still, because the Kenne Bell blower can only be turned so fast, to increase its output the larger supercharger must be used when going for more than 12 pounds of boost. Responding to criticism that its standard 1.5-liter per revolution supercharger (the 1500 blower) was a bit too small for the 5.0 engine (some say it doesn't run quite as hard as it should at the top end), Kenne Bell introduced the 2.2-liter (2200) and 2.6-liter (2600)

There's hardly an inch of the engine compartment that doesn't have some part of the ATI Procharger blower kit near it. It all starts with the twin air filters along the firewall, followed by a trip forward through the blower, then the air-to-air intercooler, out through the passenger side fender and back up to the intake manifold. Interestingly, throttle lag isn't really a concern after all that. Internally, Prochargers are pretty basic superchargers, but with an intercooler as standard, they've proved popular in hot climates.

Intercooling or Aftercooling?

Although commonly used to denote the devices used on simple supercharger systems, the word intercooler denotes a heat exchanger used between (inter) stages of a multi-stage supercharging system. On large industrial engines it is not unusual to find a large turbo blowing into a smaller turbo, which then blows into the engine. An intercooler goes between the turbos; an aftercooler goes after the second turbo. Thus, on the single-stage blower or turbo systems commonly found on Fords, the charge air cooling heat exchanger is properly known as an aftercooler.

blowers in 1997. The 2200 has the same outer dimensions of the 1500 and exchanges directly with the 1500, making it easy for existing Kenne Bell owners to move up. The 2200 should provide enough air to support 660 horsepower and 17 pounds of boost according to Kenne Bell. Like the 1500, the 2200 uses a six-rib drive belt.

The 2600 is a couple of inches longer than the 1500 and 2200 blowers, and runs all the way to the firewall on a 5.0. It is designed to deliver 780 horsepower worth of air, so it is getting away from the pure bolt-on level. It requires an eight-rib drive belt and uses a different air inlet.

Two items not previously available from Kenne Bell, a bypass and an intercooler, were also slated for availability at this book's press time. The bypass is especially important, as during deceleration inlet temps can get hot enough under poor conditions (hot days) to cause the rotors to grow and touch the case. The bypass will substantially cool the air temperature, and is best used with the 2.2-liter blower. Kenne Bell says you really don't need the bypass

with the 1.5-liter compressor. As for the intercooler, Kenne Bell thinks they're a waste of time with their blower, as the pumping losses through the cooler cancel any gains from the denser air. So, while there was talk of an intercooler to meet market demand at press time, Kenne Bell prefers to concentrate on electronic tuning as the most promising blower power-building strategy.

The fixed fuel management unit included in Kenne Bell kits over-richens the mixture when it is hit with immediate boost. This situation can be addressed with computer chips. In fact, Kenne Bell does a good job of maximizing its blowers with electronic aids such as the Switch Chip, and it's a smart way of building a torquey, tractable street engine. I should also note that while Kenne Bell likes to say its blower is silent, and indeed it makes nearly no air noise, it does make a constant, almost metallic growling from its gear drive, especially once the supercharger has many miles on it. Vastly quieter than a Vortech, the Kenne Bell can still make itself known when coupled with stock mufflers and a quiet valvetrain (no roller rockers). Like all noises,

it bothers a few people and others don't seem to care, and I mention it only in case you're big on keeping your engine dead quiet. With booming mufflers and a big stereo, no one will ever hear it.

BBK Performance

BBK joined forces with OEM supplier Eaton Superchargers to package Eaton's M90 roots blower for the 5.0 Mustang under the Instacharger name. This is the same blower supplied as original equipment on the Thunderbird Super Coupe and is reliable as sunrise.

Rather than mounting the blower on top of the intake, like the Whipple, BBK chose the familiar passenger-side mounting location frequented by centrifugals to avoid requiring a taller hood. For first-time installers, the Instacharger proves a muscle-straining installation, thanks to its pre-assembled bulk. However, the six- and nine-pound kits are competitively priced, and include a bypass valve, an adjustable fuel management unit, and a built-in 73-millimeter throttle body.

The nine-pound kit adds blower niceties like an inline booster fuel pump and a trick boost retard ignition. The latter allows ignition controlling when the retard activates and includes a built-in boost gauge with a max-boost recording feature that's pretty handy.

Kenne Bell's standard offering, the 1500 unit shown here, is plenty for the typical daily-driven bolt-on 5.0. These blowers share their drive belt with the other engine accessories and use small blower pulleys, so belt slippage can occur at higher boost settings, but typically not to the point where it's a major concern. Naturally, a variety of blower pulleys is available, so between the three Kenne Bell blowers and those pulleys, nearly any boost level can be accommodated. Bolt-on 5.0 owners will be happiest with the 1500 (1.5-liter) kit, while more sporting enthusiasts with a prepped engine can use the 2200 "Blowzilla" supercharger and its 12 to 18 pounds of boost.

Once installed, the Instacharger operates flawlessly and particularly shines off-idle and at moderate highway rpm, where early boost negates the need to downshift for passing. Just like the Kenne Bell 1500, the small-M90's limited boost potential makes the Instacharger best suited for stock and mildly modified 5.0s. The roots-design Eaton blower takes a definite last place in the heat efficiency race, too. That's why Ford intercooled the Thunderbird SC, and one reason you won't see the BBK kit banging off 10s at the strip.

The BBK and small Kenne Bells excel in everyday street driving, where they add easy power at all normal rpm. Their easy boost make even fifth gear a "full service" cog. Loaf down the freeway at 1,800 rpm, step on the throttle, and these blowers move a 5.0 right along. Do that with a centrifugal blower and the 5.0 will groan its way forward—like grass growing. Furthermore, the Kenne Bell blowers are offered in enough versions to make race-winning boost, so they are more than a casual street piece.

Accessories

Supercharging kits for Mustangs are pretty complete, but almost every installation does better with some form of accessory. In some cases the so-called accessories are really mandatory, typically with entry level kits. This is because the pressure to keep prices low means the manufacturer keeps the entry level kits' equipment list a bit too sparse. Also, many 5.0s are already modified, so it is assumed some popular pieces of gear are already on the car. In the end, the smart owner ensures he has plenty of fuel and spark retard available. It's always better to have a little less power than eight holed pistons and two blown head gaskets.

While not commonly thought of as blower accessories, good cylinder heads, headers, cat-back exhaust, and other airflow improvers are vital when considering a hard-running blower car. The less-expensive, easy-to-install street bolt-on kits from Powerdyne, BBK, Kenne-Bell, and so on make an otherwise stone-stock 5.0 run the way it should. If you're dreaming of tire-hazing and wheel-lifting performance, how-

ever, it's going to take the bigger blower and all the airflow trimmings.

Fuel
Management Units

Forcing air, or boost, into an engine is just the beginning with forced induction. Without adding a matching amount of fuel to the cylinder, engine-killing detonation will occur. Most supercharger manufacturers remedy this by plumbing a fuel management unit into the fuel return line that funnels unused fuel back to the tank.

When the FMU senses boost, it snaps the return line shut, boosting fuel pressure and increasing fuel flow through the fuel injectors. This allows smaller, emissions-legal fuel injectors to temporarily act like much larger injectors. Most blower kits come with fixed FMUs, which are often calibrated on the rich side of safety. That is, these FMUs use simple, spring-loaded rubber diaphragms that are fixed to close off the return fuel line at the first hint of boost. To adjust the boost pressure at which the FMU closes the fuel return line, adjustable FMUs were developed. They are sold by Paxton, Vortech, and turbo vendor Cartech, and allow adjusting the boost point at which they respond via an adjusting screw and locknut, which is easy enough to do.

The trick with these units is knowing what the engine truly needs fuel-wise, which is best done with a $30,000 chassis dyno and an accurate air/fuel meter, such as the industry standard $10,000 Horiba. Of course, there is always the trial-and-error school at the drag strip, which also includes exchanging diaphragms in "nonadjustable" FMUs. A smaller diaphragm nets less fuel pressure and a leaner mixture, while a larger diaphragm brings on more fuel pressure and a richer mixture. The whole thing smacks of playing hand grenade catch between you and your expensive engine.

In any case, a mechanical FMU can only approximate the engine's fuel needs and serve as an important anti-detonation protector. While savvy tuners can get a standard issue FMU

BBK makes no secret that its supercharger is designed strictly for bolt-on street driving. With a just big-enough blower, poor heat efficiency, and no intercooler, the BBK isn't a high-boost race piece, but it does make a 5.0 drive and feel like a 460. Torque off the bottom is instant, and freeway throttle response for real-world driving conditions is excellent. BBK's pricing is good, too, and the kit includes both a built-in bypass and large throttle body.

and blower combination dialed in for maximum power at full throttle, mechanical FMUs are less than perfect in the tricky transition from normal aspiration to boost. Often they provide 9.0:1 air fuel ratios in the mid-range, then lean out to max power mixture, about 12.5:1, at the power peak or redline. When you think of it, fitting a simple mechanical control like an FMU into the middle of an electronically controlled fuel system is pretty dumb.

With the advent of Dynojet dynos and chip-writing software, it has become possible to custom-tune supercharger fuel systems, and this is the way to do it right. The regular drill is to upgrade the fuel system, especially with larger fuel injectors, eliminating the FMU with its troublesome transition spikes of fuel pressure, and letting the computer chip do a much better job of maintaining the desired fuel ratio. It's an expensive, time-intensive solution that works with just that engine combination, but it works the best. Enough of this work has been done now that even over the phone the more common combinations can be accurately tuned with a chip.

Fuel Pumps

Pressure is only one part of the fuel equation. An FMU and the factory 88-liter per hour fuel pump can accommodate six pounds of boost, maybe. In fact, most insiders say the Mustang's stock fuel pump is decidedly marginal, even for mild bolt-on mods like headers and rocker arms. Part of the problem is that stock pumps vary greatly in their actual output.

Clearly then, more boost requires at least a larger in-tank replacement, like Ford Motorsport's 155- or 190-liter per hour fuel pump. However, most supercharger manufacturers, like Vortech, recommend an in-line booster pump, which works, but does so noisily. Kenne Bell offers an alternative called the Boost-a-Pump, which increases fuel flow by delivering more voltage to a stock or aftermarket in-tank pump. Paxton also has a similar device. These work surprisingly well and don't seem to hurt the pump.

For race-oriented 5.0s pushing 15 or more pounds of boost, you should consider a dedicated fuel system—bigger fuel rails, lines, and pump—from Paxton or Cartech. Running larger injectors can help stave off the need for a dedicated system by reducing the pressure requirements to achieve the same fuel flow, but then you have to watch off-boost fuel mixtures.

Injectors

Like the stock fuel pump, the stock 19-pound per hour fuel injectors found in most 5.0 Mustangs (Cobras have 24-pound per hour injectors) can work with the stock pump and an FMU to support around 6–8 pounds of boost. Anything beyond 8 pounds will likely work better with bigger injectors, plus a new FMU and mass air calibrations.

This gets to be an emissions gray area and a tuning challenge. Injectors larger than 24 pounds per hour don't come on a stock Mustang and thus could present an emissions sticky point in areas where hard-core testing exists. Still, there are many reports of Mustangs with big injectors sailing through emissions tests. These cars likely go a step beyond just FMU and mass air calibrations and rely on custom chips or electronic tuning devices like EFI Systems' Programmable Management System or Ford Motorsport's Extreme Performance Engine Control system.

Aside from emissions, it's likely a good idea for 5.0s running 10 pounds of boost to run at least 30-pound per hour injectors. Pushing more boost may require 36-pound per hour or bigger injectors. As with most EFI tuning choices, you should consult with a tuner versed in forced induction for advice on selecting the right injector flow rate for your car. There are just too many combinations to cover in exacting detail in a book.

Air Filters

All the 5.0 supercharger kits come with a version of K&N's washable Filtercharger air filter (except Kenne Bell, which uses a similar filter). These high-flowing filters include a wire mesh covering that prevents large pieces of debris from piercing the filter and being force fed to your engine after trashing your supercharger. Again, the filter included in the kits seems to be good for 6 to 10 pounds of boost. However, like most other forced induction add-ons, a larger air filter mounted inside the fender will help high-boost applications by providing a larger filtering surface area and isolation from hot underhood air (important). Reducing inlet restrictions with smooth bends is also a benefit to underfender air filters.

Don't overlook underhood heat or fan wash. The air filter must draw cooler in-fender air, or detonation could result. Underhood air kills power and is tough to tune, too. Fan wash drives the idle nuts as blasts of air off the radiator fan randomly shoot into the air meter via an open element air filter. Don't forget about electric fans. They do the same thing as the engine-driven fan.

Low Restriction Air Inlet

We all tend to forget that while a supercharger is a pressure device, its inlet side is naturally aspirated. As it turns out, most blowers breathe okay at the bolt-on stage, but when things get serious, attention to the blower air inlet helps. This is especially true of centrifugals, which aren't exceptional normally aspirated breathers.

Rick Anderson at Anderson Ford Motorsport sells his Power Pipe for Vortech customers. It replaces the stock 3 1/2-inch inlet with a 4-inch mandrel bent tube. The large tube takes up room, forcing the mass air meter and air filter into the fender, a common spot for these on racers anyway.

The Power Pipe really earns its keep on the hardest running street cars and racers, but doesn't do much—or anything—for bolt-on cars, because the stock Vortech inlet is large enough for them. Around 450 horsepower or more, the Power Pipe can unlock boost, depending on how restrictive your combination has been. On a 650-horsepower engine, the Power Pipe can be good for an amazing four pounds of boost, enough to move from the low 10s into the 9s at the strip. The Power Pipe fits Mondos, R and S Trim Vortechs, in fact, just about every centrifugal blower except the ATI.

Kenne Bell sells the Flowzilla, an improved inlet. It's not worth its substantial cost at 8 pounds of boost, but at 10 pounds of boost it adds 8 horsepower and is maybe worth the money. Move up to 400-horsepower engines with 12 or 14 pounds of boost and it really shines, bringing 35–40 horsepower to the party. Racers will pay anything for that kind of power.

Cat-Back Exhaust

Blower engines demand the best possible breathing from the exhaust. This is because extra air is forced into the engine, but there is no extra help in getting it out, and thus the mufflers and

Cogged drives look neat, but they're too noisy for the street. The air squeezing from between the belt and pulley is what causes the noise, so there isn't anything to do about it. High boost race blowers require these expensive drives, as the horsepower needed to drive the supercharger is considerable. Also, less belt tension is necessary with a cogged drive, which relieves some load off the crankshaft. Note also how the rod end bearings on this brace allow it to move freely in several planes.

tailpipes are asked to handle much larger volumes than they were designed for.

So, while a stock 5.0 doesn't respond to a cat-back except for extra noise, on a blown car you need all the least exhaust restriction you can get. High-flow cats and your choice of low-restriction cat-back mufflers and tailpipes, all in 2 1/2-inch diameter, really help.

Boost Retards

The old hot rodding trick of advancing the ignition timing is still useful with supercharged 5.0s, but as boost increases, cylinder pressures increase and combustion speeds up. Thus the spark must be retarded to avoid detonation. Remember, detonation can kill any engine, but goes from lousy news to death in the blink of an eye on blower engines. It easily results in blown head gaskets, and often worse. So, you don't want to control detonation, you must eliminate it.

Boost retards are mandatory for supercharged engines. They reel in the timing as boost pressure rises, holding detonation at bay. Most well-heeled, high-output kits offer some kind of

boost retard. However, if you plan to keep upping the boost ante, you'll need a high-output ignition with boost retard features. These are required because high boost pressures, 10 pounds and higher, actually blow out the unaided spark, causing a miss.

Octane Boosters

While not normally thought of as a blower accessory, burning high octane gas is a super help. This is especially true when running at the track, where detonation is more likely from heat, or a smaller pulley is being used. Unleaded fuels in excess of 100 octane are widely available, and octane boosters for doping premium pump gas are available everywhere. Use them.

Bypass Kits

One of the most important accessories (mandatory) for a centrifugally supercharged street 5.0 is a bypass valve. These simple, vacuum-driven parts route unused boost back to the blower inlet. They are important because they eliminate blower surge caused when the throttle blade slams shut, leaving boost crammed into the discharge tube. A

Testing Vortech's Aftercooler

Typical of the centrifugal intercoolers is Vortech's aftercooler. Hardware in the Vortech kit includes an injection-molded-plastic water reservoir with submerged bilge pump, a two-pass heat exchanger that replaces the standard discharge tube, a pair of heat exchangers located low in front of the radiator to cool the cooling water, plus enough hardware and plumbing to make it all work. The only thing missing is the required battery relocation kit. Vortech believes many owners have already relocated the battery to the trunk, so that part of the aftercooler kit is optional. This lowers the base price, of course, but doesn't change the need to relocate the battery to make room for the reservoir.

At the Drag Strip

Mike Regan, an engineer at Vortech, provided the following drag strip test results:

Test	ET	Mph
Baseline	12.75	111.5
Ice water	12.10	121.1

All drag testing done on Goodyear Gatorback radials.

Any time you can get 0.6 of a second and 10 miles per hour by pouring chilled water into a plastic bucket, do it! These numbers really whetted my appetite for the dyno test, as the 10-mile per hour gain on a car already running 111 miles per hour meant serious power gains were being made.

Running ice at the drag strip with the aftercooler is uncomplicated. Mike says the ice stays pretty cool for a couple of runs, depending on ambient temperatures. Also, by turning on the system's water pump (it has a small cockpit-mounted toggle switch) in the staging lanes, some cool-down effect can be gained. This works only with ice water. Tap water is not cold enough to provide any cool-down.

On the Dyno

Three pulls were made in each configuration—baseline, tap water, and ice water. Each group of three runs has been averaged to even out minor variations in engine temperature and other testing variables. Also, the baseline was run using the standard discharge tube, not with the heat exchanger in the way, as the heat exchanger would have caused a bit of power-robbing back pressure. All testing was done at a maximum of 11 pounds of boost; no pulley changes were made. Each run was started at 3,000 rpm.

The results were:

Test	Torque	Horsepower
Baseline	434.0	446.0
Tap Water	456.3	464.6
Ice Water	469.6	473.3

I thought the improvements were excellent, but typically, Vortech was disappointed the gains weren't larger. More importantly, listing the power peaks tells only one part of the improvement. When the baseline, tap water, and ice water runs are graphed together, the type of power allowed by the aftercooling is immediately apparent. Unlike a camshaft, rear axle gears, or other mechanical changes, cooling the air charge does not alter the shape of the torque or power curves, it simply raises them up the chart. Thus, the improvement spans from off-idle to redline, meaning the area under the curve is much greater. That's why Mike's car could gain 10 miles per hour at the drag strip.

It's also interesting to note the diminishing returns posted by ice water. The change from no aftercooling to tap water is about twice as large as moving from tap water to ice water. This is simple physics, as at some point, even with liquid helium in the aftercooling system, there can be no further lowering of the charge air temperature. Of course, with more air moving over the car, this relationship could change. Diminishing returns or not, ice water definitely makes more power, and it was fun watching the aftercooled discharge tube form fat, cold beads of condensation. The engine certainly knows what to do with that.

It's obvious aftercooling at the 10-pound level is beneficial; anyone running more boost should get even more out of it. That's because the hotter the charge air, the greater the difference between it and the cooling water, and thus the greater the rate of heat exchange.

side-effect of eliminating this drivability nightmare is a reduction in inlet temperature because the unwanted boost is no longer bludgeoned in the discharge tube. These days, most 5.0 blower kits come with at least a small bypass.

As boost levels rise, the air volume handled by the bypass rises too. Around 12 pounds or so, a high-flow or racing bypass is necessary. These are available from several sources; Paxton and Vortech units are popular.

Drive Belts and Pulleys

All serpentine supercharger belts slip somewhat. This is a good thing on a street engine, as the belt slip cushions the supercharger when rpm peaks during a shift or when there is the sudden drop in rpm that occurs on engaging the next gear. As boost pressure increases it takes more energy to spin the supercharger faster, and belt slippage increases. Around 10 pounds of boost, slippage becomes troublesome, costing boost. Several methods are used to address this condition, including tightening the belt, adding traction compound to the belt, wider serpentine belts, and cogged belts.

Tightening the belt with youthful enthusiasm is okay, but must not be overdone, or the crankshaft and front main bearing will wear rapidly. It is even possible to break the snout of the crankshaft off, so don't use a 6-foot bar and hang off it when tightening the blower belt.

Belt glue is also good stuff, but use it sparingly. McClure Motorsport offers

Three Power Runs on One

Rpm	Baseline Tq	Hp	Tap Water Tq	Hp	Ice Water Tq	Hp
3200	313.6	191.1	355.6	223.4	346.5	211.1
3300	320.0	201.1	365.0	236.3	363.5	228.4
3400	327.8	212.2	369.9	246.5	363.6	235.4
3500	333.4	222.2	375.1	257.1	377.9	251.8
3600	337.8	231.5	382.8	269.7	390.7	267.8
3700	349.5	246.2	392.0	283.6	393.2	277.0
3800	352.1	254.8	397.1	294.9	405.1	293.1
3900	356.9	265.0	402.1	306.2	407.0	302.3
4000	363.7	277.0	404.1	315.5	408.3	310.9
4100	356.0	277.9	404.8	323.7	408.5	318.9
4200	354.8	283.7	411.4	336.8	411.9	329.4
4300	364.8	298.7	423.3	354.6	425.3	348.2
4400	386.5	323.8	430.6	369.0	432.2	362.1
4500	391.9	335.8	437.9	383.5	443.7	380.1
4600	404.4	354.2	443.6	397.0	448.4	392.7
4700	413.8	370.3	450.4	411.6	454.0	406.3
4800	421.0	384.8	453.9	423.4	460.9	421.2
4900	425.9	397.4	454.8	433.0	463.3	432.3
5000	431.0	410.3	457.4	444.2	464.4	442.1
5100	429.6	417.2	458.1	453.6	466.8	453.3
5200	432.1	427.8	454.7	458.8	467.7	463.1
5300	429.6	433.5	453.7	466.4	462.4	466.6
5400	428.1	440.2	444.4	465.4	458.3	471.2
5500	422.3	442.2	433.5	462.2	450.1	471.4
5600	415.8	443.4	426.3	462.6	440.6	469.8
5700	-	-	-	-	436.7	474.0
5800	-	-	-	-	432.6	477.7

Instaboost, and the usual drag racing traction compounds normally used on tires (VHT, Track Bite, Formula V) work well too. If too much chemical is used, belt traction skyrockets, to the point where the belt sticks to the pulleys and excessive horsepower is consumed just turning the belt!

A common way to alleviate belt slippage is adding wider serpentine belts and pulleys. Most base blower kits include 6-rib belts, while high-output kits generally use 8-rib belts. Super-charger manufacturers and pulley builders like Auto Specialties also offer 10- and even 12-rib blower pulleys and belts. Limiting factors on the wider-is-better method are fan shroud clearance and high tension. It may be necessary to run a low-profile electric fan to clear 10- and 12-rib belts, and though these should be more than adequate for 10 or so pounds of boost, the eventual limit is how much tension you can put on the blower bracket, blower snout, and most importantly, the crankshaft snout.

Cogged belts are the ultimate non-slip supercharger drive. The mechanical locking action of the cogged belt and pulleys means belt slip is eliminated, but it comes at a cost. First, of course, the cog system costs money. They're also quite noisy and the belts wear more rapidly than a serpentine. Cogged belts are intolerant of misalignment, often making it necessary to machine and shim the blower, brackets, and pulleys until they're all true, and then stout brackets and braces are required to hold that alignment. The nonslip drive also means more impact loads on the blower, requiring heavy-duty brackets, strong blower bearings, and a strong blower housing to retain them, plus a racing bypass to instantly off-load closed throttle boost. Their one definite mechanical advantage is they do reduce crankshaft loads if you've been tightening the serpentine belt with a come-along.

If you look at the 1/10 or 2/10 gain in ET possible from a cog drive, it's clear that incremental speed increase is available somewhere else for less money, at least on an 11-second or slower Mustang. It's another way of saying cog drives are fine for race cars, but a bit much for the street. When you do decide to go racing, then a cog drive will give maximum blower rpm and reduced belt tension.

Blower Braces

Often overlooked in the belt slippage fight is blower and bracket deflection. Belt tension increases on the drive side of the belt with rpm, pulling the typical centrifugal supercharger forward (BBK and Kenne Bell blowers don't have this problem—just really small blower pulleys). The movement is allowed by the blower brackets, which are quite flexible. This movement is the leading cause of thrown belts, and the cure is better, and more, brackets.

Manufacturers such as Vortech offer stouter race brackets and other companies, such as HP Motorsports and Cartech, offer Heim-jointed braces that bolster the blower bracket via the block and the shock tower, respectively. HP also has a bracket to connect the

As blower boost rises, so does charge air heat. Intercooling is the answer to this, which then allows more ignition timing, or boost. With centrifugal systems, an air-to-water cooler is easiest to design and install, but there is much more to these systems than the actual intercooler shown here. Moving the battery to the trunk, a water reservoir, pump, water-to-air radiator, and plumbing are all part of the system. ATI uses an air-to-air intercooler that might be better on the street, but doesn't allow packing a water reservoir with ice for extra cooling at the track.

Perhaps the best of the big-time blower braces is the one with Vortech's Mondo. It strengthens the blower/crankshaft assembly in the same plane as the belt, so it is very efficient. Simple hand tightening of this brace is enough to offset the drive belt load. Experience has shown the most rigid blower mounts are worth the effort. Thick mounting plates and extra braces like this Vortech Mondo piece or HP Motorsports V-1 brace are smart additions.

lower end of a Vortech to the header bolts. Homemade angle iron and turnbuckle braces also work, but remember that any brace that goes from the engine to the chassis must accommodate engine movement. Most of the time solid engine mounts are necessary to reduce engine movement to workable levels with such blower braces. No matter what, the most rigid mounting possible is a benefit to any blower.

Intercoolers

As centrifugal superchargers started to make headway on 5.0 Mustangs, some tuners, like Kenny Brown, toyed with plumbing air-to-air intercoolers downwind of blowers. These helped, but suffered from perceived complexity, mild boost loss, and most importantly, high prices. The only commonly used air-to-air intercooler is the one packaged with most ProCharger kits.

That's a shame, as air-to-air intercooling is a great for a street car. It's light, relatively simple, requires no maintenance, and can provide good cooling. It does need to be very carefully designed and installed, however, or efficiency takes a real dive.

Although intercoolers were initially shunned as unnecessary in the days of the 8-pound race blowers, things are different in an age of 10- to 20-pound street boost. Vortech started things by offering an air-to-water intercooler add-on kit. These compact units retrofit to existing centrifugal installations, and offer highly effective ice water cooling for drag racing. On the street, the water heats enough to feel tepid to the touch, but by passing it through a water-to-air radiator, the cooling water still does a fine job of removing intake charge air heat. These "water coolers" are an effective bolt-on, especially for high-boost applications of 10 pounds or more as the sidebar shows.

So far the BBK blower has gone without intercooling, in keeping with its easy, bolt-on position in the market. The BBK would especially benefit from an intercooler, however, as its roots design makes air hot enough to bake a turkey. The other positive displacement blower, the Kenne Bell, generates nowhere near the heat of a roots blower.

5.0 Turbo Kits 98

Turbo Technology 101

CONTENTS

TURBOCHARGING

When moving into the high-pressure world of Pro 5.0 racing, you'll run across Turbonetics and their Big Thumper turbo. Turbonetics is not in the street business, and like most racing turbo suppliers, doesn't even offer a kit. Instead, the Big Thumper label refers to a turbo Turbonetics assembled from big diesel parts. It's good for around 1,200 horsepower on the small-block Ford, and by itself, costs the majority of what you'd pay for a street supercharging kit. Installation, plumbing, and tuning are all up to the purchaser, which is not a problem for the seven-second club engine builders like Ken Duttweiler and Job Spetter, who specialize in these units.

For full-time power production, turbosupercharging is the most powerful power adder available. By using energy already "paid for" and otherwise wasted as heat or pressure in the exhaust system, turbocharging is able to pressurize the intake side of the engine with unequaled efficiency.

So far, several factors have kept turbocharging from being more popular than it is. Speaking generally, a turbocharger is expensive, because it is a precision device operating at extreme rpm in a hot environment. After all the air inleting, compressing, intercooling, exhaust collection, wastegating, and exhausting, turbocharging means plenty of bulky plumbing. Another turbo bugaboo is underhood heat, requiring protection for the vulnerable spark plug wires, fuel and brake lines. Finally, while no one mentions it much, a good daily-driver turbo package does best with heavy iron exhaust manifolding. Along with a pair of turbos and associated gear, this means more front-end weight, exactly where the 5.0 Mustang doesn't need it.

Add all this up, consider the relatively large displacement of the 5.0 HO V-8 and it's not difficult to understand why easier ways of generating 350 to 500 horsepower have been favored. They're less expensive and perhaps more suited to the street environment.

When it comes to limit-pushing 5.0 power outputs, however—1,100 horsepower in 1990, 1,400 horsepower in 1997, and who knows how much more in the future—turbocharging always gets the job. Such racing engines have been popularized by Job Spetter of Turbo People and Kenny Duttweiler. These mega-power engines are hand-built for each application, and while not

particularly trick from a hardware standpoint, do employ the best materials for durability reasons. Thus, they aren't even remotely affordable from the street performance fan's point of view, and of course, they are hardly emissions legal or drivable. When you are ready to run 7s with your 5.0, however, a call to Kenny or Job will fix you up.

Lately, fairly serious drag racers, and not just the $100,000 rocket sled club, are trying turbos. As the centrifugals approach 30 pounds of boost, tradeoffs in the belt drive, crankshaft wear, and overall system efficiency take on new importance. After all, it's asking a lot of the crankshaft to drive around 100 horsepower a long 10 inches in front of the No. 1 main bearing. Turbocharging makes no such demands,

and offers pretty easy energy for such boost levels.

Naturally, for the street crowd there is always the sex appeal of something exotic, something racy, something completely different from the legions of blower cars roaming the streets, and turbos deliver that in spades. The major turbo performance advantage for a street car is that modern turbo systems can pump healthy amounts of boost starting in the low mid-range, then keep huffing strongly right through the engine's redline. That translates into considerably more power under the curve, and more speed from less gearing. Done right, turbo power starts early and parties hearty all the way to the end, thus out-powering its belt-driven counterparts, the centrifugal blowers.

5.0 Turbo Kits

While the lure of easy centrifugally boosted horsepower has captured most 5.0 enthusiasts, turbocharging's exotic power has long had a small following on the street. Naturally, this has led to several turbocharging kits for the 5.0, a class of power adder that seems to be gathering favor. Furthermore, turbocharging is often custom installed by local tuners using their own assembly of parts.

While not selling a kit per se, Gene Deputy at Texas Turbo outfitted many 5.0s in the late 1980s and early 1990s with streetable turbo systems, although he always maintained the simple centrifugal supercharger was the best choice for the average customer. The first 5.0 kit was a single turbo system from Corkey Bell at Cartech, also in Texas. A player for a short time was the DDMI twin-turbo kit, and today the turbo Mustang kit scene is populated by Turbo Technology, Cartech, and new-on-the-scene INCON Systems, looking to catch on with their twin-turbo kit.

Cartech

Cartech, in San Antonio, Texas, offered the first 5.0 turbo kit and is still at it. Cartech's kit has not changed much over the years, but principal Corky Bell thoroughly engineered his kit from the

Devine's Intervention

While there is always an army of supercharged and nitrous late-model Mustangs filling the Pro 5.0 drag racing ladders, at any given point there seems to be one turbo 5.0 running ahead of everyone. Gene Deputy and Racin' Jason have filled that spot, as has Bill Devine of Pennsylvania.

Bill's white 1989 GT has gone from daily driver, through hot rod to top of the heap. Although a few street-only items remain to wow the natives, such as power windows and a working sound system, Bill's car is all racer, with a back-halved chassis, four-link rear suspension, and 16x33-inch Goodyear slicks.

His twin Turbonetics turbo, 347-cubic inch A4 block engine, was built by Kenny Duttweiler, using a Crawford billet crankshaft, Cunningham rods, and 8.8:1 JE Pistons. The cam specs are secret, but said to be mild (typical of turbo engines), and breathing is done through a 90-millimeter Accufab throttle body. A special Duttweiler distributor is used to clear the air intake, ignition is by MSD, and the control system from DFI is tuned by Job Spetter, a New York City area 5.0 specialist. The driveline is built from an F&B Powerglide, 9-inch Art Carr torque converter and Mark Williams rear end. While power figures have not been released on the combination, it consistently runs in the high 7s at nearly 180 miles per hour.

beginning, so it is still capable of more power than a street 5.0 can use.

Today, Cartech specializes in custom turbo installations for racing 5.0s, and is a major source of premier fuel system components. In fact, it may well be the only outfit capable of building a complete, 1,000-horsepower fuel system for a 5.0 with off-the-shelf parts. This meshes perfectly with its turbo business because, as Bell points out, it's supplying the fuel and controlling the ignition that are the tough points of building a workable turbo system, not necessarily the turbo, exhaust manifolds, and plumbing.

Cartech does offer a pair of kits for 1986–1995 Mustangs, the Streetsleeper for streetable power and the Outlaw for track duty. Both kits are single-turbo designs, but the Streetsleeper retains all engine accessories, while its race kit requires eliminating the air conditioning and power steering. Actually, the hardware in both kits is pretty much the same, although the street kit is designed to snake around the engine accessories rather than require their removal. Cartech says its street kit is good up to 650 horsepower, at which point the race kit takes off. Neither kit is emissions-

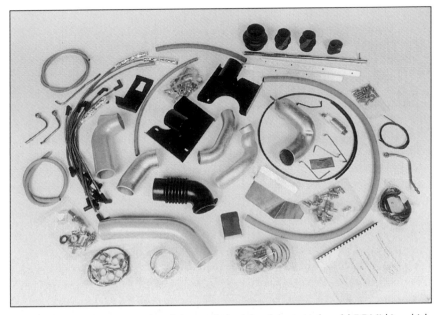

This is just a moderate portion of the total number of parts in the old DDMI kit, which came in seven large shipping boxes. While the DDMI kit is no longer available, this photo still illustrates the complexity of a good turbo installation. You might as well think of it as a reengineering of the engine. Air plumbing accounts for much of a turbo installation, additional fuel capacity and engine management upgrades account for the rest.

exempted for street duty, despite the Streetsleeper name.

Cartech doesn't specify exactly one turbo, injector, and other hardware for its street or race kits, preferring to tailor each application with the customer. That way the relative importance of torque, peak horsepower, drivability, cost, engine durability, and so on can be evaluated and accounted for. This ability to help an owner tune his turbo kit is probably Cartech's largest asset. The engineering power, long 5.0 experience, and on-hand supply of hardware will keep the customer who heeds its advice running hard with plenty of fuel and safe ignition timing. If constantly improving your car is important, then this is a big advantage.

One reason Cartech developed the single-turbo format is that single turbos are considered a power adder in Fun Ford Weekend racing, while twin turbos are categorized as double power adders, and have to run in the unlimited class. Furthermore, single-turbo systems are definitely simpler when it comes to plumbing and installation, not to mention the cost savings—two concepts that should not be underestimated.

On the downside, it's a little tougher to spool up a single large turbo than two small ones. The headers for a single turbo present something of a lopsided packaging challenge, but there's no reason a single turbo, like a single centrifugal supercharger, won't make tons of power.

DDMI

In some ways, the DDMI kit exemplifies the turbo fan's penchant for getting carried away. A very thorough kit, the DDMI proved just too much for the market to bear, and it fell short in several important ways. The price was grand. The kit was so complete it took seven boxes to ship UPS, and the extra weight of the cast-iron exhaust manifolds and turbos (100 pounds) required a step up in spring rates to retain stock handling. Installers couldn't take it, because $3,000 to hammer it into a 5.0 still wasn't enough money, and once it was running, several spark plugs were nearly inaccessible and the plug wires burned off about every 2,000 miles. Topping it all, the T-25 turbos had spun their all by 480 horsepower.

The DDMI's completeness, and packaging concerns in the Mustang

chassis, made it an installation nightmare compared to a centrifugal supercharger. Step one in the DDMI installation manual was to remove the engine so some clearancing of the inner fender and K-member could be done.

Despite all that, the DDMI was still a landmark kit. It used a relatively efficient intercooler, and strongly promoted the idea of charge air cooling. Along with the Cartech kit, the DDMI was way ahead of the centrifugal blower crowd in this regard, and helped pave the way for things like Vortech's aftercooler. With a large advertising budget, the DDMI also put the concept of turbos in front of the 5.0 market, which got many people considering an alternative to nitrous or a centrifugal blower. The DDMI did make passable street power and was suited to the buyer who wanted to have his car modified once and then forget about it, but with its weight and limited tuning range, the ever-faster 5.0 crowd didn't flock to the DDMI bandwagon, and the concern folded.

INCON Systems

The newest system for the 5.0 is the twin-turbo arrangement from INCON. Employing personnel and concepts from the old DDMI system, the INCON offering has DDMI roots, but is an all-new kit, considering the amount of new work that was done. The general twin-turbo, intercooled format remains, but the turbos are completely different, as are the air ducting, intercooler, and general hardware. Although still making its production debut at press time, the INCON system appears ready to be a significant player in the Ford scene. Aimed at the street market as a high-quality, long-lasting bolt-on, CARB exemption was pending at press time.

The two smaller turbos instead of one larger turbo mean faster turbo response, reducing turbo lag. Boost comes on considerably lower in the rev range than with a centrifugal blower; INCON says it can provide eight pounds of boost at 2,000 rpm, then

Because they've been working with high boost pressures from the beginning, and have plenty of boost capacity to make up for any pumping losses through a heat exchanger, turbo people have been way ahead of the supercharger folks when it comes to intercooling. This is the intercooler core from the DDMI kit, which was also experimented with by a few centrifugal racers. It fits low and flat to the air stream, just behind the radiator, and relies on baffles to duct the cooling air up into it. The obvious overall size and care that went into shaping the air "tanks" and fittings suggest the tricky task of designing a good intercooler. Attention to how the air flows both outside and inside an air-to-air intercooler is important.

When cost and long-term durability of a turbo installation are important, then a cast-iron exhaust manifold becomes almost mandatory. This DDMI turbo and manifold assembly is quite similar to the newer INCON system, although the INCON turbos are larger and make more power.

Another view of the DDMI/INCON exhaust manifold shows its extremely robust construction. It takes plain old iron mass like this to withstand the wild heat cycling turbo manifolds experience. So much iron, however, adds plenty of front-end weight.

Spark plug changes with the DDMI/INCON are the sort of thing one plans ahead for. Using premium plugs that don't have to be changed very often is the first planning step, and letting the engine cool is the second. INCON plans on 1 1/2 hours for a plug change on a cold engine.

easily hold that eight pounds—or much more—all the way to redline. This puts real muscle in the mid-range, reducing the need for low rear axle ratios and adding drivability and fuel mileage.

Even though the turbos are compact, there are two of them, so large volumes of air can be pumped. The GT-35BB ceramic ball bearing turbos are assembled by INCON for maximum flow characteristics using its own housings and not off-the-shelf housings from another, compromised OEM application. According to INCON this adds up to 800 horsepower worth of airflow, of which 500 horsepower can be enjoyed by the average street enthusiast. After that the fuel system requires complete reengineering, and the stock 5.0 block must be replaced with the beefy A4 unit from Motorsport or at least an old Boss 302 unit.

Obviously, considerable money and effort must be expended on the basic engine and fuel system before 800 horsepower will be generated, but it won't take new turbos. This does bring up the almost too easy way turbo systems can vary their boost pressure: simply adjust the wastegate screws. INCON says its system adjusts between 7 and 25 pounds of boost. With a claimed 78 percent adiabatic (heat) efficiency from their turbos, that much boost means plenty of air and thus horsepower.

INCON's ball bearing turbos are designed with pressure oiling and water cooling for long life. This means plumbing two oil return lines into the oil pan, plus a water loop from just behind the thermostat housing (a drill and tap operation), but combined with the heavy cast-iron exhaust manifolds, means the installation should prove OEM durable. Also, INCON says the ball bearings allow the turbines to speed up 40 percent quicker than those supported by plain bearings.

INCON has also opted for formed silicon rubber air ducting hose. This is lighter, quieter (doesn't rattle), and fits better than the cast or sheet metal alternative, and requires fewer pieces.

INCON's intercooler measures 36x6x3 1/2 inches but still allows the stock battery, sway bar, and all front-of-engine accessories. An 80-millimeter mass air meter is fitted in part of the ducting, and features blow-through operation. Mike Wesley is doing a chip for INCON to handle the electronics, including the critical mass air meter voltage curve to work with the Bosch

Dennis Lugo has had good success with Turbo Technology's single-turbo system. His older Pro 5.0 car runs easy 10s, makes big wheelies, and massive miles per hour. The general layout follows typical forced-induction 5.0 practice, with the turbo on the driver side and feeding charge air down to an air-to-air intercooler, which brings the air back up on the passenger side to the throttle body. With electronic tuning, this sort of power is available on street engines.

Driving a Turbo 5.0

Building turbo boost when staging at the drag strip calls for some driver technique, and an automatic transmission. Because of turbo lag time, the turbo driver can't wait until the green light comes on to step on the throttle. The second or so it takes the motionless turbo(s) to rev up to 100,000 rpm is just too much to give away.

Instead, the engine must be loaded prior to the launch, so when the green illuminates, all the boost and power are straining to leave. This is done by power-braking an automatic transmission (free-revving a manual gearbox won't build boost). The brake pedal and trans brakes are normally used, but timing the power buildup during the staging process is part of running a turbo 5.0 at the strip.

On the street, turbo lag is noticeable but not a concern. It's one of those things you subconsciously learn to drive around the first time in the car. Besides, with street tires on, the soft hit of turbo boost allows the car to get moving before the big power arrives.

30-pound injectors. A 190-liter per hour in-tank pump and no FMU are used. So configured, INCON says its fuel system will feed 500 horsepower through the stock fuel lines and rails. Any more and the entire fuel system must be upgraded.

Installation is still no picnic with the INCON, although engine removal is not required. A steel plate and template are supplied so the passenger side inner fender and frame rail can be marked, cut with a torch or plasma cutter, and the new plate welded in. INCON says this isn't that difficult once the exhaust header is removed. In a well-equipped home shop INCON estimates installation at 16 hours. Much of this is busy work, such as dropping the fuel tank to install the fuel pump, plugging in the electronic module to the computer, and taking the intake manifold off to install the injectors. Some is more involved, with a few holes to drill for intercooler mounting, punching the oil pan for the oil returns, and tapping

and drilling the intake manifold for the water line, not to mention the blacksmith work on the chassis. The rest is bolting on the kit. If you're a first timer under the hood, this is a definite shop job for you. Senior enthusiasts will no doubt find it a worthy challenge.

It sounds like INCON is using the same exhaust manifolds as the DDMI kit, and the heat concerns are handled with ACCEL Extreme 9000 plug wires with shielding—much better stuff than in the DDMI kit. Plug access is still difficult, but INCON says a Snap-On thinwall plug socket with integral swivel is the trick tool. Figure on 1 1/2-hour plug changes after an overnight cool-down, says INCON.

Looking ahead, INCON is planning on a new long-runner intake manifold, a staggered round design similar to the GT-40, with space for a second set of injectors, their fuel rails, and associated hardware. INCON is also planning on an electronic wastegate controller. This would allow much more precise control of the turbo wastegate, and thus yield faster turbo response.

Turbo Technology

Probably the most familiar current player in the Mustang turbo scene is Turbo Technology from Washington state. Like Cartech, Turbo Technology has settled on a single-turbo kit, with intercooler. Thanks to the cost of the turbo, intercooler, and the large amount of piping and high quality clamps, the cost of this kit is several hundred dollars above the average centrifugal blower installation. The results are well above average, though, with several advantages over a blower kit.

Some of the advantages of the Turbo Technology kit over the more common centrifugal superchargers are:

- quick, no-cost, 6-to-14-pound boost adjustment via the wastegate
- exhaust headers included with kit
- standard intercooling
- quiet operation, with "whoosh" generated only under boost
- full boost by 3,200 rpm; more area under the curve
- large mid-range torque increase

When getting serious about speed, turbos poses unique intake manifolding needs. Boost is plentiful from the mid-3,000-rpm range, but below that the low compression ratio of a dedicated turbo engine means the engine is pretty soft and can use some intake manifold runner length. Once boost ramps up, however, runner length is more a restriction to the plentiful mid-range and top-end power the turbo makes by itself. Fiddling with custom manifolds can thus make a difference on a track car.

A closer look at Lugo's Turbo Technology installation shows the T-04 turbo and tubular exhaust manifolding. Cloth header wrap on the manifold retains heat in the exhaust system and thus pipes more energy to the turbo. The trade-off is shorter header life, as they get baked inside their cloth jacket. Unless you have a specific need to protect an underhood component, avoid header wraps.

• lower shift points, so rpm-related breakages are not a concern
• improved fuel mileage, as less rear axle gear is required
• the mystique of being different

Naturally, there are tradeoffs and differences with the Turbo Technology kit. Like the advantages, these tradeoffs are mainly typical of all turbo installations:
• higher initial price
• increased underhood heat, calling for some heat-protection measures
• somewhat involved installation
• lack of a few required parts in the nearly complete kit, compared to the best blower kits
• necessity of removing the exhaust headers, if the engine has already been hot rodded, although they can be sold to recoup some of kit pric.
• poor power steering pump access

Installing the Turbo Technology system is about one step more involved than the more complete centrifugal blower kits, and is best left to the pros for the first-time 5.0 modifier. Dennis Lugo, a Turbo Technology dealer, allows 12 hours to install the kit. Highlights of the installation include relocating the battery to the driver side of the engine compartment using a longer positive cable, splicing into the mass air meter harness to lengthen it, holing the oil pan for an oil return line from the turbo (the pressure line comes from the oil pressure sending unit area), cutting and extending the power steering pump filler neck, intercooler mounting onto and forward of the K-member (some drilling, and possible welding with tubular K-members), hole sawing of inner fender for air intake hose, and heat shielding some ignition wiring.

Driving the Turbo Technology kit is exciting, with a big mid-range and top-end rush. If you want, you can pad around town without getting into the turbo boost, and because you don't need 3.73 gears to pull the beast, mileage is good. If trying for both cruising and power, it's possible to move from the stock T-04 turbine to the T-04 Hi-Fi, which spools up faster. It's the ticket for a stock 5.0 with AOD and 2.73 gears, as it gets into the boost quicker. You don't want the Hi-Fi on a modified engine, as the top end is a bit limited compared to the stock turbo.

Courteous street manners aside, the Turbo Technology kit can be set for awe-inspiring track performance. This requires good cylinder heads, intake, and bottom end, of course, but with 14 pounds of intercooled boost available from the low mid-range on up, holding on to the rear tires is the major problem. Also, as can be seen in the photos, the tubular headers allow vastly improved spark plug access compared to cast-iron headers (which are more durable).

C O N T E N T S

Why a Stroker? 103

Stroker Blocks 104

Stroker Crankshafts . . .104

Damper and Flywheel . .104

Stroker Connecting Rods
and Pistons 105

Stroker Tradeoffs 105

Stroker Tuning 106

Why Not a 351? 107

With the popularity of 347 engines, machine shops have become familiar with putting such engines together. When installing a 347 kit, relieving the lower cylinder wall to clear the connecting rod bolts is the only modification necessary. If you want to run a main bearing cap girdle, ask its manufacturer if it will clear a 347 rotating assembly—most do.

STROKERS

Racers are fond of pithy statements that sum up the realities of their sport. One of the more famous, and certainly accurate, of these is, "There's no replacement for displacement." Many have argued the point, but when it's time to hit the track or especially motor around the streets, it's true. There simply is nothing like displacement. The bigger the engine, naturally the more torque it makes, and torque makes an engine easy to drive, especially on the street. Rev the larger engine a bit and that extra torque becomes the prime factor in increased horsepower so, sure, displacement rules. Besides, you can just as easily put a power adder like a supercharger on top of a stroked 5.0 as on a stock displacement one.

There are two practical ways to increase displacement: increasing the diameter of the cylinder bores (boring) or increasing the stroke with a modified crankshaft (stroking). Typically the two methods are combined to arrive at a workable combination of bore-to-stroke ratio, rod length-to-stroke ratio (often called just "rod ratio"), and to work with piston, connecting rod, and crankshaft availability.

With the 5.0 Mustang, the way to get extra displacement is with a stroker kit, where all the details have been worked out by the machine shop. Many such kits are offered, with easily the

most popular being the 347-cubic inch variety. Other popular 5.0 sizes are or have been the 317, 320 to 330 range, and the oversized 355 and 362 varieties.

Why a Stroker?

While volumes have been written on why increasing stroke is good, and thousands of hours logged bench racing the merits of bore, stroke, torque, and horsepower, the bottom line is stroking the 5.0 is the only practical way to increase its displacement. The 5.0 block is compact and thin to keep it light. This means a 0.030-inch overbore is the maximum practical limit to the bore, and this gives only 3 more cubic inches of displacement. Even at the sometimes obtainable 0.060-inch overbore, only 6 cubic inches are gained.

So, practically speaking, to move past 306 cubic inches, it is necessary to increase the throw on the crankshaft along with a matching shortening of the connecting rod or decrease in the piston's compression height (the distance from the centerline of the piston pin to the top of the piston, or crown). This substantially increases displacement, as much more cylinder volume is gained.

Practically speaking then, 5.0 stroker kits are built around a special crankshaft and pistons, along with special connecting rods in some applications.

To finish up with the theoretical niceties, the 5.0 comes with a relatively short 3.00-inch stroke. While the compact block and crankcase architecture was built around this stroke, many other small blocks, the 350s and 351s, use a 3.50-inch stroke or thereabout. To lengthen the 5.0's by 0.400 inch to 3.400 inches is not really so bizarre, and keeps the engine well within the realm of conventional design practice.

Because the only way to increase the stroke of any engine is with a longer stroke crankshaft, the crankshaft is the heart of any stroker engine. Small-block Ford stroking was revolutionized by this cast-steel crankshaft from China. Extremely affordable and cast with the necessary 3.400-inch stroke, this crankshaft is the quick and easy way to a 347 Ford.

To think about stroking a bit differently, a 347 is a more relaxed engine than the 302, with an easier torque hit, which is especially welcome on the street with heavy cars. Convertible 5.0s are a natural for a 347, as they typically weigh hundreds of pounds more than a coupe or hatch, often employ automatic transmissions coupled to cruising rear axle ratios, and are asked to provide easy, roll-on-the-throttle power. All that adds up to a real need for torque.

Stroker Blocks

Any 289 or 302 block can be used with a 347 kit. The best production blocks pre-date the lightweight 5.0 casting; a late 1970s block is the best thing short of an SVO A4 casting. They have the extra material in all the right places, such as the head bolt bosses, cylinder walls, main webs, and skirt area. Dan Nowak of Nowak and Company prefers to use 1966 to 1980 289 or 302 blocks for this reason. Earlier five-bolt blocks work, but these should be saved for vintage owners who need them. The late-model roller block in the 5.0 Mustang works for a street 347 with moderate power gains, but these blocks are so thin an earlier or Mexican block, or a Ford Motorsport A4, is suggested for serious duty.

No matter which block is used, the lower end of the cylinders must be cleananced for the connecting rods. This is typically done by the machine shop while the engine is being bored, honed, and so on.

Offset grinding a 351 Cleveland crankshaft also makes a good 347 crank. Both the Cleveland and cast-steel Chinese crankshaft are great for any street use and will survive plenty of bolt-on strip action, just as the stock 5.0 crank does. Engines using 7,000-rpm, big compression, or heavy power adder assistance will live longer with a much more-expensive forged or billet racing crankshaft. Cleveland's cranks are easy to spot by their larger main bearings and the "step" between the number-one main and the crank snout.

Stroker Crankshafts

Stroke can be easily increased in two ways. Given a stout crankshaft to begin with, it's possible to offset-grind the connecting rod journals. This reduces the journal size, and by taking all the material off one side of the journal, the stroke is lengthened. Of course, a connecting rod with a smaller big end is then required.

With 5.0 engines, the trouble with offset grinding the crankshaft is the crankshaft. The 5.0 crank is one of the lightest production V-8 cranks in the world and doesn't have the journal diameter or journal overlap to support much in the way of offset grinding.

Obviously some other crankshaft can be used, provided it fits, of course. In the 429 and 460 Ford big blocks, for example, the only difference between the two engines is the crankshaft throw and the piston compression height. While many engine families offer a range of crankshaft throws, the small-block Ford is not one of them. There just isn't a longer stroke crank for the 260/289/302 family. Also, the 351 Windsor uses a much larger, heavier crankshaft that won't work.

So, on to plan C, which is offset grinding some other crankshaft. It happens that Ford's 351 Cleveland crankshaft shares some dimensions with the 302 and can be machined (considerably) to fit. By de-stroking a 351C crankshaft to 3.400 inches of stroke and cutting the counterweights down to fit the 302, the Cleveland crank becomes the basis of the 347 engine (that's right, the Cleveland stroke is actually reduced via offset grinding for this application). No heavy metal is required for balance, and the rest is pretty much just fitting a shorter piston and matching connecting rod.

On the street such a cast-iron stroker crankshaft is acceptable from a strength standpoint, but for true racing engines, a much stronger, custom billet crank is typically used. Just remember that whenever the word custom appears, the word expensive can be substituted.

While Cleveland crankshafts make fine 347 strokers for street/strip duty, as this book went to press an imported Chinese crankshaft had come to market via Coast High Performance, Ford SVO, Nowak, and others. It offers a 347's 3.400-inch stroke and an impressively low price. This crankshaft is cast steel, which is commonly said to be approximately twice as strong as a production cast-iron crank, but not in the same robust league as a quality forged steel or billet crank. Just the same, it's about one-third of the price of such an all-out racing crankshaft. It's plenty strong for street use and should hold up to considerable track abuse.

Damper and Flywheel

Another balance consideration is the amount of imbalance built into the crankshaft, a characteristic of the external balancing Ford uses on its small V-8s. Ford used 28 ounces of imbalance on small-block crankshafts up to 1981, then went to 52 ounces imbalance with the 1982 HO. The two crankshafts cannot be interchanged without the rest of the matching reciprocating parts, damper and flywheel, a point to consider should you need another crankshaft, or want to change a flywheel, flexplate, or damper. Cut-down Cleveland crankshafts utilize a 28-ounce imbalance, so a new flywheel and crankshaft damper are needed for a 5.0 engine

While you could assemble your own parts, the only way to go when stroking a 5.0 is with a kit. Among the many 347 kits available, some make a virtue of price, while others cost a little more and are better suited to higher output engines. The kits from Nowak & Company feature a cast-steel crankshaft, Crower or Eagle connecting rods, and Nowak pistons. Pricing and street/strip suitability is thus adjustable.

when using the Cleveland crank. This can be done by simply purchasing new parts, or the existing parts can be rebalanced locally.

The 3.400 stroker crankshaft from SVO/Coast High Performance (they use the same crank) is available in either the early 28-ounce or later 50-ounce imbalances. For 5.0 duty, you want the 50-ounce version.

Stroker Connecting Rods and Pistons

It's difficult to separate connecting rods and pistons when discussing stroker engines. Both are commonly adjusted in order to put the top of the piston in the right spot.

Thus the piston is usually compressed vertically, bringing the piston pin and ring package closer together, and the connecting rod may also be adjusted. Because pistons are standard replacement parts, and are often custom built, they're where much of the stroker action takes place.

In fact, stroker engines, and small-block Fords in general, have become so popular that Nowak's N400 and Probe pistons (sold through Coast High Performance) are viable business propositions. Both pistons are Ford specific, so they are quite light, yet they're forged for great strength and come in standard and 0.030-inch over sizes for both standard displacement and stroker Ford V-8s.

Like crankshafts, many stroker kits pirate a production connecting rod from some other application that can be machined to work with reasonable effort. Pinto 2.3-liter rods and Chrysler six-cylinder rods have long been common Ford stroker fodder. There is nothing inherently bad about such automotive cannibalism, save the obvious fact you're limited by a production part. So, when you see a kit using regular production rods, you know you don't want to go nuts with rpm or power adders. That's what premium aftermarket rods are for.

Today, most stroker kits use some form of aftermarket rod and high-quality fastener. Nowak's 347 street kit features Crower Sportsman rods. These forgings use ARP rod bolts and 12 point nuts, and will support all the power a two-bolt, stock-block 347 is going to live through. Likewise, Coast High Performance is partial to the Blue Thunder forging, which is also plenty strong. In either case, rod longevity is not a concern with any bolt-on engine.

Stroker Tradeoffs

No matter how the increased stroke is obtained, there are tradeoffs. At any given engine speed, a longer stroke increases piston acceleration all by itself. Maximum piston speed increases as well. For the street, these maximums occur well above the stock 6,250-rpm redline, so they are not much of a concern. At the track, however, racers running steep rear axle gears and big-time engine rpm bump into redline limits when stroking. This is the main reason some Pro 5.0 racers prefer 320- to 335-inch displacements. Such engines have enough greater displacement to help mid-range torque, but with a still relatively compact stroke that allows eye-watering high rpm in the lightweight 302 package. For those who want something different on the street, a 320 can have a pretty snappy personality when supported by enough head and cam, although a 347 works even better in the normal street rpm ranges.

There are even 317-inch stroker 302s for pretty much the same reason, although a big factor is that the economics of building that size were once favorable. Today, with inexpensive 347 stroker crankshafts readily available, such a small stroker is really not worth the investment on a street engine, although it may have its place in some racing classes.

In fact, there is no doubt that for the street, and even the lighter duty racing, supercharged, turbo, and nitrous crowd that the 347 is the best choice. There are two reasons for this, one mechanical, the other financial.

From a mechanical perspective, the 3.400-inch stroke of a 347 helps equal the displacement of the 350 competition, while retaining good revability. Even though it's clearly longer than the 302's, the 3.400-inch stroke is hardly big by V-8 standards, so there is no major reason to keep a 347 reined in like a tractor engine. At the same time, the larger displacement works well within the stock 6,250-rpm rev limiter; the larger displacement naturally builds mid-range torque.

Financially, the 347 has easily become the favorite stroker kit because

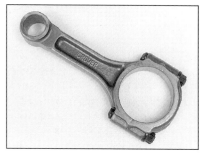

Some form of reprocessed production connecting rod works fine for a modest power stroker kit, but with good forged or steel connecting rods available at nearly the same cost, there is little reason to run anything less. This forged Crower rod has long been a favorite, as is the Blue Thunder rod, or the Chinese Eagle. All of these rods are good to 600 horsepower, which is more than any street-tired car can use.

Premium pistons from Coast/Probe or Nowak are excellent selling features of their current 347 kits. Both pistons are made in Ford-specific dies, which saves weight because a tightly shaped, Ford-only valve dish must be accommodated in the dies. These Nowak forgings show the exact dome shapes possible with such semi-custom pistons. The different domes accommodate the popular cylinder head combustion chambers.

Full-floating piston pins are desirable because there is no need to heat the connecting rod during pin installation. Heating the rods is of no concern on production or mild performance engines, but rod failures in higher-stress engines are more often than not seen right where the blue line or dark area (from heating) ends at the small end of the rod (left). Also, floating pins, like the one at right from Nowak's 347 stroker kit, are easy to assemble.

of the inexpensive imported crankshaft. Additionally, it is mechanically sound and provides the sort of power increase most people want. With increasing numbers of 347 kits being sold, the pistons and rods involved are a bit less expensive, making the 347 easily the best dollar-per-cubic-inch stroker.

Ford SVO has stepped up with all sorts of 347 cranks, crank kits, short blocks, and even complete engines, and offers stroker pistons in both standard and 0.030-inch oversized dimensions, a service also available from Coast High Performance/Probe and Nowak and Company with their lightweight, Ford-specific forgings. This is another example of the popularity of the 347. It's now easy to build a stock bore 347, then rebuild it later and bore the block 0.030 inch, and know pistons are waiting for this nonproduction combination right off the shelf. When it comes to rejuvenating a tired, high-mileage 5.0, it's tough to come up with a reason not to build a 347.

Unless you are circle track racing and are willing to pay for the final few inches of displacement, ignore anything over 347 inches. The 355 and even larger strokers are a stretch when it comes to rod length, piston compression height, and ring packaging, so such sizes are expensive to the point of not being worth the bother of a few more inches of displacement. These larger displacements were mainly developed for circle track racers, where 355 is a common class displacement limit, due to the ease of building small-block Chevys to that size.

Stroker Tuning

What many casual enthusiasts overlook is that a 347 is not a 302 when it comes time for tuning. That extra stroke affects nearly everything about the engine's tune, from its cam specs, cylinder head airflow, intake requirements, and exhaust needs, to its ignition curve and fuel consumption. I'm not trying to scare anyone off, as the stock cam is still a smart choice for a 347 street engine, and mass air metering takes care of most of the fuel requirements, but it's still smart to remember it's a 347 when power-building a 347.

In the general terms we have room for here, a 347 is just a bit "bigger" than a 302. Thus, a 347 is a little more tolerant of camming, and perhaps more importantly from a practical standpoint, works the cylinder head a little harder. By this, I mean the 347 will accelerate the air in the intake tract a little faster when the valve opens, demand more total intake air, be a little less finicky about intake runner length, and ask more of the headers and exhaust system as it expels a greater quantity of gases. Thus, a 347 will definitely want a 1 5/8-inch header, as opposed to a 1 1/2-inch version, and will respond a bit better to a long-tube than a 302. A 347

will be a bit more forgiving of large runner cylinder heads and slightly short intake manifold runners, although it won't make a box-style upper intake manifold build much more torque on a naturally aspirated engine, nor will the big-port race heads seem much better on the street atop a 347 than a 302.

Many of these effects are of small concern at the bolt-on level, but have a more noticeable effect as the engine's state of tune rises. Still, all said, it is easier to build power with a 347 than a 302. Just don't forget to think a tad bigger.

One consequence of not thinking bigger with a 347 is that the engine will sign off somewhat quicker. That is, the power and torque peaks will be a tad lower than with a 302, and once past the peak the power will sign off just a bit harder. As an example of an engine I tested was a typical combination of unported Twisted Wedge heads, Crane 2030 cam, 1.6 rockers, Extrude Honed Edelbrock intake manifold with a 70-millimeter throttle body, and 1 5/8-inch long-tube headers made 355 horsepower and 420 lb-ft of torque, with the peaks at 5,350 rpm for the horsepower and 3,750 rpm for the torque. This was a pretty happy combination, running as high as 106 percent volumetric efficiency around the torque peak, but upstairs the volume efficiency dropped off, and while the engine would overrev the power peak nicely enough, it was clear the combination was somewhat undercammed, and could make more power yet at the top end.

Why Not a 351?

The natural extension of stroking is to replace the 302 with a 351 (5.8 for a 5.0). This is good thinking, and a great swap, even if it is beyond the scope of this book. There are, however, tradeoffs to the 351 swap to consider before falling madly in love with it.

As always, more costs money. It takes considerably more money to swap in a 351 than it does to fit a 347 kit to a 302. This is because the 351 engine must be bought outright, plus the price of several associated parts specific to the job, such as headers. Furthermore, your current hot rod intake manifold, distributor, headers, front engine dress, supercharger brackets, and so on won't fit the taller and wider 351, and hood clearance is a problem. All this costs money to resolve, not to mention time.

The 351W is also a much beefier engine than the 302. This is good if you are going for tons of power and longevity, but it does have a detrimental effect on handling because that beef weighs. The Mustang is already nose heavy, and the brawny 351 doesn't make it any better. This is especially true of road racing Mustangs, although obviously the 351-powered 1995 Mustang Cobra R-model does pretty well with an iron block, aluminum head 351 over the front axle. Front axle weight is also a handicap at the drag strip, and when all the bench racing

347? What 347?

The best thing about a stroker engine is it fits in just about anything and no one knows the difference. To take a more extreme view, stroking a 289 to 347 cubic inches gives gobs of torque and serious horsepower, but externally it will still appear as a 289 right down to the Powered By Ford valve covers. Naturally, the increased torque from a 347 will stress anything downstream or attached to it, such as transmissions, rear axles, and radiators. Given their light-duty cycles, 5.0 street cars tolerate the extra heat and torque from a 347 without a problem, with the more highly tuned and harder driven examples wanting some reinforcement in the driveline and cooling.

No doubt the ultimate stroker kit for 5.0 Mustangs is a 351 Windsor. Definitely more expensive than a 5.0 stroked to 347 inches, the Windsor offers a big step up in physical strength in the short block, plus the potential to go well into big-block cubic inch territory, should you ever decide to stroke it. Sighting across the intake manifold of this S351 Saleen, it's obvious the taller 351 requires a slightly higher hood.

clears, most of those looking for more cubic inches go with a 347. Those going whole hog with a 351 often end up stroking that engine, so obviously they're not saving any money! They are, however, going seriously fast.

Just in case you're leaning that way, a quarter-inch of stroke, to 372 or so cubic inches, makes for one rowdy son-of-a-gun. It's possible to go up to the low 400-inch range with a 351, but it's

expensive, looks a bit funny from an internal architecture point of view, and isn't exactly the last word in sparkling top-end revving.

Don't forget, there are still more performance parts for the 302/347 than for the 351, especially when it comes to intake manifolds and headers. So, if you like to drive your 5.0 more than fabricate parts for it, stick with the 302/347 combination.

Cylinder Block	108
Boring	109
Sonic Checking	109
Honing with Block Plates	110
Align Boring and Honing	110
Decking	110
Lightening	111
Crankshaft	111
Balancing	111
Rear Main Seal	112
Knife-Edging	112
Oiling	112
Oil Pans	112
Connecting Rods	113
Deburring and Shot Peening	113
Aftermarket Connecting Rods	113
Pistons	114
Dome Shape and Deburring	114
Balancing	115
Head Bolts and Studs	115
Crate Engines	115
Crank Kit	116
New vs. Rebuilt	116
Stock vs. Modified	117
Cost	117

One area where racing all-out engines require extra machine work is in the lifter bores. Typically these are not as well squared to the camshaft as desirable, meaning the machinist can unlock some horsepower by truing or sleeving the lifter bores. This is not necessary on street or even moderate performance engines, so don't worry about it. If you want to do something in the lifter valley, grinding the pebbly cast-iron surface smooth with sanding rolls and a die grinder will aid oil drain back, but this is pretty much a nicety as well.

SHORT-BLOCK PREPARATION

While the purpose of this book is to guide the owner through bolt-on modifications, it makes sense to briefly address the short-block because of the increasing age of the 5.0 fleet. Today many 5.0 owners are faced with either rebuilding or replacing their now high-mileage engines, and this number is only going to grow. So, to assist you in deciding how to handle the short block, I'm including this below-the-head-gasket overview.

Just in case the term short block is unknown to you, it is the block and everything inside it—crankshaft, connecting rods, pistons, camshaft, and timing gear set.

Working with the short block means working with a machine shop, so let me point out the importance of keeping a good relationship with your machine shop. You are buying their machining services, of course, but you'll also be paying for their experience, and most of the time, some or all of the parts they'll buy for your engine. While the costs of having an engine machined are seemingly astronomical, most machine shops make a modest profit for their rather substantial labor, so don't resent their prices. Also, when shopping for a machine shop, a good reputation and slightly higher prices are always better than bottom-of-the-barrel prices. Machining engines is not going to the shelf and pulling off the box with the matching number, it takes intelligence, experience, attention to detail, and expensive machinery, so it's going to cost something.

People also talk about "blueprinting," which is one of those catchy phrases that no one knows the meaning of. Blueprinting is the process of machining every aspect of an engine until it meets the exact value listed in the design of the engine, and not just letting it fall into the acceptable range for that part. There is no official designation or agreement on precisely what blueprinting is, but the more tolerances are machined to their nominal value, the more blueprinting is being done. You can see that truly blueprinting an engine would take tremendous effort, which is one reason a full-house Winston Cup or Trans Am engine costs the best part of $50,000. Warning buzzers should sound when the term is spotted in advertising for cheap parts. I prefer to see more precise descriptions of the machining steps involved.

Cylinder Block

Short-block servicing begins after removal from the chassis and disassembly. Any remaining gasket material is scraped off, and the parts cleaned so they can be inspected. Most machine shops use a jet tank to clean parts. The jet tank is an upright, closet-like locker. Inside the parts rotate on a turntable while hot soapy water is sprayed at high pressure on them. Once out of the tank, the parts are hosed off with fresh water as a rinse and cool-down.

Boring

Restoring the cylinders by boring them larger and fitting oversize pistons is a major engine-building step. Cylinders wear mainly because the force of combustion, pushing outward on the piston rings, wears the cylinders more at their tops than the bottom, tapering the cylinders. It is noteworthy, however, that the greater wear at the top of the bore is due, as much as anything, to the fact that the piston comes to a dead stop at TDC (top dead center), so the slight hydrodynamic "wedge" of oil that floats the rings in the bore breaks down. That happens at BDC (bottom dead center) too, of course, but there is plentiful oil there, while at the top end, the microscopic oil film gets burned off every time the plug fires. Cutting the cylinders oversize to restore a round cylinder with fresh material exposed on the walls is the cure.

Machinists enlarge the cylinders by boring and honing. Boring is a cutting operation that is followed by honing, a stone-grinding step. Honing is necessary to remove the material disrupted by boring, and is also more accurate and easier to fine control, as it is tough to remove less than 0.020 inch by boring. Sometimes large amounts of material are simply honed out with a power hone.

While the machinist can enlarge the cylinders to any size, the availability of oversize pistons and rings, along with how thick the cylinder walls were cast, limit the engine's overbore capacity. The typical featherweight 5.0 block won't go over 0.030-inch overbore, with the occasional thick one making it to 0.040 inch (going from 0.030 inch to 0.040 inch is typically done with a power hone).

In practice, lower mileage 5.0 blocks, those with 40,000 miles on them or so, often clean up at 0.030 inch, but the more usual 100,000 mile block invariably takes a 0.030-inch cut. This doesn't mean the cylinders are actually worn this much (.007–.008 inch of taper is typical), but when enough material is bored out to clean up the wear, keep the cylinder square with the crankshaft, leave 0.003 inch of stock for honing and then factor in for the

available piston diameter, it's going to be 0.030 inch over.

One thing to keep in mind when considering boring or power honing is that boring can cut the cylinder any way the machinist wants while honing can only enlarge the existing hole. That's why power honing stock cylinders to 0.030 inch isn't normally done. Boring restores the cylinder's squareness in the block and doesn't exaggerate any abnormalities that may have found their way into the block.

Sonic Checking

Chances are great you won't need to sonic check a 5.0 block, but I'll mention it just in case. Sonic checking is a specialized ultrasound test. It determines the thickness of the cylinder walls by holding a stethoscope-like sensor against the inner cylinder wall. No cutting or drilling is done. Measurements are made at three levels in the cylinder, at both the thrust face and sides of the cylinder. The thrust face is the side loaded by the piston during the power stroke (inner and outer cylinder walls, perpendicular to the piston pin), while the sides are those surfaces inline with the piston pin. The thrust faces take more load and must be thicker than the side walls, which can be relatively thin.

Sonic checking ensures that adequate material will remain after boring, and checks against core shift. Core shift occurs when the molds at the foundry moved slightly relative to the rest of the block molds, resulting in cylinders overly thick on one side and dangerously thin on the other. Sonic checking is vital if large overbores are planned for displacement increases.

Fords are not known for their thick cylinder walls (to say the least), so don't expect to find enough material to build a 360-cubic inch 5.0. When all boring and honing are done, you'll need at least 0.080-inch thick sides and 0.120-inch thrust faces. You don't need to sonic check for 0.030-inch overbores, but above that, it becomes an increasingly good idea. Sonic checking is also smart if you're building for maximum power (and should be using the thick-walled

Nowadays, and especially with a lightweight engine like the 5.0, there is no excuse for not power honing with torque plates. Getting the cylinders truly round and square is where the horsepower is at in the short block, so don't skip on this step.

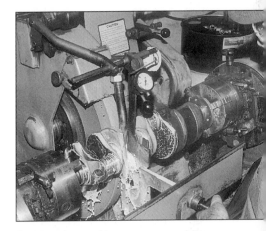

Because the machines are so expensive and specialized, your local machinist will send your crankshaft out for grinding. This is another reason why you want to deal with a good machinist; he'll be making many decisions for you, and you don't always want the least expensive option. Like anything else, there is crank grinding, and then there is taking the time to do it right.

Due to its compact counterweights, the small block Ford crankshaft does not easily accept much more in the way of piston or connecting rod weight. When beefy, high-rpm reciprocating parts are needed, heavy metal for balance purposes is often needed, too. The round, lighter colored plug on this counterweight is a single slug of sintered tungsten, a heavy metal. Tach-twisting naturally aspirated engines will many times require five to seven such slugs, an expensive proposition, and a good reason to stick with a lower rpm power-adder engine.

One way to make a lighter crankshaft is to cut down the amount of counterweighting. This is what Ford did in 1982, when it reengineered the 5.0 HO engine. The stub of a counterweight right in front of the No. 4 main bearing is a full counterweight on earlier cranks. Swapping cranks is possible, but will require matching flywheels and harmonic dampers, cutting down the counterweights, and an oil sleeve repair kit.

While 5.0s go long and far on their stock aluminum oil pumps, most machinists like to see a step up to an iron aftermarket version. The extra volume and pressure (no more than 60 psi) aid oiling and support any future oil coolers or other pressure-robbing accessories. The deeper gear case of the pump at right identifies it as a high volume pump.

A4 block anyway). Max effort engines need thick-as-possible cylinder walls.

Honing with Block Plates

Once bored, the cylinders are then honed to their final size. A standard rebuild calls for honing without block plates, but it's worth the extra cost to have the block honed with deck plates. Deck plates are thick metal slabs with holes in them to allow access to the cylinders. They bolt on in place of the cylinder heads, to simulate the stresses on the block when the heads are installed. Because the 5.0 block is a lightweight casting, with thinner decks and cylinder walls than previous 302 cylinder block, honing with plates is an excellent idea.

Keep in mind that no matter whether deck plates are used or not, the grit of the honing stones used must match the type of piston rings being used. Chrome rings call for a rougher finish than that used with the more common moly rings. Just be sure you and your machinist understand each other, and that he knows which rings you are using.

As an aside on piston rings, with today's accurate machine tools, the cylinders really come out round. This and continuing ring material improve-ments have allowed fine cylinder wall finishes, meaning the rings seat almost instantly. Final seating still takes place after a bit of WOT running, but the point is, you should not put up with an oil smoker. If you have one, something is wrong.

Align Boring and Honing

It's a bit difficult to think of cast iron as plastic, but it is. As the engine block heats and cools over years of operation, it shifts and wiggles into a slightly different shape as it relaxes the stresses poured into it when cast by Ford. One place where this matters is in the main bearing bore alignment. Because the 5.0 block is lightly built around the main caps, the main bearing bores are most often out of alignment by 100,000 miles. Even the beefy SVO A4 blocks rack out of shape, but mainly because they use steel main caps on the center three mains, and cast-iron caps on the end two.

When the main bearing bores are out-of-round or misaligned, they are made round and true by honing, or boring in extreme cases. Align honing equipment is fairly common (align boring tools are rare, and require honing after boring), and align honing a 5.0 block should be considered standard procedure for any performance rebuild.

Align honing is done by removing the main bearing caps, grinding .0001 inch or so off their mating surface, then reinstalling them on the block. The block is fitted inside the honing tank, where a special set of stones is passed through the bores while cutting lube is squirted onto the job to cool and carry away debris. The stones restore the bearing bores to round, and ensure the bores are aligned with each other.

If your stock block is so badly misshapen or egged out that it needs align boring, pitch the block and start over. A good core block in the wrecking yard is less money and will rebuild into a better engine. Align boring, aside from being expensive (you have to pay to both bore and hone), moves the crankshaft centerline closer the camshaft, causing oil seal and timing chain issues that are best avoided. Bore if you must, but remember you don't want to. Use a new block if at all possible.

One nice thing about align honing is that once it has been done, it doesn't seem to need doing again. That's because a seasoned block (one that has been heat cycled numerous times) has settled down and won't lose its shape.

Decking

The area the head gasket sits on is called the deck. Like all the major surfaces in the 5.0 block, it moves around with heat cycling because the block is so light. If you're beginning to wonder if "just enough" engineering is such a great thing, you're getting the idea. It's much nicer to work with 1960s-era blocks, or the modern A4 racing block, because their greater mass keeps things from wiggling around so much.

Anyway, milling the block's deck flat is called decking, and is a really good idea on any 5.0 rebuild. The machinists say it needs to be done almost every time anyway, so count on it.

Besides being light, 5.0 blocks use only four head bolts per cylinder, causing larger, more spread-out loads in the block deck than five-bolt designs. It's another reason why it's unusual to find a flat 5.0 block; most have a 0.002-inch dip between the cylinders, even the A4 blocks. The cylinder head bolt holes are already counterbored, so that trick won't help the distortion.

Interestingly, Ford 5.0 blocks are really good in keeping decks perpendicular to the bore, so it's rare to find them tilted to the outside of the block. They'll tilt end-to-end, and one deck may be higher or lower relative to the crankshaft, but the perpendicularity is invariably good.

Make sure your machinist squares the decks to the crankshaft centerline when decking. This evens the piston-to-deck and compression heights and flattens the decks for head gasket sealing, making it a good blueprinting procedure. With a 5.0, you want to do everything to keep the head gasket sealed.

Lightening

You may have heard serious drag racers lighten their engines, just the way they do the rest of the car. On the block, this involves cutting off various lugs used at the factory for locating the block in the boring machinery, and generally thinning material wherever it can be safely removed. The crankshaft is massaged, flyweight pistons are used, and titanium valves rule.

All this is fine for racers, but they're in the habit of spending time and money as if there were no tomorrow, and they are using A4 blocks. Everything about the stock 5.0 engine is already painfully light, so don't even think about putting it on a diet. Besides, the reciprocating weight only comes

This comparison of a stock rod bolt, at left, and its ARP replacement, at right, gives a good clue as to the benefit of a superior rod bolt, which in the 5.0s case, is just about any bolt! The larger bearing area under the good head bolt is clearly visible.

into play above 6,000 rpm, too high to worry about with a bracket or street/strip engine.

If you want to do some special steps, polish the lifter valley with sanding rolls to aid oil drain-back, and deburr all sharp edges that could form stress risers.

Crankshaft

Unless your 5.0 has been abused (low oil level), the crankshaft will take surprisingly little work to refurbish. During a standard overhaul, the crankshaft journals are polished to remove varnish and restore the proper surface roughness, and that could be all that's necessary. A Magnaflux test will tell if the crank is cracked and needs to be replaced. Cranks from stock engines are rarely cracked, but hard running can do the dirty deed, so it's smart to invest in this check before spending machining dollars.

A quick check with a micrometer tells the machinist if the journals are out-of-round or tapered. If so, the crankshaft is ground undersize and matching main and rod bearings are used during assembly. Typically the journals need be ground 0.010 inch

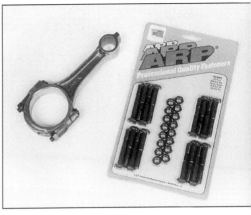

Honestly, for the vast majority of bolt-on performance 5.0s working within the stock 6,250-rpm rev limiter, the stock connecting rod outfitted with good aftermarket rod bolts is all that's necessary. Getting the bolts is easy; several companies offer high-strength hardware for 5.0s in kit form, like this hang card from ARP.

undersize, although 0.020–.040 inch undersizes are possible. For performance street engines, it is nice to stay at 0.010 inch or less, but it doesn't really seem to matter much if you go all the way to 0.030 or 0.040 inch under on street engines. The combination of damage to the crankshaft and available bearing sizes will determine how much to grind the crankshaft.

Crank grinding is done on specialized grinders using large-diameter stone wheels. Such machines are too expensive for all but specialty shops, so expect to have your crankshaft sent out for grinding.

The other standard machinist job is to chamfer the edge of the oil holes in the crankshaft journals (sometimes called "spooning"). This is a hand-blending operation that aids oil flow. Another area to watch is the fillets, the radius where the journals turn up into the counterweights. Quick and dirty crank grinds sometimes get these areas too wide, forcing the crank into the edge of the bearing, or too narrow, weakening the crank and promoting cracking.

Balancing

The entire rotating and reciprocating assemblies in an engine are balanced to work with a minimum of engine-wearing vibration. When the engine's stroke is changed, or when piston and

111

Even with all the machinery, there is still plenty of handwork to make things right. The big-end mating surfaces of these stock rods are being sanded smooth prior to fitting new bolts and resizing the big end.

connecting rods of different than original weights are used, the crankshaft must be rebalanced to accommodate the new weights.

When building stroker engines, or when using heavy pistons, it quickly becomes necessary to add heavy metal to the small-block Ford crankshaft because of the small diameter counterweights. This is quite expensive, so be sure to talk your grandiose engine building plans over with your machinist before buying parts.

Rear Main Seal

Ford changed from a two-piece to one-piece rear main oil seal in 1982 as well. You may run across this with a replacement 5.0 crankshaft. Because the larger counterweights on the 1981 and earlier crankshaft can be cut down to allow it to work in the 5.0, and because there are occasional shortages of 5.0

cranks, such cut-down cranks are in the 5.0 parts stream. To use these cranks, a crankshaft repair sleeve is required, and should be included with the crank.

Knife-Edging

As the crankshaft spins inside the engine, it encounters resistance from oil suspended in the air. Racers used to knife-edge, or grind the edge of, the crankshaft counterweights at an angle to aid the crank in cutting through this heavy mist. This really just slings the oil sideways, where it gets knocked around by another part of the crank. Today, the leading edges of the counterweights are shaped into blunt, rounded forms, like the nose of an airliner. It works better than the knife edge.

For any street or street/strip engine, such measures are not cost-effective, so don't spend the money on them. They really benefit only high-rpm racing engines.

Oiling

Once your engine is inside a machine shop, it seems inevitable someone there will try to sell you a high-volume or high-volume and high-pressure oil pump. This is part of the old, "more is better" school of hot rodding, and often isn't necessary. The small-block Ford V-8 oils quite well from the factory, and giving up some horsepower to a larger oil pump, and running that higher load through the oil pump drive should be done only after determining it is necessary.

That said, the 5.0 oil pump is aluminum, and after 100,000 miles, it will have increased clearances, mainly from debris running through it. Moving up to an affordable aftermarket cast-iron pump (Speed Pro, Melling) that's had its end clearances set means you'll be getting a fresh pump that is more durable and offers a reasonable step up in pressure. Stock, the 5.0 puts out 45 psi, while the common aftermarket pumps make more like 60 psi. Such a pressure increase ensures full oiling at all times, and isn't such a boost that it is worthlessly beating the oil into a hot froth. The cast-iron pumps are more durable, too.

If you're trying to save money on a street rebuild that'll see the occasional quick blast down an on-ramp, then a stock pump with its clearances checked will do. You want to check the clearances, however, as they're sloppy from Ford. As oil coolers and remote oil filters are added on a race engine, more oil pressure is definitely needed from the pump to make up for the pressure drops in the cooler, lines, and fittings.

What you want to avoid on street engines are high-pressure (anything over 60 psi) pumps. Street engines don't benefit from high oil pressure; it just heats the oil and costs horsepower to drive. The old rule of 10 psi of oil pressure per 1,000 rpm is still pretty valid. As long as you're staying within the 6,250-rpm rev limiter, it's likely 45 psi of oil pressure will do and 60 psi will take care of all the tire-spinning antics a crazed high schooler in his first V-8 can dish out. After all, tens of thousands of 5.0s survived blowers and nitrous with the stock pump. Leave the 80–100-psi pumps to the guys running Clevelands.

Another small-Ford feature is a rather dainty oil pump drive. Again, these thin rods seem to live just fine from the factory, but a stronger aftermarket replacement is a good match to a high-volume pump.

Oil Pans

Probably more important to a hard-driven 5.0 than an oil pump is a better oil pan and windage tray. All this is to control windage—the storm of oil droplets swirling around the crankshaft—increase oil volume, and, most importantly, keep oil around the oil pump pickup at all times.

The stock pan lets the oil swarm all over the crankshaft. You get away with it when running stock, but if you rev it, bad things happen, such as aerated oil, insufficient oil in the sump so the pump momentarily runs dry (very bad!) and power is lost to whipping the oil. It's said this seems to occur starting at 6,000 rpm, which is another reason why the 6,250 rpm rev limiter is the 5.0's best friend.

Even the tamest daily driver benefits from a windage tray, which is a sheet metal baffle (or occasionally a wire mesh screen) fitted between the crankshaft and oil pan. It keeps the crankshaft windage from frothing the oil; or at over 6,000 rpm, winding up around the crankshaft in a dervish-like petroleum cloud. Windage trays are inexpensive, so they're a no-brainer to select. If you choose to run a stud girdle (a great idea on high-powered or stroker 5.0s), then you probably won't be able to fit a windage tray as well. Luckily, the bulky stud girdle itself probably serves some windage-reduction function.

Next is a better oil pan, an addition anyone with the money should automatically invest in. Specialized drag 5.0s can run a drag-race-only pan, while all the rest, meaning slalom, road race, hot street, even the hard-driven daily drivers, should use a road racing oil pan. Canton makes a good pan with a diamond shaped set of spring-loaded gates to keep the oil pickup submerged at all times. It'll certainly give you considerably more confidence when slinging around the cloverleafs at full-chat.

You may have to spend a couple of minutes fitting one of these pans to your block as the welding process always seems to tweak things slightly, but that's about it. Also, the new pan will include a matching longer oil pump pickup.

Connecting Rods

Connecting rods are a highly stressed engine part, and are frequently replaced in race engines merely because they've been run a certain amount of time. Because the stress on the connecting rods is directly proportional to engine rpm, working within the stock 6,250 rpm rev limit means the stock rods can be reused at rebuild time. Such rods need to be resized, straightened, and have stronger aftermarket nuts and bolts installed. Collectively, these actions are known as rod reconditioning.

Rod resizing is a normal part of all engine rebuilds. The pistons are pressed off the small end of the rod and the large ends (caps) are removed. The frighteningly small, stock 5/16-inch rod bolts are pressed out, too.

Typically there is no wear on the small end of the connecting rod because the pressed-in pin and rod don't move relative to each other. The big end, however, is normally slightly elongated from being hammered up and down on the crankshaft several million times. This is cured by grinding a small amount off the parting surfaces of the caps, then fitting new bolts, refitting the caps, and honing the now distinctly out-of-round big end round again. This restores a round big end.

In the old days people used to fit larger 11/32-inch Chevy rod bolts to these connecting rods, but that isn't necessary. Trying to bore the diameter out and get the register correct is the really tough part of this operation. But today we have superb, high-strength bolts. A set of high-grade, stock diameter bolts will handle everything a stock rod is good for. The usual source of good bolts is ARP, but there are others.

Finally, connecting rods get slight twists and bows in their beams during normal use, and the machine shop will bend them straight as part of rod reconditioning. This is done cold with nothing more than a long pry bar. It looks barbaric, but is the proper way of straightening.

Deburring and Shot Peening

Any stress in the connecting rod will concentrate at sharp corners or bends. Dings and cuts in the rod's beam can be trouble, especially at higher rpm, and should be smoothed out. This is done with belt sanders, hand filing, and sanding rolls mounted in die grinders.

Shot peening introduces a residual compressive stress in the surface of the material, increasing its fatigue resistance. It is done by masking off those portions of the rod that should not be exposed to the steel shot (big and small end bores), then blasting the rod with steel shot.

Deburring and shot peening are usually done together. They're a bit of overkill for the typical bolt-on street engine, but are recommended when running the stock rods under high rpm, such as a racing class where stock rods

are required. Such protective steps are belts and suspenders for a street car.

Aftermarket Connecting Rods

When the stock connecting rod is the slightest bit suspect for some sort of performance duty, it is typically replaced with an aftermarket rod these days. The cost of an aftermarket rod is more than doing all the bolt and shot peening tricks to a stock rod, but they're not that much more expensive, and even the entry level aftermarket rods are much stronger than a prepared stock rod. Furthermore, a new rod is new, while a used rod is part way through its cycle life. If you haven't owned the rods since new or know their history, then you don't even know how much life is left in them.

One of the best buys in aftermarket Ford rods are Eagles. They come with nice bolts, accurate sizing and weight. Essentially a Chinese copy of the superb H-beam Carillo from the United States, Eagles cost a bit more than a set of prepped stock rods, but are even stronger than good forged rods like the Crower Sportsman. The Crowers were very popular well into the early 1990s, but have been undersold on price by the Eagles. Still, the Crowers are another fine rod, and strong enough for most 5.0 builds. If you like to buy American, then they're a good way to go.

Another option is what I'll call the Manley rod. A slightly nicer version of the old Boss 302 rod, it's a forging, with a ribbed cap, and 3/8-inch bolts. They're not that much less in price than an Eagle, and definitely lack the sex appeal of that H-beam rod, but again, are enough rod for most hot street and strip engines. Blue Thunder is another fine connecting rod that pretty much falls into the same category, with the twist here being that the Blue Thunder is also the latest Ford SVO rod.

You may run across aluminum rods, but only pure racing engines should use them. They aren't as durable as a steel rod and require periodic replacement, so they're not a fiscal practicality on a street engine. Besides, the reduced weight of an alu-

Even a stock rod picks up some sex appeal once its been smoothed with a sanding roll and given good bolts. The stock rod at right is still showing the forging parting line and its naturally pebbly surface. Note that the small balancing pad atop the small end is untouched on the prepped rod. That bump may look superfluous, but removing it will only ruin the engine's balance. Leave it alone.

minum rod is wasted at anything less than very high rpm.

Pistons

Except in special cases, forged pistons should be used. Good as hypereutectic pistons are, forged pistons are stronger, and the only sane choice for an engine that will see any form of forced induction. Nearly all 5.0 HOs built for speed eventually acquire some form of forced induction, so forged pistons might as well be considered mandatory. Forged pistons were original equipment up to the 1993 Cobra, so anything less at rebuild time would be a step down for these engines anyway. The only time the less-expensive hypereutectics should be run is on naturally aspirated daily driver engines. Their main advantages are less cost and quieter running, because they can be run more tightly in the cylinder.

When it comes to hypereutectic pistons, Ford's replacement offering is so-so. Keith Black hypereutectics have a much better reputation, and are the only brand name of hypereutectic piston that engine builders specifically mention as one they'd consider using. They also generally agree that 6,000 rpm and no forced induction are good hypereutectic limits.

It's also a common misconception that hypereutectics are lighter than forg-

ings, but this isn't true. As a cast piston, they must have some material thickness to build strength, so they tend to be a tad heavy, which on stock-type engines isn't a concern, but is increasingly important as engine speed rises over 6,000 rpm.

As for forgings, Ford's forged replacement pistons are pretty good, and considered tougher than the commonly available TRW replacement part. The Ford piston uses metric-sized rings, which limits size availability, but this shouldn't pose a problem with any normal combination. TRW's common and cheap 2240F street piston has a slot in it for oil drainback, which weakens it. The Ford piston has drilled oil drainback holes, which is stronger. TRW has racing forged pistons available, which is what you want, should you decide to use a TRW.

Another step up in price brings you to custom pistons from JE, Ross, Venolia, Wiesco, and others. Most of these are Chevy or universal piston blanks machined to Ford specification, although JE and others have semistandard piston lines that often work right off the shelf.

However, Nowak and Probe both offer Ford-specific pistons. Forged from the beginning to be Ford small-block pistons, these blanks are then machined into very light yet still strong pistons that feature valve reliefs for all the big-valve heads, save for the Street Heat and Twisted Wedge. The upright valves in those heads call for flycut pistons with all but the smallest cams. Finally, the price on these Ford-specific pistons is not bad, either. They're a great choice for an engine project.

So, what are the considerations with forged pistons? The light ones are great for reducing the stress on the connecting rods, and all of them expand and contract more than cast or hypereutectic pistons. Thus forged pistons need more piston-to-wall clearance, often up to 0.008 inch, which can lead to rattling while they warm up in the morning.

To reduce noise and control the piston a little better, not to mention the ability to advertise a radically tight clear-

ance, several piston manufacturers have splayed the bottom of the skirt. This makes a pair of small pads that run pretty tightly, around 0.0025 inch. Still, the rest of the piston stands off about 0.006 inch, so these pistons don't have true cast-piston clearances.

Actually, all my talk of tight piston-to-wall clearances perpetuates the common desire to run the pistons as tight as possible, and that's not necessarily a good thing. Clearance minimums are just that, minimums, and should be opened up when heat and load go up. A street car that sees pretty light duty has little trouble keeping a good oil film on the cylinder and 180 degrees of water temperature. Burn off some of that oil, watch the temperature rise and the pistons can gall as they contact the cylinder wall.

So, run the pistons toward the tight end of the scale plus 0.001 inch for daily driving and the occasional on-ramp blast, then another 0.001 inch looser for nitrous or a blower. Shoot for something 0.001 or 0.002 more open than dead tight, and you'll be doing well.

Dome Shape and Deburring

The finish on modern pistons is fine out-of-the-box, so the vast majority of 5.0 engines are assembled without a touch of handwork on the pistons. However, when getting truly serious with the short block for racing, such as a 14:1 drag engine, attention to the piston dome is worthwhile. The machinist will likely hand-fit the piston dome to the combustion chamber shape, and definitely massage away all sharp edges with small files and sanding rolls.

This sort of stuff is for all-out competition engines, and the only reason I bring it up here is to point out you don't need to spend the money or time on it. This is especially true today, when the popularity of forced induction means piston domes are typically pretty flat and not the series of mountain ranges found in some naturally aspirated engines.

Smoothing the domes is still a nice touch, however, as it reduces the chance of forming a hot spot on the piston dome which can set off preignition. If you've got the time and want to bond

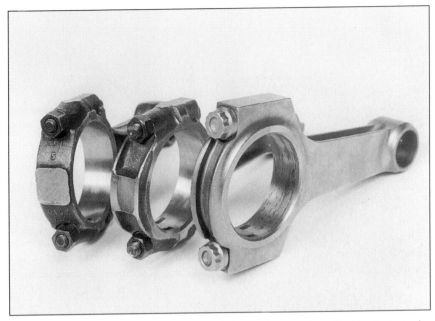

At left is a stock rod, in the center is a forged aftermarket part, identified by the twin ribs running down the cap. The cap may look thinner than stock, but is considerably stronger. At right is an H-beam Eagle rod. There's little doubt about its strength, but the boxy big end does require more clearancing problems when building a stroker.

with your 5.0, smoothing the piston domes won't hurt.

Another possibility is that the machinist may deburr the skirts while inspecting the pistons. They're mainly looking for any protruding edges.

Balancing

Local shops can dynamically balance the entire reciprocating assembly, and this is an excellent thing to do to any engine. The engine will run more smoothly and last longer when balanced to close tolerances.

You may also be forced into balancing when changing pistons, rods, or other rotating or reciprocating parts because of differing weight, so you may not have much of a choice.

Furthermore, by custom machining standards, Ford's balance on 5.0s can be improved upon. Typically the balance is poor at the front of the crank while the back is a little better, and generally it's inconsistent all over. When it comes to aftermarket parts, steel billet balancers and flywheels would just as soon vibrate out of the balancing machine as rotate there nicely, so make sure you get them balanced.

This comes into play when changing flywheels and clutches. Most of the time clutches are okay, but aluminum and steel flywheels can be real shakers and need to be match balanced to the rest of the engine.

With the imbalanced Ford flywheel you can spin the old flywheel, then match this imbalance on the new flywheel. Or, a dummy crankshaft can be employed, so both the old and new flywheels can be balanced to it.

Fluid dampers should have the crank balanced without the balancer because of their floating weights. But the bottom line to balancing is get your engine balanced as an assembly if at all possible.

Head Bolts and Studs

All 260–302 Ford small blocks use 7/16-inch head bolts, while the beefier 351W and SVO A4 blocks sport 1/2-inch bolts. For years small-block head bolts were reused without problems, but somewhere in the early- or mid-1980s, Ford seems to have changed its bolt specification, and now all good shops replace the head bolts. When it comes to quality automotive fasteners, ARP is about the only game in town, although

there are other good outfits. With ARP's excellent distribution, chances are you'll end up with their stuff. They sell their hardware from small sets all the way to complete engine kits. What you really need are the head bolts, although the complete engine kits look neat and provide all-new, clean hardware, if that's important to you.

Because the 5.0 engine uses only four head bolts per cylinder, proper clamping load is sometimes difficult to achieve with high cylinder pressures. This is why it's been popular to drill and tap the cylinder head bolt holes for 1/2-inch bolts. With the availability of good hardware in the stock diameter from places like ARP, it's faster, cheaper, and easier to simply install a new set of aftermarket bolts and skip the expensive, time-consuming drilling and tapping.

Replacing the bolts with studs is smart on a race car, on which the cylinder heads are removed with some regularity. With studs, the threads in the cylinder block are not run every time the head is taken on and off, saving the threads. With bolts, it's possible to wear out the block from loosening up the head bolt threads. For a street engine, bolts are better: They're easier to install and work around.

Crate Engines

Crate engines have been around for ages, but have gained considerable popularity with the aging 5.0 Mustang fleet. No doubt the largest reason for this is the escalating cost of rebuilding engines. As machine tool costs rise into the stratosphere and the price of parts is tagging not too far behind, the cost of rebuilding an existing engine has gone from something the average guy would have to save up several months for, to something you can get a bank loan on.

Crate engines have not risen in price as much because of the economies of scale associated with volume buying and production. Larger machine shops can keep their expensive machines busy by building engines in quantity, and their ability to buy pistons, bearings, and so on in bulk helps too. In essence, these crate

Mild street engines that must run quietly do well with hypereutectic pistons. Those from Keith Black are the most highly regarded, much better than Ford's, in fact. Just go lightly with the power adders when running hypereutectics.

TRW is a very popular source for forged pistons because its huge volume keeps the cost down. Those huge volumes come from using more or less universal forging dies, however, so these are not the last word in lightweight pistons. TRW offers two general families of forged pistons, stock replacements and lightweight or racing pistons. The stock replacement parts use an oil drain back slot, while the racing parts feature oil drain back holes, as seen here. The holes are preferable because they lend a bit more rigidity to the piston skirts. TRW recommends larger piston-to-wall clearances for the racing pistons, but they're the ones you want, due to their strength.

offerings are limited-edition production engines, hence the cost savings.

An associated concept is the popularity of brand-new engines sold over the counter. Years ago such engines were considered too expensive, but with the factory offering short blocks, long blocks, and complete engines (at least as long as they make 5.0 engines), the advantages of bolting in a completely new engine, factory-correct and ready to go, have outweighed fiddling with a wornout engine in the machine shop. The obvious disadvantage here is that the engine is still either stock or near stock, so if you're looking for more performance, custom machining and assembly are necessary.

What Is a Crate Engine?

Let's start by defining a few terms. A short block is a partial engine assembly consisting of the block, crankshaft, connecting rods, pistons, rings, camshaft, timing chain set, and little else.

A long block is a short block with the cylinder heads attached, so it also includes the cylinder heads, lifters, pushrods, rocker arms, and associated small parts.

A complete engine is just what it says, a long block plus manifolding, induction, distributor, spark plugs, plug wires, water pump, brackets, and many other small parts.

Note there is no textbook or legal definition of these terms. That means you must read the fine print when ordering such an assembly, as a long block may or may not include a flywheel and clutch, or it may not have a single piece of sheet metal on it (oil pan, front cover, rocker covers). A complete engine probably doesn't have an alternator, air pump, and serpentine belt on it either. On the other hand, sometimes all these items are included.

Crank Kit

There's another option closely related to crate engines, the crank or rebuild kit. This is essentially a short block minus the block itself. Thus you get a ready-to-go kit made up from a combination of new and machined used parts. The cost is low because you don't have to pay a machine shop to do the assembly, yet the more difficult machining steps have been done. All that's left is for your local shop to machine your block, followed by your careful assembly.

New vs. Rebuilt

Something else you want to pay attention to is whether the assembly you are considering is all new, or built from a mixture of rebuilt and new parts.

All-new partial and complete engines are by definition Ford Motor Company's private reserve. No one else makes all the parts, so only Ford Motor Company can offer assembly-line new engines. As long as the supply of 5.0 engines from Ford SVO holds out, this is a great way to go. Obviously the parts are 100 percent all new, so all of their service life is ahead of them. Perhaps even better, these parts were assembled in the Ford factory using production machines and labor, and have gone through Ford quality control. These things cannot be duplicated by anyone outside of Ford, so that makes an all-new engine or assembly the best possible replacement part.

Even so, these parts are typically not the most expensive, either. The factory's huge buying power allows this to happen. The combination of all-new parts, factory assembly, and affordable price is a tough combination to beat.

Don't forget a new clutch at rebuild time. There is no cheaper time to install a clutch than when the engine is out of the chassis, and the increased power from a new engine may overpower a clutch that was borderline with the old engine. Two popular street/strip options are the weight-assisted Centerforce and Ford SVO's "King Cobra." Both offer relatively light pedals for their clamping loads. Racier engines want something more robust, like this McLeod combination.

Rebuilt engines and assemblies reuse the major factory pieces, such as the block, crankshaft, and connecting rods (probably), then add new pistons and possibly new cylinder heads and small parts. These assemblies range from wonderful to so-so, depending on the source, but it's tough to say which is which. Certainly the larger outfits, such as AER and RHS, do a fine job, but that's not to say some of the smaller, local shops don't provide good assemblies, either. Some do and some don't. You'll have to decide for yourself. Ask lots of questions, look around if the shop is local, and make certain of what you are buying. At least with a local shop you can go back to them if you have a problem. Just make sure they'll work with you before you spend the money.

A relatively new variation of the used vs. new question comes from performance houses that are using all-new,

but not necessarily Ford-sourced, parts in their short blocks and complete engines. It's too early to tell if all of these parts meet acceptable durability standards, but it's probable they do. Naturally, such all-new engines do benefit from having zero time.

Stock vs. Modified

Both Ford and the aftermarket offer stock and modified assemblies. The modified ones are what we're interested in, as they have the better performance parts already installed and are easily the better buy for hot rod work. Ford's GT-40 and 351 GT-40 long blocks are excellent examples of modified assemblies. They're also great buys and built from all-new factory parts.

Large aftermarket rebuilders excel at modified engines and assemblies. Companies like RHS offer a large variety of engine combinations, especially

when it comes to camshafts, cylinder heads, and intake manifolds, so you can shop for the combination you are looking for without having to either have it custom built locally or accept the more standardized offering like the GT-40 engines. Many of the Ford specialists offer engines, of course. Places like Benett, Coast, DSS, JBA Racing Engines, Nowak, and so on know these engines extremely well and can get you further down the performance road for less money than the local hero shops.

Cost

When figuring the cost of a crate engine versus a rebuild, don't forget to factor in the associated costs. One of the biggest reasons to go with a crate engine is the time savings. In some cases, you can drive your 5.0 home from work on Friday afternoon, then drive it to work again Monday morning after installing a new engine. If you rebuild an engine, you'll have to drive something else while your Mustang is tied up for weeks in the machine shop. You'll also have to store the immovable chassis somewhere, too.

If you mail order an engine, you could save on sales tax, which can be considerable. On the other hand, shipping could eat up all the other savings, so do your figuring as closely as possible.

One cost that's tough to figure is quality. For any enthusiast, the cost of a new engine should be looked at over the life of the engine. Better engines last longer, plus the disruption of changing engines costs money. This all adds up in favor of somewhat more-expensive assemblies initially, which last longer and run better than the blue light specials headlined in some advertising. Cheaper parts coupled with quick and dirty labor are no bargain two years down the road, and especially if the engine leaks or fails to perform to expectations 10 minutes after it is installed.

Stock Cylinder Heads . .119

Odds and Ends 125

Cylinder Head
Preparation 127

Porting 129

Screw-In Studs and
Guide Plates 132

**C
O
N
T
E
N
T
S**

Ford enthusiasts haven't always
been so lucky, but today there's a
huge number of cylinder heads
available for the small-block. Most
of the new heads are aluminum,
which saves about 40 pounds off
the front axle.

CYLINDER HEADS

No other engine part so fundamentally improves the 5.0 HO for performance duty as freer-flowing cylinder heads. Cylinder heads are critical because they contain the intake and exhaust ports, plus the valves and combustion chambers. Most importantly, though, they contain the ports, including, as we've previously noted, the restrictive exhaust port. Improving the exhaust flow is the key to unlocking 5.0 performance, and a set of aftermarket cylinder heads will definitely do the job.

On any engine, the intake and exhaust ports are critical, because they play a huge part in controlling the amount and quality of the airflow through the engine. The port size and shape are important factors in the volume of airflow. At least equally important are the size and shape of the valve seat and the port area just above the valve seat, called the bowl. These areas, along with the valve shape and valve job angles, play a large part in the control of the hugely important factor of air stream velocity. Filling the cylinder is done partially with large areas for the air to flow through, but also very much by accelerating the airflow to high speed over the valve seat.

Because the cylinder head contains all these important areas, it plays a huge role in both the engine's ultimate power output and its power personality. The stock 5.0 HO is optimized for torque. Given natural aspiration and stock displacement, no other combination of parts produces as much low-rpm torque as the stock engine. This makes the HO easy to drive in traffic and around town, plus it keeps fuel mileage up.

The downside is that the stock head is restrictive at higher rpm, choking horsepower. In fact, the stock heads are one of the main reasons why a showroom stock 5.0 explodes so hard off the line, but then runs out of breath as the tach climbs to 5,000 rpm. The bottom-end torque is great for everyday street driving, but the limited top end does slow the car down at the track, and perhaps worse to the enthusiast, gives the engine a grunty, weight-lifter feel. Sportier driving calls for a bit more top-end horsepower, which aftermarket heads deliver.

Of course, changing the cylinder heads to improve top-end power means the very bottom-end torque suffers. The more horsepower-oriented a cylinder head design is, the more low-rpm torque and around-town drivability it will lose. Luckily, unlike with old carbureted engines, the 5.0's long-runner

intake manifold keeps good torque on hand, even with fairly aggressive cylinder heads. It isn't necessary to put up with a soggy daily driver, just to have good power up to 6,000 rpm.

On the other hand, the 5.0's popularity has driven Ford performance into the mainstream, with many offerings bombarding the enthusiast and his pocketbook. Today there are small-block Ford cylinder heads for every purpose, and it takes some doing to sort them out. That's part of what we'll do in this chapter.

Stock Cylinder Heads

There have been many cylinder heads fitted to 221-302 and 351W small-block Fords by Dearborn. For decades there were no aftermarket alternatives, and hot rodders settled on the largest-valved 351W cylinder head as the best performance choice in an in-line valve small-block head. You'd also see the occasional canted-valve Boss 302 or Cleveland head, but these worked best only when optimized for all-out top-end power as they simply killed torque.

Those days are long gone. Today Ford fans have a bewildering choice of lightweight aluminum and stout iron cylinder heads to choose from. The tamest of these equals or exceeds the best stock casting in power output, and they're the better financial deal as well. It costs a bit more to prep a set of used stock castings in the machine shop than it does to simply buy a set of better performing aftermarket heads and bolt them on, so there is no reason to bother with the old stuff. Leave it for the restoration crowd.

Just to set the record, however, the modern 5.0 engines used the mom and pop small-block cylinder head from 1979 to 1985, then made do with the hopeless masked-intake valve version in 1986 before moving to the ubiquitous 1987–1995 head, best known by its E7TE casting number. Just in case you must tinker with stock heads, the E7TE is easily the best cylinder head of the bunch. With so many of them being replaced by aftermarket castings these days, you might end up with a good

used set to put on the shop truck or older daily driver. They make a nice step-up in power in such applications.

GT-40

In 1992, Ford introduced the GT-40 cylinder head through SVO, then fitted it to the 1993–95 Mustang Cobras as well, so you know it is a 100 percent true bolt-on. On the production cars, the head was sold only in cast-iron form, but SVO carries it in an aluminum version, too.

SVO calls their aluminum GT-40s "Turbo Swirl" heads because of a lip cast into the combustion chamber, something not found on the iron version. It promotes swirl for better mixture distribution. There are a few other minor detail differences between the Turbo Swirl aluminum and iron versions of the GT-40, and the aluminum heads make a tad more power. Both are solid street parts, with good low-rpm torque capacity coupled with another 1,000 usable rpm. When heavily ported, they can make respectable horsepower, but if big miles per hour and low times at the track are the goals, other heads are considerably better. On the street, the GT-40s are good choices for their low cost and moderate power boost while retaining factory drivability and bolt-on ease.

A late variation of the iron GT-40 head is the GT-40P found only on 1996 and later 5.0 Explorers. Moderate improvements in porting and a slight variation in spark plug placement make the "P" head the best of the iron GT-40

By casting a fence of material around the intake valve of the 1986 5.0 cylinder head, Ford engineers gained a high-swirl combustion chamber, but murdered airflow in the bargain. These heads are hopeless from a performance standpoint and must be avoided. Fitting an aftermarket head and mass air to an 1986 Mustang really wakes it up.

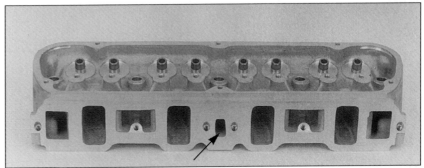

Unless a cylinder head has air (Thermactor) injection port (top) and an exhaust heat crossover passage (bottom) it is not a street cylinder head. On the other hand, the presence of these two ports is no guarantee the head carries an EO number, but chances are good it does. The air injection helps burn excess hydrocarbons and has no effect on performance. The 5.0's modern EGR system is shut off at WOT, so it too is not a performance consideration. The EGR draws its exhaust gas from the crossover passage.

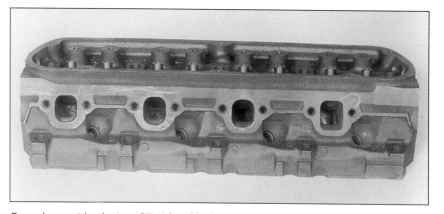

From the outside, the iron GT-40 head looks a lot like the stock E7TE casting, but it runs much better. The iron GT-40's big advantages are easy bolt-on architecture, high build quality, and low cost. But in the airflow department, it trails its newer competition, mainly due to a constricted exhaust port. It's still a good bolt-on street head.

Ford gave the GT-40 aluminum head the "Turbo Swirl" name because of this swirl-inducing ridge in the spark plug side of the combustion chamber. It evidently doesn't hurt anything, as with slightly revised porting, the aluminum version makes a bit more power than the iron head.

heads, but that still puts it at the lower end of performance small-block heads. The "P" head is a great step-up for most normally driven street 5.0s, and in the hands of a skilled head porter will probably go faster than it has any right to, but it is still all too easy to buy a lightweight aluminum head that offers even more airflow. The biggest difference is cost. GT-40Ps are offered by a few shops at very low prices, so if cost is very important, a set of these could be a smart move.

The latest iteration of the aluminum Turbo Swirl is the GT-40X. Again, this is a cleanup of the original head, so it isn't a revolutionary improvement over the straight Turbo Swirl. It is an improvement, however, and the top of the line of GT-40 heads, and a great power builder for any street engine. It offers OEM level fit and finish, meaning it will bolt right on and all the bolt holes that are supposed to have threads in them do, and it will easily support 350 horsepower in popular supercharged applications, so it's a good way to go with a street engine.

J302

Ford SVO's original aluminum cylinder head was the J302. Never granted an EO number, the J302 nevertheless was a fine street head. It bolted directly to the 5.0 engine, required no special pieces to work, had no durability problems past the earliest batch, which proved porous, and boasted some of the best low valve lift flow figures of its day.

If the J302 had a failing, it was that they were pricey compared to the available iron heads and didn't perform as well as the then TFS High-Port cylinder head—last known as Will Burt Street Heats. So, with no street emissions legality, nor killer race head flow capacity, the J302s were eventually replaced at SVO by the GT-40 and others. The head was taken out of production by its developer and manufacturer, Alan Root, years ago, so these are swap meet parts

today. If you run across a used set, they'd make a fine low-buck head for a bracket or nonemissions street car, but they won't run with the best of the current crop of aluminum castings.

Finally, the J head, as it was called by Ford insiders, had provisions for two different header flange bolt patterns (four bolt holes per exhaust port, with the second set staggered at 1 and 7 o'clock). The wider, vertically staggered pair allowed aggressive porting and a larger pipe diameter to match; this is still a good idea and can be machined into the "bigger" heads on the market today if you're going all out.

Windsor by World Products

World Products offers several versions of its small-block Ford head, but all are affordable price leaders. A curious footnote to World Products heads is they are often referred to as "DARTS" on the street, but this is officially the name of the same company's small-block Chevy head. The heads are properly, if cumbersomely, known as "Windsors" and "Windsor Jrs." by World Products.

World Products introduced the iron Windsor head first. This is a large port, big-valve head that makes good power on larger or high-rpm racing small blocks such as 351Ws or strokers; they are not streetable except on radical street rides for the 302, so don't buy these for daily driver duty. Deep-breathing stroked 5.0s, 351Ws, and high-winding strip engines can use these heads effectively, but they do require a bit of setup to run right. Sold with 2.02-inch intake valves, which have been moved slightly from stock Ford locations, the Windsor head poses a valve-to-piston issue with the stock 5.0 pistons. Flycutting the pistons is the answer, which can be done in the block with a special tool.

World Products likes to keep costs low, and these heads have been sold with very light-duty valves, springs, retainers, and keepers. Replacing these items, especially the ball-point pen springs, is a must. Most folks simply buy the heads bare, then add valvetrain

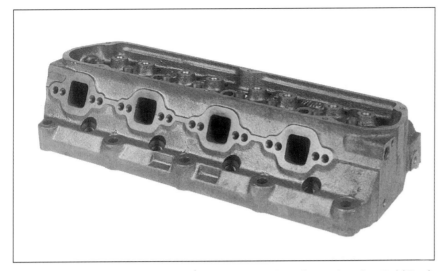

Probably the heaviest 5.0 head ever built, at 47.5 pounds each, Windsors by World Products have the beef to take any sort of cylinder pressure you can throw at them. This is the big-valve, big-port version; both it and the more street-friendly Windsor Jrs. feature a double-header bolt pattern. The wider pattern headers are considerably better for spark plug access, which is not a strong point with these heads. You can also occasionally find these heads in aluminum.

parts from a reputable cam company, along with a stainless-steel valve.

Spark plug access has also been an issue with some short-tube headers, as the plugs have been moved from the stock location. It depends on the header, however, as the Windsors offer two header bolt patterns. Those headers using the wider bolt pattern have the better spark plug clearance.

Windsor Jrs.

Because the larger Windsor ports and big valves are too much for the majority of the 5.0 market, which runs stock displacement 302s on the street, World Products released the Windsor Jr. It uses smaller 58-cc combustion chambers, smaller 170-cc intake port volume, and smaller valve sizes than the Windsor. Naturally, some top-end power capability was lost due to the smaller ports and valves, but only on the big-inch, high-rpm applications where its big brother, the Windsor, shines.

For the more popular bolt-on applications, the Windsor Jr. outperforms its big brother. This is because the air velocity is higher in the smaller ports; the compression ratio is higher too. It's also financially easier to take because the piston flycutting issue has been resolved in your favor.

The same hardware and header considerations apply to the Jr. as to the Windsor, and these heads have screw-in studs and guide plates like the Windsor. Thus, new rockers and hardened pushrods are required.

Both cylinder heads have been built in aluminum and iron versions, and there are no differences other than the material. All World Products heads are beefy parts, built with plenty of material. This makes the heads heavy, but able to withstand detonation well and last a few passes through the head milling machine. Also, World Products hasn't been overly aggressive in the Ford market, so you won't see these heads in every speed shop advertisement. The aluminum examples are especially tough to come across, as World Products races to keep up with business, especially with its Chevy parts.

Edelbrock Performer and Victor Jr.

There wasn't any doubt left the 5.0 had come of age when aftermarket giant Edelbrock tooled up for small-block Ford head production. As part of its series of heads, intakes, and cams, Edelbrock offers five versions of its bolt-on small-block Ford head, all in aluminum. The heads are the Performer for nonemissions early Fords, Performer 5.0,

Performer RPM, Victor Jr., and Victor.

The Performer 5.0 is optimized for bolt-on 5.0 use, and comes out of the box assembled and ready to go. While usually slightly higher priced than its bolt-on competitors, the Performer 5.0 heads are well machined, assembled with quality components, feature thread inserts to protect the parent aluminum casting, and make very good horsepower. They also respond easily to porting to make even more power. Their architecture is faithful to the 5.0 engine, so all accessories, such as headers, intakes, and valvetrain, bolt on without hassle. They are an excellent choice for a bolt-on street 5.0, and are often rated as the first choice for such duty by machinists and engine builders.

The Performer RPM is a bit more aggressive, and is aimed at bracket racers and others who have moved well beyond streetable power, but who don't need to spend the long dollars on an all-out racing engine. The same, but more so, can be said about the Victor Jr. This head follows the stock architecture like the Performer series of heads, so it bolts up like a stock replacement part, but it is a pretty serious race head that doesn't care much about low-end torque and is not emissions exempted. Don't consider it for a street car.

Edelbrock Victor

All that needs saying about the Victor from Edelbrock is it is a full-race head. Almost no 5.0 part bolts to this head, with its uniquely shaped and raised ports. It requires a shaft-mount rocker valvetrain, spacers to mount the intake manifold, custom exhaust manifolds, and special pistons. In fact, about the only thing "stock" about this head is that it will bolt to a small-block Ford block. At that, it's a full-on piece that barely runs below 4,000 rpm, so don't even think about it as a bolt-on.

Where the Victor shines is in speed-for-money. With flow figures that approach the full-boogie Yates head, but at substantially lower cost, the Victor gives the Pro 5.0 racer another good tool. Still new at press time, initial reports on the Victor say it flows great

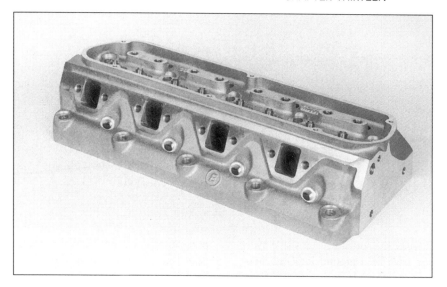

Edelbrock has been aggressive with its 5.0 cylinder head offerings, and it's paid off. This Performer 5.0 head is a great way to go on most bolt-on 5.0s, with the Performer RPM and Victor Jr. ready for more track-oriented street/strip cars. A good head out of the box, the Performer 5.0 responds very nicely when ported just on the exhaust side, and like all Edelbrock hardware, enjoys excellent build quality.

Thanks to the large machined rectangles around the exhaust ports, the Street Heat cylinder heads are easy to identify. Known at first as TFS heads, then a Will Burts, these heads are excellent power builders and run fine on the street, even though they never had a EO number (CARB exemption) or provisions for air injection. Now out of production, many of these heads are still in circulation, and they're still a power force to be reckoned with.

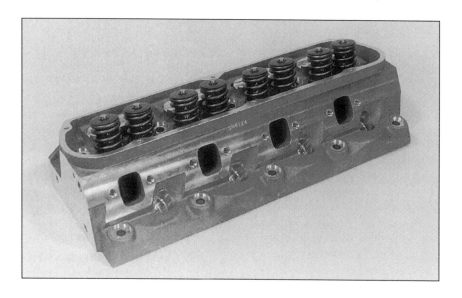

For outright airflow and overall power building, the Twisted Wedge is tough to beat. Very affordable to purchase and blessed with excellent ports and a compact, high-swirl combustion chamber, the Twisted Wedge has been dogged by spotty build quality and an overly aggressive valvetrain geometry that typically requires the substitution of bronze valve guides. An easy power maker, the Twisted Wedge is best built using Summit/Trick Flow valvetrain parts to reduce side-loading the valve stems.

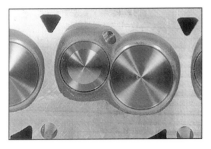

The shallow Twisted Wedge combustion chamber is both compact and open at the same time. An ingenious mixture of airflow from the port and swirl-inducing ledges, this chamber is a big part of the Twisted Wedge's power capability.

out of the box and likes a light cleanup in the porting booth, but is difficult to impossible to improve upon when ported aggressively, thanks to its quite large ports.

Will Burt Street Heat

Here's a hard-charging cylinder head with some history. Originally designed by Trick Flow Specialties (TFS) and built by Will Burt in iron and aluminum versions, the head was commonly known as simply the "TFS" or "TFS High Port." When TFS was bought by Summit Racing, the rights to this head passed to manufacturer Will Burt, who dropped the iron version and produced the aluminum casting through 1997. It's a nonemission, raised port design that has stood up to nearly 10 years of newer competitors with its excellent power production and responsiveness to porting. For years the "TFS" was the head of choice in 5.0 circles, a status that's pretty much fallen to its replacement, the Twisted Wedge, in street applications.

Running the Street Heat requires some considerations, as it was designed to run just on the edge of bolt-on, streetable status back in 1990. The raised exhaust port is just high enough to want a special header. Some people seem to get by with a standard header, but it does pull the exhaust pipes up against the floorboard. A handful of header makers offer a specific part number for the Street Heat heads in 5.0 Mustangs.

With moderate camshafts, no piston flycutting is necessary with Street

Heats, but once valve duration gets around 215–220 degrees at 0.050-inch valve lift, the piston-to-valve clearance gets close. A B303 cam clears, but that's about it. Considering the type of engines these heads get bolted on to, piston flycutting should be part of the plan. These heads also require guide plates, hardened pushrods, and screw-in studs.

Capable of great airflow, these cylinder heads ran okay straight out of the box, but were really designed for porting, with generous material in the port castings. This allows the machinist to shape the port as necessary, and many sets have been ground into real monsters. Another plus is the standard Street Heat intake valve seat accepts valves from 1.94 up to 2.08 inches. The exhaust is a large-enough 1.60 inch. With a little bowl work, chamber cleanup, and a valve job, these heads can flow 250 x175 cubic feet per minute.

Some of the fastest 5.0s have run these heads, and they remain a good choice in the mid-range and higher power ranges. More bolt-on friendly heads are a smarter choice for the more casual street application. Currently out of production, Street Heats are still surprisingly available, as many were put into circulation.

Twisted Wedge

After his success with the Street Heat, designer Rick Smith turned his talents to a new street head design, the Twisted Wedge. The Twisted Wedge uses a unique, 61-cc, craftily shaped combustion chamber with valves rotated and moved to the center of the cylinder to improve breathing. The spark plug has also been moved closer to the center of the cylinder.

The combination of good, high-velocity ports and small combustion chamber makes the Twisted Wedge quite a beast right out of the box. It's not the easiest cylinder head to port, but it flows so well as cast that most tuners never have to worry about it. As a bolt-on, the Twisted Wedge is far ahead power-wise of any of the stock-type heads like the GT-40 offerings, and is noticeably ahead of the Edelbrock Per-

former out of the box, flowing more like a Performer RPM or Victor Jr. As all these heads pass through a competent porter's hands, the differences become much closer. Still, the Twisted Wedge has become the head to beat powerwise for street engines, and it makes superb bolt-on power. If you are running treaded tires, the Twisted Wedge makes about as much as you can use right out of the box.

Another major part of the Twisted Wedge story is its low cost. Summit knocked the market on its ear with its price, which was hundreds of dollars below the going rate for an aluminum head at the time. The resulting jump in market share was predictable; but there have been some prices to pay along the path to $1,000 pairs of assembled aluminum heads.

One is build quality, which is passable these days, but has been spoiled by the occasional hole that isn't drilled deep enough, no thread inserts, and a generally machine-shop morning-after look when they unwrap from the box. None of this is deal-busting, but these heads can be aggravating to work with when the headers won't go on without a stack of washers under one of the bolts or the valve cover hardware drags its way in. Just make sure you run a bolt through all the holes and give the accessories a dry fit before dropping the heads onto the short block. Then if a hole does need a tap run through it, you can easily do it on the bench.

More important is the Twisted Wedge valve guide wear situation. Some shops have reported incredibly rapid valve guide wear, on the order of 500 miles of running, before needing new guides and valves. Other shops report no problems. Trick Flow has gone to extensive lengths in attempting to re-create and study the conditions that have resulted in rapid guide wear, and has concluded mismatched parts are the culprit. The Twisted Wedge head, like the TFS Street Heat head before it, was designed close to the limit for maximum power. Thus the valvetrain geometry is more critical than the easier-going bolt-on heads, and particular

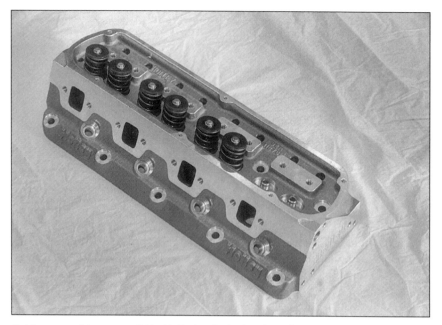

Sold as part of its system II kit, Holley's cylinder head combines many good features of standard small-block Ford head architecture. The high exhaust bolt placement relative to the port allows some porting room.

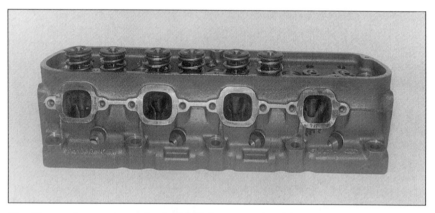

The Chevy exhaust ports make the N351 Sportsman head from SVO unique. The ports give the head great exhaust flow, but mean purpose-built headers are required to match both the port outlet shape and bolt pattern. This has to be the most powerful cast-iron Ford head with inline valves, but it's hardly a 5.0 bolt-on part.

attention must be paid to ensuring the rocker arm sits correctly on the valve tip and that the pushrod length is correct. Some shops argue the Twisted Wedge valvetrain geometry is so skewed that even with careful attention to setting up the rocker arms, spring heights, pushrods, and so on, it is impossible to get the geometry within their acceptable guidelines, and at best, valve guide wear will be higher than normal.

To make setting the Twisted Wedge valvetrain geometry easier, Trick Flow began packaging rocker arms,

pushrods, and other valvetrain parts in late 1997. Simply buying their recommended parts package is the easiest way to be sure the valvetrain is to specs. Otherwise, a knowledgeable machine shop can set up your combination, but such a shop should be thoroughly familiar with Ford performance in order to get this right.

TFS also says the original PC valve stem seals they used were a bit tight for their iron guides, and the later Viton umbrella seal is better, as it lets a little oil onto the valve stem. The best option,

albeit considerably more expensive, is to remove the Twisted Wedge's iron valve guides and substitute more forgiving bronze guides. This is a good move when looking for the ultimate solution, as the bronze guide sheds heat to the cylinder head better than the stock iron guides. You'll find most higher-end machine shops push this work pretty hard, as they don't want the heads coming back anytime soon.

A nice characteristic of the Twisted Wedge is that it is pretty forgiving of valve-to-piston clearance. Although big cams are going to get close, as always, with the moderate cams used on 325+ horsepower normally aspirated and moderately supercharged 5.0s, Twisted Wedges typically don't require piston fly cutting. TFS says the maximum cam with a flat-top piston is 224 degrees duration at 0.050-inch lift, with 0.540-inch maximum total valve lift and 112 degree lobe separation.

The bottom line with the Twisted Wedges is they're power builders, and worth working with if street power is the goal.

Also, it's worth noting Summit Racing bought Trick Flow Specialties after the Street Heat head was released, but before the Twisted Wedge came out. So, the Twisted Wedge has always been offered through Summit Racing under the Trick Flow Specialties name, while the older TFS Street Heat continued for a while by its original manufacturer, Will Burt. Though both were designed by Rick Smith, they are two very different cylinder heads.

Twisted Wedge R

While the Twisted Wedge has gone plenty fast on race cars, TFS put the Twisted Wedge valve and combustion chamber concept into a "bigger" head for dedicated racing duty. With over 200 cc of intake port volume and exhausts to match, the Twisted Wedge R is plenty large enough for hot racing engines, and too big for street use.

As many tuners will tell you, for nonemissions, big-power applications, the Twisted Wedge R head is tough to beat. The price is easy to take, the airflow

Used Australian Cleveland heads are brought into the United States by the gross, rebuilt, and offered at competitive prices. Although a great breathing head, and not a bad way to go when purpose-building an engine for carbureted track duty, its manifolding requirements keep it from being a wise 5.0 bolt-on head. There are many dedicated 5.0 heads that will make this much power, and with aluminum's weight advantage.

is great, and the chamber helps build power. Like the standard-issue Twisted Wedge, this is a head you want to have prepped by a good head shop using quality valves and guides.

The Twisted Wedge R is quite similar to the standard head, including the compact combustion chamber, valve angles, and so on. The major differences are in the larger ports and available intake valve sizes that can be run. A dual exhaust bolt pattern is also fitted, to allow larger flanged racing headers or stock pattern flanges.

Holley

Holley's SysteMAX II kit has given Ford enthusiasts one of the newest street-oriented cylinder heads. Built by Brodix for Holley, the new head is offered only as part of the SysteMAX II kit, which replaces nearly everything from the head gaskets up. This makes it difficult to pass judgment on just the head alone, but it seems clear the Holley gear is on par with the Edelbrock Performer RPM or maybe Victor Jr. level, which puts it in very good company. Initial reports on SysteMAX II give it high marks for top-end power, but also a soggy bottom end that hurts street drivability. Much of this may be the SysteMAX II camshaft.

The Holley gear is built around Ford architecture, so there should be little trouble substituting different manifolds and so on. In fact, the lower intake is based off the 302 truck intake, the upper intake is an improvement of the Saleen/Vortech piece, and Holley doesn't offer headers, so the exhaust must interchange with stock as well. The valvetrain poses no special needs, either.

Brodix

Besides building a cylinder head for Holley, Brodix offers its own cylinder head, the Brodix Track 1. It's completely different from the Holley casting. The Track 1 is an ultimate street or bracket racing head, and comes with a large 68-cc combustion chamber and a big 2.08x1.60-inch valve package.

Like many aftermarket heads, the Brodix takes liberties with the valve placement, and coupled with the large intake valve, these heads require piston notching with stock pistons. Once past that chore, however, the Brodix is a bolt-on, and allows stock manifolding. One unusual characteristic of the Brodix is its thick 0.750-inch deck. This allows substantial milling, for almost any usable combustion chamber volume and thus compression ratio.

While the Track 1 had not been out long enough at press time to evaluate, preliminary specifications showed substantial airflow, with every indication these heads would be super power builders. The 195-cc intake ports are rated at 260 cubic feet per minute of flow at 0.700-inch valve lift, with Brodix saying this can be ported to over 300 cubic feet per minute, which is big flow indeed. Of course, to take advantage of all this airflow, you'll need the matching camming and manifolding.

Brodix offers the heads bare or assembled, and all come with phosphor-bronze guides. The assembled heads feature swirl-polished stainless valves and large 1.55-inch valve springs. In all, they're really a bit much in the strict sense of a street bolt-on, but if track duty calls, they look promising.

Avenger/Canfield

Understanding this head is simple. Although a product of Canfield and also sold by Ford Performance Solutions as the Avenger, this head is functionally the TFS "Street Heat" piece. The Canfield/Avenger and Street Heat castings differ just a hair, but in all major respects, they are functionally identical and share the same advantages and concerns.

Of course, the Canfield is just barely different enough to point out a few things. The exhaust port, which is said to be slightly improved, features a dual-pattern header bolt pattern, and the intake port roof is slightly raised. This higher roof makes a SVO's GT-40X intake manifold gasket the one to use with the Canfield head, as the GT-40X intake port is slightly raised as well.

Furthermore, large-valve versions of the head are offered. Panhandle Performance markets a large-valve Canfield head, with special emphasis on the exhaust port. The idea is to run this large exhaust valve head on big blower, turbo, or nitrous engines, where extra exhaust capacity is sorely needed. Ford Performance Solutions also has a couple of variations of the casting with CNC chambers, large valves, and the like. This includes a so-called R-version with high-quality valves, titanium retainers, and other premium equipment. No matter which version, the Canfield/Avenger head is noted for its reasonable price, and with its Street Heat breeding, it certainly has good horsepower potential.

Odds and Ends

Several cylinder heads merit mention because they will work on the 5.0

Cylinder head decks are milled for a variety of reasons, but the most typical is to clean and flatten the head's mating surface to seal with the head gasket. Expect to lightly mill even new heads out of the box, as many aftermarket heads have poor surfaces as supplied. This is a step you can skip with some of the better, more expensive heads, which are nicely machined from the factory. Let your machinist be your guide.

HO engine, but aren't popular for various reasons. I'll mention them here for identification purposes. None are bolt-on parts, and they make no fiscal sense, but it's still likely you'll run across them.

N351 Sportsman

This iron head from SVO is aimed at carbureted Saturday night circle track racing. It's a race head with no EO exemption, but is not so radical that it couldn't easily be streetable in a lumpy-cam sort of way. A bolt-on to the 5.0 block, the main bugaboo to using the N351 in a Mustang is the head's unique exhaust manifold bolt pattern. At press time, header selection was limited to a pair of long-tube designs, and it's doubtful any short-tube headers will ever be

developed for this head, which features an especially good, Chevy-style exhaust port.

The N351 builds great power and would make a fine bracket race head, especially if the rules require an iron casting. The N351 is reasonably priced, too. All you'll need to do is find or build the necessary headers.

Cleveland

Ford's small-block production head with the most power potential is the canted-valve Cleveland. It comes in the so-called "four-barrel" and "two-barrel" variations. The huge four-barrel intake ports run like gangbusters at 8,000 rpm at the race-track but are too big for the street (never mind that's where they were sold), while the smaller

two-barrel ports are better on the street, but suffer on the exhaust side. All Cleveland heads are cast iron and have been left behind in flow and torque by modern 5.0 street heads.

The main practical trouble is that the Clevelands were built to go on Clevelands, not Windsors, and all the two engine families share is the cylinder head bolt pattern. The valvetrain, water passages, and intake and exhaust manifolds are all Cleveland spec, and while special carbureted intake manifolds have been available to mate Cleveland heads to 5.0 blocks, it still takes some machine work and special parts to get them working. The one place jumping through all the Cleveland hoops might be worth it is an old-fashioned style bracket car where the desire was deep rear axle gearing, tach-twisting rpm, and sparkling high-rpm power for running down the other guy at the big end of the track, but there really are better ways to do this nowadays.

Australian Cleveland

Australian heads are still offered in the Ford magazines. As the name suggests, these are used heads salvaged out of Australia and cleaned up for sale here. They are the best combination of usable ports in the all-iron Cleveland head family, and are indeed good running heads. Of course, all the Cleveland conditions apply to getting them running on a 5.0. They aren't EOed or aluminum and they don't support EFI intake manifolds; they are best run on carbureted engines for those reasons.

C302

Ford's NASCAR racing head in the 1980s was the C302. An updated aluminum canted-valve variation on the Cleveland theme, the C302B version is the most numerous of these. Sold with tons of material cast into the ports, the C302s were designed to be hand-ported; not an easy thing to get just right in this head, it turns out. The C302s can really scream at the track, but have been superseded by the Yates inline valve heads for checkered flag duty, and are much too finicky, expensive, and lacking in low-

BHJ's special tool makes cutting Loc Wire receiver grooves accurately easier than machining them manually. Because so many shops seem to have trouble getting these grooves properly cut, you may want to ensure your shop has a BHJ tool. Should you inherit a poorly cut set of grooves, the best option is to mill the heads until the grooves are gone, as recutting the same grooves is tough.

rpm torque for any street use. Manifolding these is a custom proposition on an EFI engine, too.

Yates

Ford's current NASCAR head is one developed by Robert Yates Racing. These are impressive top-end breathers, but have no place on a street car. The Twisted Wedge has a passing resemblance to the upright valve angles and extremely compact combustion chamber of the Yates head. Twisted Wedges are the castings to use if you want to explore this school of airflow theory. Yates heads are also extremely pricey and have unique manifolding requirements (read: "expensive custom headers and intake").

Cylinder Head Preparation

While some of the bolt-on 5.0 heads are literally ready to bolt on when they come out of the box, there's plenty more to do if you want, and some heads really need some attention before they

go on an engine. A good machine shop can make your new heads run better, or sometimes longer; the shop can also rebuild used heads.

Milling

To ensure a flat head gasket sealing surface (deck), cylinder heads are cut in a specialized mill. This is a standard rebuilding step, and is commonly done with new heads, too. On a new head, milling 0.003–0.005 inch off the deck ensures a dead-flat surface (blueprinting), while a deeper cut, up to 0.050 inch, raises the compression by reducing the size of the combustion chamber.

To put it in perspective, a 0.035-inch cut on a GT-40 decreases the chamber 7 cc (from 65 cc down to 58 cc). You'll get about the same from any of the popular inline small-block heads with a similar combustion chamber. Milling Twisted Wedge heads would give even more compression, as the chambers are small to begin with anyway.

Heads really should not be milled more than 0.050 inch because it changes too many angles. If you need that much compression, it's time for new pistons. Also, be advised more than 0.020 inch of head milling narrows the distance between the heads on a V-8 to the point where the intake manifold must also be narrowed to fit. Otherwise, the intake stands up high between the heads, and the ports, water passages, and bolt holes don't line up. Naturally, all this adds expense.

A head can also be set in the mill at an angle to take more off one side than the other (angle milling). This is an expensive racing trick done for reshaping the combustion chamber. It's not necessary on a street engine for standard rebuilding or most hot rodding.

Angle milling does give two good results if you're racing. First, very small combustion chambers can result for high compression, and second, it stands the intake valve up a bit for improved flow. On a Street Heat head, for example, the 22 degree stock intake angle can be decreased to 20 degrees and the chamber squeezed down to 50 cc with a 0.200-inch angle cut. Naturally, angle

milling makes a mess out of everything else. The pushrod holes will need elongating, as may the head bolt holes, the intake manifold will also need an angle cut in addition to a standard cut due to the narrower engine. The valvetrain may need a different pushrod, too.

Getting back to everyday reality, expect to pay for a light milling pass after porting the heads. Working with a grinder around the heads inevitably results in an accidental nick, which is cleaned up with the milling machine. For the same reason, but even more so, porting should be done before the valve job or milling.

Combustion Chambering (CCing)

Combustion chamber volume is measured by filling the chamber with a known amount of oil. This somewhat tedious process is the only way to know the exact combustion chamber volume, and thus the true compression ratio. It is also used by racers when machining all the combustion chambers to the exact same chamber volume.

You rarely need to do it on a street engine, although the "get it perfect" engineers in the audience are fond of it as a check. This would also be an important step when blueprinting, as the idea is to get all the combustion chambers exactly the same size (and shape). With the advent of CNC machining along with seat and guide machines, machine work has become much more accurate and repeatable, which has reduced the amount of CCing being done. Typically what it uncovers these days is an inconsistent head casting—not enough to worry about on a street engine.

O-Ring and Loc Wire

Because 5.0 engines vent excess cylinder pressure generated by detonation by blowing out the head gaskets between the four head bolts, O-ringing the block or Loc-Wiring the cylinder heads has become popular.

O-ringing the block is a time-honored hot rodding method of ensuring the head gaskets don't leak cylinder pressure. A groove is cut around the cylinder bore, then filled with a strand

Unlike O-ring grooves, which typically travel in a figure 8 pattern between two cylinders, Loc Wire grooves are simple circles that surround the combustion chamber. A wire imbedded in the Loc Wire head gasket fits inside the groove to provide a very positive seal. Some shops don't have much trouble fitting Loc Wires, but others do. Many enthusiasts have forgone Loc Wires and gone back to the basics, that is, O-ringed blocks, to avoid blown head gaskets.

Small-block Fords use only four head bolts per cylinder, which has too often been blamed for blown head gaskets. Actually, attention to torquing details using a quality gasket and keeping all surfaces clean, flat, and square goes far to maintaining head gasket seal. The rest is detonation avoidance. Of course, stronger head studs and Loc Wire gaskets, as seen here, are good investments when moving up the cylinder pressure scale with more boost, nitrous, compression, and rpm.

of relatively soft, thin wire. When the gasket and cylinder head are installed, the wire O-ring concentrates the clamping load of the cylinder head, forming a gastight seal that is nearly impregnable to attack by combustion pressure.

Loc-Wiring the cylinder heads is essentially O-ringing the heads. A receiver groove is cut into the head, which accepts the steel ring in the Loc-Wire head gasket. Special tools are available to make this job easier, and any competent machine shop should be able to do it. I recommend you find a shop that is familiar with the operation, as it can be fouled up, and unfortunately, often is. It is necessary to accurately place the receiver grooves, and to cut them to the proper depth to avoid causing gasket leaks.

This also holds true when buying heads (mail order or over the counter) that were cut with Loc Wire receiver grooves at the factory or shop. These grooves must be 0.010-inch deep, and unbelievably, are often much shallower due to sloppy work. This keeps the head from crushing the head gasket, with the usual result of filling the engine with cooling water. I've seen this put that oily, goopy water-oil mix everywhere from the oil pan to inside the throttle body. Because the engine really should

come apart to inspect the bearings after such a disaster, this is a dumb mistake you want to avoid.

Finally, it is possible to run both an O-ringed block and Loc Wired heads, although it's definitely not needed or even desirable. It's important that the ring materials not overlap at any point, or they will raise the head. Theoretically, at least, O-ringing will also greatly increase the fatigue life of the head bolts/studs, because the stiffer joint reduces the cyclic stress variation in the fasteners.

Valve Job

From a power standpoint, the most important job a machine shop normally performs on the cylinder head is a valve job. A valve job is when the machinist grinds or, more typically, cuts, the valve seats and valves. Modern guide and seat machines use cutters for these operations, resulting in more accurate work than the old free-hand grinder and stones.

At a minimum, three angles are cut into the seat to establish the seat itself, plus the top and bottom angles. The top and bottom cuts are important to blending the air smoothly around the valve

seat. The accuracy and consistency of the machinist work are vital here, as it is possible to cut the seat too deeply (especially when having to clean up a botched cut), sinking the valve seat. This murders low-lift flow, as the valve is effectively sitting down in a cup, or well, that is formed by the combustion chamber.

It's difficult to overemphasize the importance of the valve job to airflow, as it is where the port, seat, and valve all come together. The airflow between the valve and seat is critical to accelerating the air just as the intake valve opens, and the airflow is greatly affected by the seat and valve shape, as it has to bend around the two. When it comes to getting maximum power from a set of heads, putting on the valve job is not a time to play amateur hour.

Because air won't bend over 9 degrees without going turbulent, a series of angles are used to bend the air around the valve. For 90 percent of all heads, the standard 30-45-70 degree three-angle seat is preferred. The 45 degree cut is the angle the valve seats against, while the 30 degree cut provides the blending angle on the combustion chamber side of the valve seat and the 70 degree cut

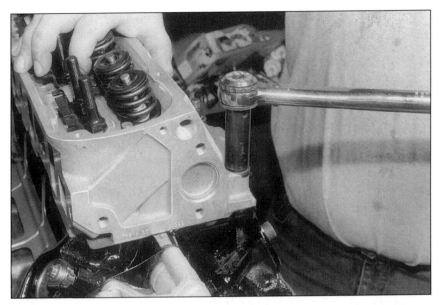

There have been almost as many cylinder head torquing sequences published for the 5.0 HO engine as there are cylinder heads. The end result is that the shorter head bolts should be final torqued to 65–70 lb-ft, while the longer head bolts need 75–80 lb-ft. The torquing pattern is simple—start in the middle of the head and alternate your way out with 25 lb-ft pulls, then bring the bolts up in 10 lb-ft increments from there.

smoothes the flow on the port side of the seat. When shopping for head work, you really want a shop with a head and seat machine, which quickly and accurately provides these cuts. This isn't to say a stone grinder can't do good work, as in the end, it always comes down to the quality of the machinist and not so much his tools. Still, the quality-oriented machinists have all stepped up to head and seat machines by now.

You may also hear about five-angle valve jobs. These are for racing heads, on which the extra expense is deemed necessary. Many a five-angle valve job is a three-angle with an additional pass by a single cutter, which provides a sloping cut into the 30 degree angle on the combustion chamber side of the seat. Because the cutter has a radius at its outer end, it gets counted as two angles, for a total of five. Such five-angle jobs are unnecessary for any street engine and are marginal for many bracket and mild competition engines, so stick with a three-angle valve job unless you have a specific reason for a racing engine.

As for the valves, they typically get a 44 or 45 degree cut to establish the seat. A 30 degree or so cut on the stem side of the valve seat will help flow and

is worth the effort. New valves are usually ready to go out of the box, but a used valve will require grinding to restore the seat.

The machinist may also grind the top of the valve, where the rocker arm contacts it, to shorten the valve for geometry reasons. If the valve is too short, lash caps may be fitted. These are small hardened cups that slip over the stem.

To check his work, the machinist may lap the valves. This is done by spinning the valves in their seats with an abrasive lapping compound between the seat and valve face. This smoothes any very small irregularities in the surface of the seat and valve, and leaves a visible trace on the valve and seat the machinist can inspect and measure.

A valve job is also required when larger valves are fitted, of course. If the valves are really large, then larger valve seat inserts, the blank steel rings the seats are ground into, must be fitted. Stock heads use an induction hardened seat on the exhaust, and the parent cast iron for the intakes. Aluminum heads use hard seats on both valves. How large a valve can be fitted onto an existing seat depends on the width of the seat, but on the typical 5.0 head new seats are usu-

When prioritizing your porting, remember that the exhaust side is where the most gains are to be had (even though John Bridges is working on an intake here). This depends on the casting, but for street/strip engines, the exhaust port is definitely where the action is. By improving the exhaust port relative to the intake, the flow balance of 5.0 heads is invariably improved, boosting engine efficiency more than just the increased flow from the improved port would indicate. You might say it allows you to get more out of your headers and cam.

ally required. Installing new seats is extensive, expensive work, and it is nearly always financially better to purchase a better cylinder head with larger valves to begin with.

Porting

Like any mass-produced part, only so much attention can be lavished on the cylinder heads by the manufacturer. For basic street engines, the accuracy of the ports in modern cylinder heads is good enough, with some heads noticeably better than others. However, any cylinder head can be improved by porting, which is the reshaping and smoothing of the ports using hand-held grinders and polishers. When it comes

Valve Seat Replacement

When fitting oversized valves or after multiple valve jobs, it is often necessary to install new valve seats. The larger valves simply require the larger seat, of course. But even with stock diameters, after many valve jobs the valve seats are "sunk," meaning the valve sits so low in the seat the surrounding cylinder head material masks the valve, killing airflow. With the constant development and low prices of Ford heads today, take a hard look at buying new heads if a bunch of the seats are sunk. The cost-benefit analysis may come out in their favor. Otherwise, there is nothing wrong with fitting new seats.

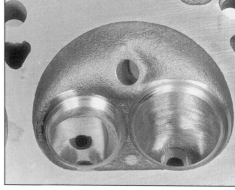

This pair of before and after shots illustrates the typical bowl cleanup. At right, marks from Ford's tool path are plainly visible on the intake port bowl wall, including a sharp lip where the cutter stopped. After porting, both bowls have been slightly enlarged, their sides straightened, the sharp edges and rough surface texture removed, and the valve guide bosses narrowed.

to racing, porting is mandatory, and on the street, porting makes the difference between a real charger and just another 5.0 with heads, intake, and headers.

It's also worth pointing out that exactly how a set of heads should be ported can depend on many variables, such as camming, compression ratio, and so on, with the porting work ranging from a quick cleanup with a sanding roll to a full-on competition job requiring days of tedious reshaping of the ports and intake manifold runners into twisting, tapering works of art. Typically such expensive, specialized porting is the realm of all-out racers; the more affordable off-the-shelf mail-order porting jobs offered on bolt-on style 5.0 cylinder heads are still well ahead of the unported castings, however. Such affordable porting is really the result of CNC machinery.

A good head porter can seemingly work magic on most heads, transforming them from so-so castings into real power houses. There's little porting can do to help with ports that are too large to begin with, however, and tiny, convoluted or highly variable ports can only be improved so much. Luckily, 5.0 performance heads carry a wide range of cast-in port shapes, so finding a set that will port nicely for a particular combination should not be difficult. Making a decision like this is where a good

machine shop is worth everything. Just remember to buy the parts from them after picking their brains; otherwise they won't be there the next time you need some help with your Ford.

There's also a flip side to porting with some of today's better Ford heads. The Twisted Wedge, for example, flows so well out of the box, and requires fairly extensive porting work before any meaningful improvement is made that porting them for bolt-on street use is tough to recommend. Edelbrock Performer 5.0 heads, on the other hand, respond very nicely to cleaning up just the exhaust port, which should be done on any application.

Conventional porting is done by hand using an air-powered die grinder with carbide cutting tips and rolls of abrasives, called sanding rolls. An assortment of cutter shapes is necessary, and great care and experience are necessary to

reach the desired shape. Just what that shape is depends on seemingly everything from the camshaft, compression ratio, rear axle ratio, valve size, intake manifold, the phases of the moon, and what color your valve covers are. The porter's experience is his guide, a highly specialized and guarded knowledge gained from years of shaping, flowing, and dyno testing cylinder heads. Porting is also time-intensive, tedious work. One slip of the grinder and a valve seat or chamber can be ruined, and all things considered, porting work is pretty cheap for the time spent—at least until you have to write a check for it!

There are various levels of porting work. Often a shop offers several stages, such as I through IV. The first stage is often called a cleanup, where the porter knocks off obvious casting flash protrusions, smoothes the bowls, and maybe blends one radius. The next stage includes all that, plus some straightening of the port walls perhaps. The next stage builds on the earlier work with what is often called a full port job, where the roof, floor, walls, bowl, short side radius, the valve guide, and port opening are fully worked over. The port may be enlarged, which is invariably done by grinding open the port roof. This straightens the port, unlike grinding on the floor, which would tighten the short turn radius, leading to turbulence and ruined airflow. The port may also be "relocated" by the machinist, typically meaning the port is raised and straightened to the limits of the manifold or gasket.

The final level of porting is for full-on race engines, and usually results in a little more flow for a lot more work. Such effort may include simply spending more time on the short turn and bowl to relocating the port more substantially, to the point where the intake manifold must be ported or even welded and ported to match. Like most "good, better, and best" purchases, the "better" is typically the most cost-effective porting approach. You'll want to port nearly any cylinder head, limited only by the cost or when running the real cylinder head airflow animals on mild bolt-on daily drivers. Run-around street engines benefit the most from light porting; progressively more intricate porting is necessary as you move up the racing ladder.

Practically speaking, the GT-40 exhaust port especially needs plenty of work, and excellent street results have come from porting just the exhaust side of the Edelbrock Performer, even though its as-cast exhaust port is well ahead of the GT-40 already. As for the stock E7TE casting, a good porter can take the exhaust from 120 to 165 cubic feet per minute, while the intake can improve from 165 as cast to touching 200 cubic feet per minute. Compare these figures to those of some of the more aggressive 5.0 aftermarket heads and you can see why there is no substitute for a good head when getting serious about airflow. It's not too tough to buy another 50 cubic feet per minute that way.

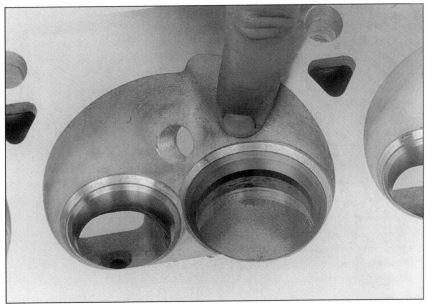

Because air is so easily diverted, even small edges can disrupt smooth airflow. The minor lip where the parent aluminum of this Turbo Swirl head ends and the valve seats begin is a concern. After very carefully guiding a die grinder around the lip, the machinist has eliminated the edge, without tagging the valve seat. There's also bowl cleanup showing in the intake.

CNC Porting

Computer Numerically Controlled (CNC) machines are computerized milling- and lathe-type machines that are computer controlled. While quite expensive (about the cost of a modest house), CNC machines are extremely accurate, with inhuman repeatability. They can cut the same amount from the same spot on piece after piece of work, and do so rapidly.

Once a program is written for a certain cylinder head, a CNC machine can whittle out nicely ported heads like so many hot cakes. The trouble is, cylinder head castings vary widely, enough that most CNC work is a basic port job, which can then be finished by hand. Obviously, this reduces the cost, and allows development of camshafts, intakes, and so on to match the port job, which in effect, has become a short mass production run. CNC porting also allows tighter matching of mani-

folds to the heads, as the port can be precisely located with relative ease by a CNC machine.

Extrude Honing

While hand-porting has been around for decades, Extrude Honing is relatively new to the automotive scene. An aerospace process that uses pressure machinery to push a gritty paste through passages, Extrude Honing is ideal for smoothing complicated internal passages.

Surprisingly accurate and capable of many different types of finishes, Extrude Honing is super for reworking the long, twisting passages of the 5.0 upper intake manifold. The same job by hand requires cutting the manifold open to gain access with a grinder, then re-welding the intake when finished. Extrude Honing does the same job faster and more consistently.

Extrude Honing is also used to port cylinder heads, and it does a passable job. However, even though Extrude Honing can take a little more off one side of passage than another, it can't match the precise reshaping possible by hand porting. Extrude Honing is cost effective on a large-run basis, however, and what smoothing and shaping it does are helpful in improving power production. I recommend Extrude Honing for EFI intake manifolds and possibly as a quick port job on cylinder heads, keeping in mind that hand porting is still better for the cylinder heads when looking for much more than "cleanup" power increases. Extrude Hone offers 5.0 parts on an exchange basis, which speeds turnaround time compared to hand-porting, and is a good option when time is a concern.

Port Matching

A form of abbreviated porting is port matching. This is the process of accurately locating the opening of a port, so it exactly matches the intake or exhaust manifold that mates with it. The reworking extends into the port to a depth of about an inch. The idea is to smooth the transitions in the inlet and exhaust tracts.

How much benefit is possible from port matching depends on the head. The E7TE stocker has a bump just inside the intake port that acts like a ski ramp. Put there to accommodate a pushrod hole, the bump is easily ground out during port matching, making it a good option on those heads. Edelbrock Performers, on the other hand, come CNC port-matched out-of-the box, so there is no need or benefit from port-matching them in the field. That benefit was paid for when you bought them.

It's important to realize that port matching is worth only so much under the best circumstances, and after cleaning things up, moving on to a full port job is best. Also, if the intake manifold and port runner are wildly mismatched, hogging out the cylinder head to match is a bad idea. Intake tracts that have the cross section of a gopher snake enjoying a heavy lunch do not flow as well as they

When a machinist fully ports, the port shape is often considerably changed. This once somewhat oval iron GT-40 exhaust port illustrates a typical transformation. Such reshaping will typically extend the entire length of the port on a full porting job, or may be found just at the port exit when port matching, which is what we're looking at here.

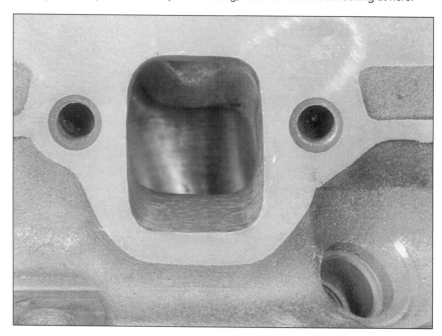

could. The idea is to gently funnel, or taper, the air all the way from the throttle body into the valve bowl and past the valve into the cylinder, so ballooning a section of the air path is no good.

There's also the problem of changing parts someday. When another intake manifold is bolted on, the carefully executed port match is off, which can leave exposed lips facing the wrong direction. It is much better to have even a large mismatch where the airflow opens into a larger section of the port than to have a small lip sticking into the air stream, causing turbulence. Therefore, it's best to leave the intake manifolds smaller than the head ports and the headers larger than the exhaust ports. If no parts changing is anticipated, this issue is of no concern.

Screw-In Studs and Guide Plates

The stock 5.0 valvetrain uses a nonadjustable, bolt-down 1.6:1 rocker arm with a sled fulcrum and solid tip. The disadvantages of the stock arrangement are high friction from the sled fulcrum and solid tip, a bit less than a true 1.6:1 ratio (and ratio inconsistencies from rocker to rocker), and nonadjustability save for the rather inconvenient method of changing pushrods. Advantages of the stock system are low cost and quiet operation.

From a cylinder head perspective, the valvetrain consideration is drilling the stock or stock-type heads for screw-in studs and guide plates. This used to be a common machine shop operation, but today there are so many bolt-on options for the stock and stock-type cylinder heads that there's no need to mill the rocker arm pedestals down to accept guide plates, plus drill and tap the rocker bolt hole in the rocker pedestal oversize to accept a heavy-duty rocker stud. (The stock rocker bolt hole is 11/16 inch, while aftermarket rocker studs use 3/8-inch threads.) Anyone that serious about the valvetrain has already moved on to an aftermarket head, which comes ready for rocker studs and guide plates.

Of course, it's possible you'll run across a set of stock heads that have been milled for studs and guide plates, which means you must run hardened pushrods and matching rocker arms. It's an additional expense, but you'll benefit from a free-running valvetrain.

Port matching involves marking the exact dimensions of the desired port outlet's shape, then grinding it to match the lines. Machinist's dye and scribe lines make the shape easy to see. This GT-40 exhaust port is fully ported, but the port matching layout is easily seen.

Both intake and exhaust gaskets typically fit with some allowance at the top of the port. This allows the machinist to open the port at the roof and still have a proper gasket seal. Opening the port roof straightens the air path and is always desirable; the floor is never enlarged, because near the port exit the airflow is relatively slow and lethargic.

C
O
N
T
E
N
T
S

Camshaft Terminology .134

Camshaft Strategy 138

Normally Aspirated . . .138

Supercharged Engines .139

Turbocharged Engines .140

Nitrous Oxide 141

Popular Camshafts 141

5.0 Lifters 143

5.0 Pushrods and
Rocker Geometry 144

Rocker Arms 144

Rocker Installation and
Adjustment 145

Rocker Arm
Adjustment 146

If you can see the lifter valley, telling a flat tappet block from a roller lifter example is simple. The giveaway is the obvious machining of the top of the bores on roller-lifter blocks. Flat tappet camshafts can be used in roller blocks without modification to either block or cam, but only flat tappet cams and lifters may be used in a flat tappet block unless a conversion kit is used. Crane Cams offers what you'll need.

CAMSHAFTS AND VALVETRAIN

When Ford introduced the 5.0 HO engine in 1982, even though its internal components were changed significantly from those of earlier 302 engines, the engines were still equipped with a conventional flat-tappet hydraulic cam and lifters. Then in 1985, Ford introduced the now-familiar hydraulic roller cam in the four-barrel carbureted HO Mustang engine. All subsequent 5.0s in 1986 had the same style roller cam and lifters. There were also several non-HO roller cam applications like the Thunderbird engine, which has a significantly different cam profile. All 5.0 engines built after 1985, including non-HO engines in passenger cars and trucks, can accept either conventional hydraulic cams or stock and aftermarket hydraulic roller cam components. Engine blocks prior to 1985 require special machine work or additional components to use a hydraulic roller cam.

The roller cam and lifter components differ from conventional hydraulic

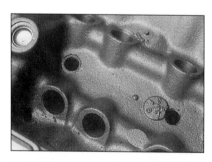

cams. The roller cam itself is of steel construction, not the cast iron used previously. Also, the roller lifter assembly is taller than the standard flat tappet lifter, requiring a change in the block construction around the lifter boss area to accommodate the lifter and antirotation guide bar arrangement.

Furthermore, all roller cam-equipped engines require a special steel distributor drive gear that is compatible only with the roller cam gear, since a cast-iron gear on a roller cam gear will fail in just a few hours of operation. Previously, racing roller cams required an aluminum bronze alloy gear to prevent galling on the drive gear, but these would wear out quickly. Since the 5.0 engine was to be used on the street, Ford engineers developed a special steel gear that yielded the long-term durability required. Initially these gears were only available from Ford dealers, but several different configurations are now available through the Ford SVO.

While all the engines from 1986 to present have the roller cam and lifters, the rocker arms have remained the standard stamped steel, bolt-down type, nonadjustable fulcrum design common to all the small-block engines. Because we're dealing with Fords, there must be an exception, in this case the Mustang Cobra engine, which used 1.72 ratio aluminum roller rocker arms. The standard pushrods used with the hydraulic roller cam are shorter in length than earlier engines, due to the taller height of the lifter, and are nonhardened.

Camshaft Terminology

Selecting a new camshaft to increase power in a stock engine, or to complement additional engine modifications, requires some different strategies, depending on the engine's final configuration.

Unlike many camshaft specifications, lobe or valve lift is easy to measure using a dial indicator. Lobe lift is most easily obtained by measuring off the pushrod, while valve lift is obviously obtained at the valve. Don't be surprised if measured valve lift doesn't come to the theoretical value obtained by multiplying the lobe lift by the rocker arm ratio; tolerances and flex usually rob a thousandth or so.

When seriously camshaft shopping, it is important to understand some of the common camshaft terminology and to be aware of a few hidden factors when reviewing published specifications.

Cam Card

This is the cam data card, which is included with the camshaft from most cam manufacturers. Normal information would include the gross valve lift, total or "advertised" duration, lobe separation, lobe lift, opening and closing events measured at 0.050-inch lobe lift, recommended valve spring closed and open pressures, and other miscellaneous information the cam manufacturer deems pertinent.

Lobe Lift

Lobe lift is the actual height of the cam lobes measured at the lifter, without lash. If this measurement varies more than 0.001 inch from the cam card, the cam is bent or possibly not made correctly. You may want to check more than

one pair of lobes to determine if the whole cam is off the same, or if there are significant variations lobe-to-lobe.

Also realize that the cam may be perfect, and the variations you measure are due to lifter bore location variances that are common in production blocks. Zeroing in on misaligned lifter bores is a job for a good machine shop, as is the expensive, labor-intensive job of bushing the lifter bores back into perfect alignment with the rest of the engine. So, while production tolerances can allow lifter offsets on blocks to be as much as 0.120 inch (which can lead to measurable valve-to-piston clearance issues with mega-lift, long-duration cams most often found on naturally aspirated racing engines), there's not much to be done about it unless you are running a full-out race engine. Only then is the cure worth the pain.

Valve Lift

The cam cards and catalogs usually list gross valve lift, which is just the lobe lift multiplied by the theoretical rocker ratio. Consider that rocker ratio variances in different brand rockers, valve stem length, pushrod length, and location geometry will affect the actual net valve movement, which is what really matters to you and the engine. The only way to tell for sure what the net valve lift is, is to use a dial indicator and measure at the valve with all the components assembled, with the correct lash.

Total Duration, Advertised Duration

Back in the 1950s when cam manufacturers wanted to get a marketing advantage over another manufacturer, they'd rate the cam duration by simply measuring the duration at a lower lift point, for instance 0.005 inch instead of 0.010 inch at the tappet. This would let them advertise the cam as having 300 degrees duration instead of 290 degrees, while the cam would essentially be the same. Because all of the different manufacturers measure their camshafts at different points (and at different points for different profiles), comparing two cams on the basis of total duration or adver-

tised duration is a poor, inaccurate way to select for duration. Just ignore advertised duration numbers. They are essentially meaningless.

Duration at 0.050-inch Tappet Lift

This has become the most universal way of comparing cam timing duration as most cam manufacturers now list the opening and closing events at 0.050 inch of tappet (lifter) lift on the cam card. This information is used for proper cam phasing to the crank, called "degreeing the cam."

A few cam cards do not list events, just duration and lobe center, while others do not list duration, just the opening and closing events. But for most enthusiasts, there is no need to go further than lift at 0.050 inch. It's the accepted measurement of cam lift among engine builders, cam manufacturers, racers, and so on. So, when comparing profiles, you can be reasonably sure a cam with 230 degrees duration at 0.050 inch is "smaller" than a cam with 240 degrees duration at 0.050 inch.

Lobe Center

Some of the most misunderstood and misapplied terminology in the selection and installation of camshafts is "lobe center." When lobe centers are discussed, there is a difference between the lobe center the cam is ground on and the lobe center at which the cam is installed.

The center line of the lobe is the maximum lift point, and the cam is ground with a fixed separation angle between the intake and exhaust lobe centerlines. This separation angle is built into the cam, and is given in actual degrees, not crankshaft degrees. For example, a cam card says the cam has a 112 degree lobe separation. If you were to lay a protractor on the side of one intake lobe and measure how many degrees it was from the intake maximum lift point to the exhaust maximum lift point for the same cylinder, you would measure 112 degrees.

However, all of the camshaft events and durations are given in crankshaft (not camshaft) degrees, meaning the opening points, closing points, total

The only way to know the valve events are happening in proper time with the crankshaft is to degree the camshaft during installation. This is not as hard as it looks and makes all the difference in how your 5.0 will run.

you aren't alone, so don't let it bother you. But it does help to understand the relationship of the camshaft lobe center-lines—how widely spaced the intake lobes are spaced from the exhaust lobes—when comparing cams. You may also have heard this referred to as lobe or valve overlap, which isn't quite the same thing either. Overlap is the period, expressed in crank degrees, when both valves are open together. Overlap depends partly on the lobe centers, but also in the duration of each lobe—how far around the base circle the lobe starts and ends. Such lobe separation affects idle quality and where in the rpm range the camshaft will make power. The wider this lobe center, the more top end the cam will enjoy, and the less idle quality you'll enjoy.

Straight Up

Do not confuse lobe separation with installed lobe centers. "Straight up" is a term that assumes the cam is installed so the intake lobe centerline and exhaust lobe centerline are equally distant from TDC. Most (but not all) camshafts are ground in such a way that when installed in an engine with standard timing components, the intake lobe centerline will be closer to TDC, thus pushing the exhaust lobe centerline away from TDC. This makes the valve events occur earlier, therefore the cam is considered to be advanced. This is normal and desirable. Lining up the dots on the timing chain gears is not "straight up." The cam must be "degreed in" using a degree wheel and dial indicator to determine proper cam installation.

Why is degreeing a cam important? A cam profile is designed for a particular purpose, and while advancing and retarding the cam can fine-tune the characteristics of the combination, if you trust all of the potential manufacturing variances to be correct and install the cam without checking, the cam may not perform at all the way you intended, due to the valve event timing being way off.

Consider all the parts that must be correct for everything to line up: The keyway in the crank, the slots on the crank gear, the dowel hole in the cam

duration, and duration at 0.050-inch tappet clearance are based on measurements taken from a degree wheel installed on the front of the crankshaft. When the cam is installed in the engine, there will be a lobe center location specification that refers to the angle, in crankshaft degrees, between each lobe centerline and TDC. Because the cam only rotates half as far as the crank, the measurement listed for the installed intake or

exhaust lobe center position from TDC can be similar to or the same as the lobe separation angle number, leading to confusion. If the lobe separation angle was listed in crankshaft degrees like all the other specifications, the two numbers would be different enough that no one would confuse them.

If you have to read the previous paragraph three times to understand the different uses of the term "lobe centers,"

Naturally aspirated camshafts tend to get brutal when the engine is tuned for racing. Explosive valve opening ramps, big lifts, and week-long overlaps are common with such cams, which, in turn, mean rapid valvetrain wear. Valve springs and guides are frequent victims of these aggressive cams. Luckily, the requirements for workable idle vacuum and moderate lift keep naturally aspirated street cams within reason for longevity.

drive gear, and the dowel location in the cam, and that the cam manufacturer is working off of the factory blueprint. For example, if the cam dowel location installed to compensate for a "factory" retard built in to the original cam gears is used by the camshaft manufacturer, then if you install that cam with a different aftermarket timing set with a different dowel hole location, the cam will not be installed correctly and the engine performance will suffer.

Having the cam installed out of proper location may also cause a valve-to-piston clearance problem. Advancing the cam causes the intake valve to open earlier and so be closer to the piston as it rises up the cylinder on its way to TDC. Retarding the cam increases the intake clearance, but decreases the exhaust clearance, which brings up a common misconception regarding gross valve lift and valve-to-piston clearance. Everyone wants to know "how big" a cam can be used in their 5.0 engine based on valve lift, although the gross valve lift has only a relatively small influence on the actual valve-to-piston clearance. Most camshafts are designed to be installed in the engine with the intake cam lobe center located somewhere

Flat tappets are simple but high-friction devices. Ford developed roller lifters to increase fuel economy, but the associated benefits are not inconsiderable. Lobes worn flat are no longer a concern, cam break-in is not critical, and the geometry possible with the combination of lobe and roller lifter makes more aggressive ramps possible. The downsides are cost and weight, although rpm must rise well above the factory 6,250-rpm rev limiter before the extra weight is a concern.

between 102 and 112 degrees after TDC. At this point the piston is more than half the stroke distance down in the cylinder and not close to the valve at maximum lift. The speed and shape of the opening side of the intake lobe, and the closing side of the exhaust lobe, affect how far open the valves are when the piston is traveling up at around 30 degrees before and after TDC. The difference in cam profile design between two different cam manufacturers could

Pressurized air from a supercharger means significant airflow begins soon after the intake valve opens, effectively making the camshaft "bigger." This phenomenon helps make supercharging a smart choice for street engines; not only is the power good, but the drivability associated with smaller camshafts makes the typical bolt-on blower car a pleasurable daily driver. Stick with the stock cam and concentrate on other power improvements as long as possible with a street blower car.

create a situation where a 0.500-inch gross valve lift rated cam with fast opening action would hit the piston, and a different profile design with even 0.550-inch gross lift that used a slower opening action would actually clear the piston. Never assume an aftermarket cam will yield adequate valve-to-piston clearance without checking. The only time you can skip this step is if there is evidence from your machine shop or the manufacturer of the cam, confirming that the particular combination of cam and cylinder head you are using has already been proven to have adequate clearance. Still, installation must be correct, since even a stock cam can hit if the cam is installed wrong.

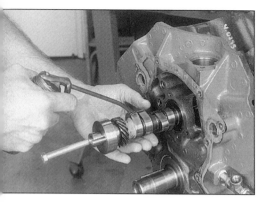

Unlike a flat tappet cam, which requires moly lubrication and careful break-in, 5.0 roller cams are installed with nothing more than oil lubrication and no break-in. Also, used cams and lifters may be freely interchanged, a sure disaster with a flat tappet cam.

Camshaft Strategy

Cam profile selection is still one of the least understood and most challenging areas of engine performance. Whether you are an experienced engine builder, or a street enthusiast, selecting a cam for your engine can be difficult without a clear idea of how and why a new or different cam will improve performance. Camshaft timing that would optimize a normally aspirated combination would not be the correct cam for a supercharged application, and compression and bore/stroke changes will change the configuration required for optimum performance. If you are not comfortable choosing a cam profile yourself, most of the aftermarket cam manufacturers have technical personnel that can give you general guidelines as well as specific recommendations for your particular requirements. This is a service more enthusiasts should take advantage of.

Normally Aspirated

The only way air gets into a naturally aspirated 5.0 engine through the intake port is due to the pressure difference between the local atmosphere and the cylinder. This pressure difference is created by movement of the piston down the bore on the intake stroke. Peak airflow velocities and the volume of air captured in the engine are integrally related to the port and valve sizing, manifold efficiencies, engine stroke, and rod ratio.

Ideally, the cam would open the valve fast and far enough so the airflow in the port keeps up with the flow demand being generated by piston movement, and after peak flow is achieved, would close the valve at the point where the maximum volume of air is captured in the cylinder before piston movement forces it out again, referred to as the reversion point.

Because atmospheric pressure is the only force pushing air into the chamber, most performance and racing cams have the intake lobe centerline positioned somewhere between 102 and 110 degrees after TDC regardless of lift and duration. Installing the cam much earlier than 102 will usually incur valve-to-piston interference problems without much gain in power (a smaller camshaft may be indicated), and installing the cam later than 110 usually kills mid-range torque without significant gain in top-end power (a larger cam may be indicated). During the intake cycle, the intake opening point is probably the least sensitive point in the cam cycle since the piston is nearly stopped as it travels through TDC. The actual net valve lift and airflow at about 75 to 80 degrees ATC (after top center) is critical since this is where the engine flow demand and piston speed is highest, and the closing point is the most critical to making proper power because that is the point at which you capture the mixture and start compression.

In general, the shorter the intake duration, or the earlier the intake valve closes, the higher the effective compression and torque will be at lower rpm ranges. The greater the intake duration, or the later the intake valve closes, the lower the effective compression will be and the engine must be operated at a higher rpm to achieve proper cylinder filling.

During the exhaust cycle, ideally the valve would open after all the usable heat and work energy has been extracted on the power stroke. The valve would open fast and far enough so the majority of the residual gases can escape the cylinder before the upward piston

Ford's flat-bar lifter retention system works well with moderate cams and rpm, but with more than .375 inch of lobe lift, or racey rpm levels and small base circle cams, the flat bars hang up and break. The cure is aftermarket lifters.

movement, avoiding a loss of power. Since 50 to 60 percent of the exhaust gases escape during the short time between exhaust valve opening and BDC, there will usually be a high velocity pulse generated, which can be utilized in a smart header design to scavenge the residual exhaust gases, as well as provide some leftover energy to help start the intake flow at TDC overlap, if the tuning of the header diameter and length is proper.

In general, the shorter the exhaust duration, or the later the exhaust opens, the better the exhaust port and exhaust system needs to be to properly evacuate the cylinder before the intake valve opens. The exhaust lift and duration can usually be increased relative to the intake profile without significant detriment to the power range of the engine, and can help overcome inadequate exhaust port flow or a poor exhaust system.

Typical 5.0 camshafts designed for daily driving street performance will have 0.480-inch to 0.512-inch gross valve lift, 204 to 216 degrees intake duration, and 210 to 224 degrees exhaust duration (both at 0.050-inch tappet lift), lobe separation angle of 110 to 114 degrees, and the cam installed with the intake lobe center positioned at 106 to 108 degrees ATC.

If you have a stock cylinder head with stock valve diameters and no porting, a "split pattern" cam is best, where the exhaust lift and duration are slightly larger than the intake. It's better to move up to aftermarket heads or ported stock heads, with a single-pattern cam, where the intake and exhaust profiles are the same. The natural bias the engine wants for cam timing is then created by the lobe separation and the 4 to 6 degree advance created by standard timing components.

Supercharged Engines

In a supercharged application, some mechanical device pushes air into the engine. If the supercharger is a positive displacement type, the pressurization occurs right away, and boost only climbs slightly through the power band. If the supercharger is a centrifugal type, the turbine has to achieve some rpm before significant boost is achieved, so boost is much more rpm dependent. In either case, air is being forced into the engine largely independent of atmospheric pressure, with important camshaft consequences.

Contrary to the naturally aspirated engine, because the supercharger is present and developing pressure in the intake manifold, air will usually start flowing immediately after the intake valve opens and the port will now experience increased airflow at low- to mid-valve lift values. This does not occur when naturally aspirated, because the piston is barely moving at this point. So, with the supercharger, there is not as much need to open the valve as early or as far.

If the intake opens too early on a blown 5.0, significant fuel mixture may be wasted as it blows right through the chamber during the overlap period, when the exhaust and intake valves are both open at the same time. A supercharged engine is not as sensitive to where the lobe center is, since airflow is not quite as dependent on port and manifold efficiencies. So, a proper intake lobe for a supercharged engine would not need as much lift to flow even more air than normally aspirated as the low lifts are better utilized. Plus, it can use a later lobe center location, say between 110 and 116 degrees ATC, without loss of power since the airflow is keeping up

with piston movement better. Also, the retarded lobe position allows the valve to stay open longer because the pressurized intake makes the reversion point occur later in the compression stroke even at low engine speeds.

Positive displacement superchargers (Roots type, B&M, BBK, Kenne Bell, Eaton, etc.) provide airflow in direct proportion to the drive speed, the flow characteristics of the blower, and the size of the engine. All other things being equal, a given size blower will produce differing amounts of boost pressure on engines of differing displacements, and I understand that their internal leakage will depend to an extent on the "head" they are working against,

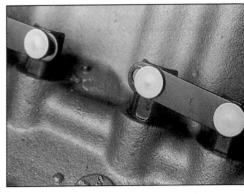

Aftermarket 5.0 lifters are joined together with flat straps. This race-oriented retention system allows essentially unlimited lobe lift, rpm, and small cam base cams. This engine is using a conversion kit to use roller lifters in a flat-tappet block.

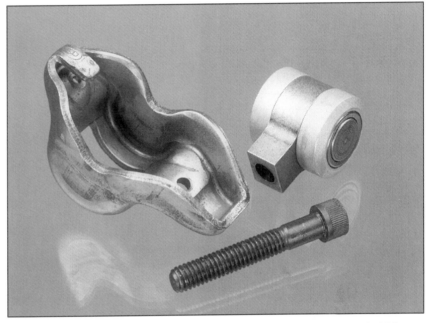

By far the greatest friction in the 5.0 valvetrain is in the stock rocker arm's sled fulcrum. The friction is eliminated by the roller trunnion in common aftermarket rocker arms, with tests showing the roller trunnion freeing 12 horsepower in reduced friction. If aluminum rockers are too pricey for you, then Crane offers this drop-in roller trunnion which is a direct replacement for the stock sled fulcrum. Crane also has low-cost stamped-steel rocker arms with either plain or roller tips.

and that this will arguably affect the "flow characteristics." But surely this last is a very minor effect over the practical range of displacements under consideration here. This means that pressure is present in the intake manifold as soon as the throttle is opened, and very high cylinder pressures can be achieved throughout the rpm range. Cam timing can usually be increased without signif-

icant loss of torque or drivability; however, the very high pressures possible at low speeds can easily lead to detonation.

Centrifugal superchargers (Paxton, Vortech, Powerdyne, etc.) depend on the mechanical drive to reach a critical speed relative to the turbine efficiency to start significant boost pressure in the intake manifold. This usually means the larger supercharger cams will decrease

Most roller rocker arms are built on aluminum extrusions. Their bulky outline results from having to add plenty of material to maintain strength. Bulky looks or not, they are relatively lightweight for good rpm potential, and they invariably sport roller tips and roller bearing pivots, called trunnions. This pair happens to fit the N351 Sportsman head, but they nicely represent the typical 5.0 rocker arm.

The major dividing line in 5.0 valvetrains is between the stock-style bolt-down rocker arms, like the pair at right, and the stud and guide plate system, laid out at left. The bolt-down rockers use the stock 5/16-inch fastener size and are an inexpensive method of gaining aluminum roller rockers. The stud and guide plate system steps up to larger hardware and is a stronger system for use with higher spring pressures. The cylinder head is wearing a slightly different stud and guide plate system, and the rocker arms illustrate the difference between castings, on the left, and extrusions, at right.

low-speed torque and drivability until the supercharger reaches the proper velocity, and engines equipped with too large a cam will have the same low idle vacuum and poor low-speed drivability as if the cam was installed in a naturally aspirated engine. Such killing of low-rpm torque may be a benefit in a high-horsepowered drag racing 5.0, where traction is at a premium. The reduced low-rpm torque may allow the tires to hook better before the big rush of boosted power hits. Otherwise, this loss of low-speed torque hurts fuel economy and drivability.

As a general rule, it is accepted that if the exhaust port can flow somewhere between 70 and 80 percent of the intake port flow, then the exhaust can be tuned to keep up with the power levels achieved in the engine via proper header and camshaft tuning. With a supercharger, the exhaust environment is now much harder to control, because the engine is burning air and fuel as if it were a larger engine.

On a pure airflow basis, theoretically a stock 5.0 with seven pounds of boost (a typical baseline configuration for an aftermarket supercharger) is processing 50 percent more air than a normally aspirated 5.0, so theoretically for the exhaust system to keep up it needs to be able to flow as if it were operating on a 50 percent larger engine. This is not com-

pletely true because there are losses in the intake port, compressor efficiency, and heat. Still, there is no mechanical device to help scavenge the exhaust, so the port, valve, and header are still operating in a naturally aspirated environment. Increasing the exhaust lift and duration, as well as utilizing wider lobe separation angles, helps the engine reduce pumping losses induced by the increased volume of the burnt mixture on a supercharged engine.

The exhaust lobe will usually need to open earlier to give the engine more time to "blow down" the cylinder pressure as the theoretical loss of heat energy due to early opening is more than offset by the pumping losses generated when the piston is trying to push out the remaining gases around 75 degrees BTC (before top center). Since the exhaust port on most 5.0 heads can only achieve, at best, 80 percent of the normal intake port flow, the lift and duration need to be as much larger as makes sense for drivability and reliability. Indeed, most supercharged applications respond nicely to a split profile that favors the exhaust. Furthermore, since the intake lobe is usually retarded fur-

ther than normal, an even wider lobe separation angle is required to position the exhaust lobe properly. Thus, on paper, a perfect supercharged engine would have an exhaust port and cam profile that would flow in direct proportion to the intake airflow achieved with boost. In reality, however, a certain amount of exhaust pumping losses are unavoidable due to port inadequacy.

Typical 5.0 cams designed for bolt-on supercharger applications will have 0.480-inch to 0.530-inch gross intake lift, 216 to 224 degrees intake duration (at 0.050-inch tappet lift), 0.512-inch to 0.540-inch gross exhaust lift, 220 to 228 degrees exhaust duration (at 0.050-inch tappet lift), and a lobe separation angle of 112 to 116 degrees, with the cam installed with the intake lobe centerline between 110 and 114 degrees ATC.

Turbocharged Engines

In turbocharged applications, the intake manifold and port operate as if conventionally supercharged, so the intake cam design for turbos is nearly the same in terms of lift requirements, lobe center location, and intake valve closing

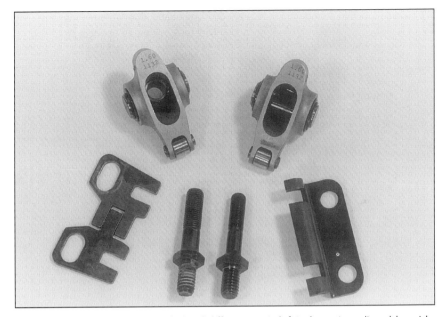

Studs and guide plates come with detail differences. At left is the racier, adjustable guide plate coupled with a 7/16-inch stud; at right is a nonadjustable guide plate and 3/8-inch stud. The heavier stud will resist higher spring pressures before yielding. The bulkier adjustable guide plates from Isky often need a bit of massaging with a grinder to fit on the end cylinders, but work well and adapt to many different Ford heads.

point. The turbocharger is unique in that under boost the exhaust tract is pressurized all the time, and the exhaust system present in most turbocharged installations consist of "log" type manifolds feeding directly to the drive turbine in the turbo, excluding any possibility of any significant exhaust scavenging.

The speed and efficiency of the turbo depend on the blow-down portion of the engine cycle, not the action of the piston pumping out the air. Since the exhaust flow is limited by the manifolding, and the turbine speed is dependent on high-temperature, high-pressure pulses, most of the work gets done before the valve is 70 percent open. Also, since significant high temperature and backpressure are present in the exhaust manifold, any significant overlap allows the pressurized, high-temperature exhaust to contaminate, oppose, and heat the inlet charge during overlap. Therefore, street turbocharger camshafts tend to be single pattern, low-lift cams with wide lobe separation angles and low duration on both the intake and exhaust. Turbo cams have been built with split patterns that favor larger intake profiles than the exhaust, to take advantage of the extra power available due to the efficiency of the turbo over conventional superchargers, but remember that the extra power produced is over and above the pumping losses generated.

Typical 5.0 cams designed for bolt-on turbocharger applications will have 0.460-inch to 0.500-inch gross intake lift, 212 to 220 degrees intake duration (at 0.050-inch tappet lift), 0.460-inch to 0.500-inch gross exhaust lift, 210 to 218 degrees exhaust duration (at 0.050-inch tappet lift), and a lobe separation angle of 114 to 116 degrees, with the cam installed with the intake lobe centerline between 112 and 114 degrees ATC.

Since the cam profiles indicated for best results under supercharged conditions are retarded relative to naturally aspirated applications even at lower engine speeds, and most purpose-built supercharged engines have lower compression for octane tolerance, engine operation without boost can be very disappointing. If you are planning for a supercharger or turbocharger and you cam the engine accordingly, do not be surprised if the engine makes less power than stock if you don't have the supercharger installed, or whenever running off boost. This is one reason many casual street blower combinations use popular naturally aspirated cams; all around they work better and are easier to pass through emission testing.

Nitrous Oxide

As far as the engine is concerned, nitrous oxide behaves similarly to a positive displacement supercharger, because the moment the solenoids are activated, additional oxygen and fuel are present in the chamber, instantly increasing the torque and power at whatever rpm the system is activated. Cam timing for this application is thus very similar to a positive displacement blower cam, including the extra exhaust lift and duration indicated to allow the engine to expel the burnt mixture. One twist, however, is that the charge temperature is usually much lower with nitrous than even an intercooled supercharger application, so the cam lobe centers can be closed up and the intake lobe location advanced slightly, all because there is less likelihood of detonation with power levels similar to supercharging.

Typical 5.0 cams designed for bolt-on nitrous applications will have 0.480-inch to 0.520-inch gross intake lift, 210 to 220 degrees intake duration (at 0.050-inch tappet lift), 0.490-inch to 0.530-inch gross exhaust lift, 216 to 226 degrees exhaust duration (at 0.050-inch tappet lift), and a lobe separation angle of 110 to 114 degrees, with the cam installed with the intake lobe centerline between 108 and 110 degrees ATC.

Popular Camshafts

Considering the lack of significant lift or duration of the stock 5.0 HO cam compared to many aftermarket cam profiles, the power results attainable with it are surprisingly good. While Ford engineers chose not to fully exploit the lifts and durations possible with the hydraulic roller cam technology, the stock cam has very good idle characteristics and drivability, and is easy on valvetrain components even with high ratio rockers. The stock cam has found favor in retro-fitting to non-HO applications (specifically the 5.0 F-150), and the wide lobe separation works well with bolt-on superchargers and tur-bocharger applications.

One comment I've heard from nearly every 5.0 tuner is there are far too many 5.0 owners eager to install more cam when they should stick with the stocker. Daily drivers are best with the stock cam, and even some higher performance applica-tions do okay with it. Of course, as more and more power is desired, then a larger cam is a must, but until then the stock cam gives more low-rpm torque, a better idle, passes emission testing easier, and returns more miles per gallon of fuel. Don't be in such a rush to get rid of it, or you could end up with a bucking, gas-swilling hog that drives you nuts.

So you will know what you are working with on a stock engine, here are the stock camshaft specifications:

Production 5.0 Hydraulic Roller Camshaft Specifications

Application	Cam Lift intake/exhaust	Duration at 0.050-inch tappet lift	Valve Lift 1.6 rockers	Valve Lift 1.7 rockers	Lobe Separation
5.0 HO Mustang	.278/.278	210/210	.444/.444	.473/.473	115
5.0 Thunderbird	.238/.247	183/191	.381/.395	.405/.420	107.5
5.0 Cobra	.282/.282	209/209	.451/.451	.479/.479	118

Besides the production camshafts, Ford SVO offers several cams that cover a reasonable range of applications, primarily oriented to normally aspirated engines:

SVO 5.0 Hydraulic Roller Cam Specifications

SVO p/n	Cam Lift intake/ exhaust	Duration at 0.050-inch tappet lift	1.6 rockers	Valve Lift 1.7 rockers	Valve Lift Separation	Lobe Recommended Intake Lobe Center
M-6250-B302	.300/.300	224/224	.480/.480	.510/.510	118	107
M-6250-B303	.300/.300	224/224	.480/.480	.510/.510	112	107
M-6250-E303	.311/.311	220.5/220.5	.496/.496	.529/529	110	110
M-6250-F303	.320/.320	226/226	.512/.512	.544/.544	114	109
M-6250-X303	.338/.338	224/224	.541/.541	.575/.575	112	107
M-6250-Z303	.345/.345	228/228	.552/.552	.586/.586	112	107

More variety and greater range of profiles are available from other manufacturers, including Crane Cams, Lunati, Competition Cams, Crower Cams, and others, most of which are designed to be used in general application street performance engines:

Aftermarket 5.0 Roller Camshaft Specifications

Crane p/n	Cam Lift intake/ exhaust	Duration at 0.050-inch tappet lift	1.6 rockers	Valve Lift 1.7 rockers	Valve Lift Separation	Lobe Recommended Intake Lobe Center
364111	.278/.293	198/208	.445/.470	.473/.498	112	112
444111	.331/.331	208/216	.530/.530	.563/.563	112	107
444126	.302/.311	214/220	.483/.498	.513/.529	112	107
444121	.333/.340	216/220	.533/.544	.566/.678	112	107

Lunati p/n	Cam Lift intake/ exhaust	Duration at 0.050-inch tappet lift	1.6 rockers	Valve Lift 1.7 rockers	Valve Lift Separation	Lobe Recommended Intake Lobe Center
51013 (?)	.278/.298	209/213	.445/.477	.473/.507	112	108
51013 (?)	.326/.326	215/224	.522/.522	.564/.564	112	108
51014	.312/.318	218/220	.500/.510	.530/.541	112	108

Lunati p/n	Cam Lift intake/ exhaust	Duration at 0.050-inch tappet lift	1.6 rockers	Valve Lift 1.7 rockers	Valve Lift Separation	Lobe Recommended Intake Lobe Center
51017	.336/.336	218/228	.536/.536	.569/.569	112	108
51012	.340/350	232/242	.544/.560	.578/.596	108	104
51018	.340/360	242/252	.560/.576	.595/.612	110	106

Comp Cams p/n	Cam Lift intake/ exhaust	Duration at 0.050-inch tappet lift	1.6 rockers	Valve Lift 1.7 rockers	Valve Lift Separation	Lobe Recommended Intake Lobe Center
35-410-8	.333/.333	206/206	.533/.533	.566/.566	110	106
35-510-8	.333/.340	206/216	.533/.544	.566/.578	112	108
35-308-8	.333/.333	210/215	.533/.533	.566/.566	114	110
35-522-8	.353/.359	232/240	.565/.574	.600/.610	112	108

Crower p/n	Cam Lift intake/ exhaust	Duration at 0.050-inch tappet lift	1.6 rockers	Valve Lift 1.7 rockers	Valve Lift Separation	Lobe Recommended Intake Lobe Center
15510	.332/.332	212/212	.531/.531	.564/.564	114	110
15511	.292/.304	218/224	.468/.486	.496/.516	114	110
15512	.310/.320	222/228	.496/.512	.527/.544	112	108

The cams listed here are a small example of the seemingly endless variety of possible cams, plus all aftermarket cam manufacturers offer custom cam grinds. They allow you to select whatever profile desired.

5.0 Lifters

Conventional racing solid roller lifter construction has each pair of lifters joined together with some type of flat bar and pivot in order to keep the lifter from turning and so keep the roller correctly aligned with the cam. Ford's 5.0 hydraulic roller lifter has a flat ground on each side of the lifter, and the flats are captured by separate guide plates that are held down against the block by a flat spring arrangement bolted to the valley of the block. This system has proven to be very reliable and inexpensive to produce, although a couple of limitations and weaknesses must be addressed when installing a large aftermarket cam profile in the 5.0L engine.

When 5.0 engines are rebuilt, the lifters are commonly reused if the rollers are not obviously scored or otherwise rough. Since there is no break-in required when replacing a roller cam, the lifters may be used again and again on different camshafts without a wear problem. However, the roller assembly that is installed in the lifter contains many small needle rollers, and over time the needle rollers will pit and wear due to debris in the oil. Also, any time the valvetrain exceeds the valve spring limit and the lifter experiences "valve float," the needle rollers are pounded and flats develop, leading to eventual failure. The hydraulic plunger in the lifter body may also cease to hydraulically adjust properly due to buildup of oil-borne deposits, and replacement lifters are only slightly more expensive than conventional flat tappet lifters, so the lifters should be replaced if time or mileage of the engine is high, regardless of the condition.

The guide bars that keep the lifter from turning are a hard cast material, and under high stress loads can develop cracks and fail. When the guide bar is no longer controlling the lifter orientation, the lifter is free to rotate sideways, with cam and lifter failure following immediately. Under normal conditions, the guide plates are held against the block and do not move, and are often overlooked as a replacement item when an engine is rebuilt, since they rarely show any significant wear. Engines with much high rpm history, or with significant street mileage, should have the guide bars replaced along with the lifters to avoid costly failure of new cam and related components.

There is also a practical limit on the amount of cam lobe lift the lifter and guide bar can accommodate, roughly 0.375 inch. Higher lobe lifts will either ram the lifter against the guide bar at maximum lift, breaking the guide bar, or if the base circle of the cam is adjusted to avoid contact with the guide bar at maximum lift, the guide flat of the lifter will drop below the guide bar when the lifter is down. Either condition will cause a cam/lifter failure, so if large valve lifts are required, the rocker arm ratio needs to be adjusted instead.

As an alternative to the Ford-based lifter and guide bar arrangement, Crane Cams is now offering a hydraulic roller

Keeping the rocker arm well positioned on the valve tip is basic to valvetrain geometry. When the valve is closed, the rocker arm tip should rest approximately centered on the valve tip, with the rocker about level or the tip slightly down. If the pushrod is too short, the tip will be closed to the intake manifold; when the pushrod is too long, the rocker arm tip is too far toward the headers. Don't forget to observe the valve/rocker tips as you rotate the engine by hand. Geometry problems often show up in midstroke.

lifter set constructed just like a solid roller with each pair of lifters joined together. This lifter does not have the same lobe lift limitation or potential failure weakness the stock 5.0 parts have, and will work well in street and performance applications up to 6,500 rpm, especially for retrofit of hydraulic roller cams into blocks other than 5.0.

5.0 Pushrods and Rocker Geometry

The stock pushrod is a fairly strong part, and can accommodate reasonable increases in lift and spring load as long as a bolt-down or other self-aligning rocker is used. If reusing stock pushrods in a rebuild, examine the ball ends for wear, and check for straightness before installation. Pushrods are commonly changed when there is a need to correct the rocker geometry with a shorter or longer length, to properly preload the lifter in nonadjustable rocker applications, or to change to a different (hardened) material to accommodate pushrod guide plates found on aftermarket cylinder heads.

When the rocker configuration of the cylinder head being used requires pushrod guide plates, hardened pushrods are an absolute requirement. Use of a stock or other nonhardened pushrod with the steel guide plate will cause failure in a couple of hours of

This valve/rocker combination is showing a well-adjusted relationship. Getting to this point is much easier if you can mock up the engine and use an adjustable pushrod to measure the necessary pushrod length. While adjusting the valvetrain with pushrod length is a pain, it is the only adjustment we have with bolt-down, nonadjustable rockers.

engine operation. Inexpensive hardened pushrods are available from SVO, as well as SpeedPro. The more expensive chrome moly pushrods used for racing are available from a wide range of vendors. If these racing pushrods are required, wait to order your pushrods until the heads are installed or at least until you can perform a trial assembly of the head and valvetrain on the block, and determine the proper length needed for correct geometry.

While most 5.0 engines use a bolt-down rocker of some kind where the rocker height is fixed, the popularity of aftermarket heads frequently requires special attention to rocker arm geometry. Ideally, the roller tip of the rocker would stay in the middle of the valve during the lift cycle to keep side loads to a minimum, but this is not possible. During the lift, the roller tip travels across some area of the valve tip, and that area should be somewhere in the middle of the tip surface. If the roller reaches the edge of the valve tip, premature guide wear, valve stem wear, or even a broken valve can result. If the roller tip is too close to the inboard side of the valve tip, a longer pushrod is indicated. If the roller tip reaches the outboard edge of the valve during lift, then a shorter pushrod is needed. Determining the correct pushrod length can be done by trial and error, but it is much quicker if some sort of adjustable pushrod is used while the new valvetrain is mocked up for the first time.

Rocker Arms

Replacement of the stock sled-type rocker with a roller rocker assembly has become one of the most popular "bolt-on" modifications. Benefits include an increase in true lift due to manufacturing quality and consistency, reduction in guide wear by use of a roller tip, and reduction in oil temperature from friction reduction. Along with these benefits, numerically higher rocker ratios are available to provide increased lift and some valve duration on stock and performance cam profiles. There is a wide availability of aftermarket roller rockers for this engine in several price and quality ranges, as well as various adjustable and nonadjustable configurations.

The stock 5.0 rocker is a one-piece steel stamping, and is fairly light and strong compared to its cast-steel predecessor found on earlier 302 engines. Advantages are that under normal conditions these rockers will run reliably and quietly for many thousands of miles. Its limitations are lack of adjustability, valve spring load limitations when increased cam lifts are to be used, plus increased wiping load on the tip of the valve when lift and spring loads are increased.

A nice alternative to the stock rocker is the Comp Cams "Magnum" series rocker for the 5.0, which is constructed using a cast stainless rocker body with hardened steel ball pivot, plus an integral roller tip. Advantages are the long life and quiet operation associated with a conventional ball-and-cup-type pivot, decreased side load on valve stems, easy lash adjustment, self-alignment on the valve tip so no guide plate or pushrod modifications are required, and reduced likelihood of interference with the valve covers or breather baffles due to their compact dimensions. Limitations are that once the valve spring loads exceed 325 pounds, the ball pivot's squeezes out the oil film and the ball will gall in the rocker.

The most popular rocker is the bolt-down roller rocker pioneered by Ford SVO. This is essentially a conventional roller rocker, but the center trunnion is drilled for the smaller 5/16-inch diameter bolt used to attach the stock rocker on a 5.0 head, and instead of riding up and down on a stud, the rocker is bolted to a special steel or aluminum pedestal, which in turn holds the rocker at the correct height and keeps it oriented in line with the valve tip. Crane Cams, Comp Cams, Omega, and Probe are just a few of the manufacturers who offer this type of rocker. Its advantages are a simple installation without machine work to the head, all the advantages of a roller rocker in reduced friction and stem loading, higher ratios available for increased lift and duration, and possibly increased cam lift and spring loads.

Disadvantages are lack of easy adjustability for proper geometry or lifter preload with standard length pushrods, relatively small fasteners when spring loads get very high, increased valvetrain noise in street applications, and rocker body-to-valve cover interference, due to the larger size of the rocker. Some rocker manufacturers (Comp Cams, Omega, Yella Terra) offer a bolt-down rocker with an integral adjustment in the pushrod cup, making pushrod length and lifter preload easier to set. These rockers are hard to beat for ease of installation and adjustment, although they usually cost more than regular bolt-down rockers and have even more interference problems with the valve cover, due to the addition of the adjuster.

Quite a few of the new aftermarket 5.0 aluminum and cast-iron heads are equipped for conventional rocker studs and pushrod guide plates. Aftermarket sources for stud-mounted roller rockers are plentiful, and cover a wide range of prices and materials. Rocker arms are available in aluminum, stainless steel, and chrome moly, and are usually available for either 3/8 or 7/16-inch diameter studs. Street and performance applications generally only require 3/8-inch studs; if high lifts and spring loads are to be used, the 7/6-inch stud is less likely to flex and bend under high loads. Rocker ratios from 1.5 to 1.7 are easily available, allowing for mixing and matching intake and exhaust rocker ratios to optimize camshaft requirements. Disadvantages are the same as other full roller rockers, mainly increased valvetrain noise and clearance problems with standard valve covers.

For extreme duty—the high rpm, high spring pressure applications associated with racing engines—shaft mount rockers are the setup of choice. Each rocker is individually mounted to a steel block attached to the head, and adjustment is accomplished with a pushrod adjuster. This type of rocker is very rigid and capable of tolerating the very high spring loads used in solid roller racing cams without the use of a stud girdle.

These rockers are usually only manufactured for so-called racing heads, and combined with their high setup cost, typically make these not a good choice for a street car.

Rocker Installation

When installing rockers for the first time, ideally you would set up a cylinder with a couple of low-tension checking springs that would allow you to hold the components in the same position that they would be in while running, yet allow you to easily open and close the valves manually and observe the valvetrain action. The roller tip should be perfectly centered over the valve side to side, as viewed from the outside end of the rocker tip. On stud-mounted rockers, the guide plates need to be moved under the studs or even cut and repositioned to align the rocker properly. Manufacturing variations in guide plate, stud hole, and valve guide location make it likely that some type of realignment will be necessary. Alignment of bolt-down or shaft-mounted rockers is more difficult, since the rocker location is fixed by the assembly of shaft and C-clip, and is not easily changed. If the side-to-side alignment will not allow at least three-fourths or more of the roller tip to rest on the valve tip, you will probably want to use a different rocker system.

Once the side-to-side positioning is determined, the roller tip needs to be checked to make sure the tip is flat to the valve tip and not cocked to either side. A stud-mounted rocker has some play, which allows the rocker to "float" a little and find its own way. However, if it is cocked more than the clearance to the stud allows (or the rocker is a shaft-mount), the mounting pads need to be remachined, valve guides checked for proper alignment, or the mount pedestals machined to bring the roller tip square with the valve.

Once the rocker is centered and square, the geometry can be checked and adjusted. As a general rule, the total travel of the contact point should be centered in the valve, so there is no danger of the roller tip falling off of the end

There are no power improvements from stainless-steel valves, but they are stronger to withstand higher rpm, and more durable to last in the hotter high-performance environment. The reduced diameter stem between the head and guide-bearing area aids airflow. Valve spring, retainer, and keeper upgrades follow the higher demands of more aggressive camshafts, and are best bought as part of a cam kit. That ensures the cam, springs, retainers, and keepers are properly matched.

of the valve during the valve events. An easy way to determine the contact pattern is to paint the end of the valve with machinists' "blue" black paint or even thick grease, mount the rockers as they would run in the engine, and rotate the engine several times to wear away the dye or paint. Remove the rockers and you'll see a shiny band where the roller tip has run in contact with the valve tip. If the band is biased toward the outside of the engine, lower the centerline of the rocker by using shorter pushrods, or machine the rocker mount if using a fixed-height pedestal mount rocker until the pattern is centered. If the pattern is inboard, increase the pushrod length or use spacer shims to raise the centerline of the rocker pivot.

Another rule of thumb that works pretty well is to adjust the rocker height so the roller tip is exactly centered in the valve at half the maximum lift. This

may work well if you are not at one edge of the seat or maximum lift. If the best pattern you can achieve still brings the roller tip close to the edge of the valve tip, you may have to use lash caps to increase the valve tip area.

If bolt-down rockers are used and need to be raised for tip geometry or lifter preload, rocker pedestal shims are available. If the rockers sit too high for proper geometry or do not preload the lifter properly, the support pedestal needs to be machined. Since you are moving the center of the rocker, it does not take much material removal to accomplish preload. A simple formula for determining how much to remove from the pedestal is to measure the lash between the roller tip and the valve, add 0.065 inch to that total, then divide the total by the rocker ratio twice. This amount removed from the pedestal will remove the lash and provide for about 0.040-inch lifter preload.

An example may help. Let's say the rocker moves 0.020 inch from the valve tip to roller. Add 0.020 inch to 0.065 inch = 0.085 inch. Divide 0.085 inch by 1.6, then divide again by 1.6 = 0.033 inch, which is how much to remove from the bottom of the pedestal.

Rocker Arm Adjustment

There are several methods for installing and setting lifter lash or preload. The simplest is the "Exhaust Opening-Intake Closing" method, which can be used for any engine, hydraulic, or solid-lifter setup. Simply start with the first cylinder on whichever side of the engine is convenient, typically cylinder No. 1. Turn the engine over by hand or with the starter with the plugs removed and observe the action of the pushrods. When the exhaust pushrod starts to move up from the closed position (exhaust opening), stop and install the intake rocker for

that cylinder. Most hydraulic cams require about one-half to one full turn of preload after all lash is removed to properly hydraulically adjust when the engine is running. Bolt-down rockers should have about one-third to three-fourths of a turn of lifter preload to full torque for proper adjustment. If setting a solid lifter cam, set the valve lash using feeler gauges.

Once the intake rocker is installed and adjusted, continue to rotate the engine, and now observe the rocker arm you just installed. The intake rocker will soon begin to open. Watch the rocker and when the intake valve has completed its full cycle, stop when the intake valve is just about to close (intake closing). Now install and adjust the exhaust rocker the same as the intake. Once both rockers are installed, move to the next cylinder and turn the engine over until the exhaust just begins to open, and repeat the procedure. You can quickly install all the rockers and set the lash/preload properly before starting the engine for the first time without many readjustments to correct clattering rockers.

Setting proper hydraulic preload can be tricky if the procedure is not followed. The idea is that if the plunger in the lifter is depressed somewhere into the middle of its travel range, oil pressure will fill the lifter and allow the lifter to adjust properly. Some lifters have a very weak spring under the pushrod cup, and some care needs to be taken not to depress the plunger so far that it is bottomed out and the valve is held open. Not only will the engine not run right, but damage may occur if there is valve to piston interference. Thus it's best to adjust the valve-train when the intake manifold is removed. That way you can see the lifter plunger while twirling the pushrod in your fingers. Together, the two inputs will let you know when the plunger is starting to depress.

C O N T E N T S

The Basic Engine 147

Truck Speed/Density 148

Camshaft 148

Mass Air Conversion . . .148

Induction 149

Forced Induction 149

Exhaust 150

5.0 TRUCKS

When it comes to the basic engine, there's nothing fundamentally different about the 5.0 small-block V-8 that came in F-Series pickups, Broncos, and Explorers. All the basic concepts surrounding 5.0 Mustang engine improvement transfers to the truck engine, with the major difference being the near universal need to add mass air metering if you really want to hot rod it. Unlike the Mustang, Ford trucks are nearly all speed/density.

The Basic Engine

All major truck engine hardware is the same as on the Mustang. In fact, if you go back to the 1984 and earlier models, the engines are the same. Since 1985, no matter what the brochures say, the truck block will accept a roller cam, a characteristic that even applies to some 1984s. Apparently Ford was going to install the roller cam in 1984 trucks, but had piston breakage problems that put the program

mainly back to 1985. Since then, all 5.0 trucks have had roller cam blocks, even though the engines continued to use flat tappet cams. Also, 1985 was the first year for fuel injection in the trucks.

While we're on the subject of roller cam blocks, which have taller lifter bores than flat tappet blocks, some Lincolns and T-Birds have roller cam blocks, too. Not all, but some, so don't automatically discount these "mom and pop" engines when combing the wrecking yards for rebuildable cores. By simply having a roller camshaft and lifters installed, these blocks can be converted to roller cam use.

So, if you're looking for a 5.0 engine to build from scratch, trucks are a good place to look. A truck engine could be cheaper than a Mustang engine, and if you're building a second engine for your Mustang, then you don't need all the 5.0 HO-specific manifolding and so on. In fact, the short

Paired with F-150 weight, the 5.0 engine comes up a bit short of torque. Worthwhile, affordable modifications to 5.0 trucks are found mainly in the exhaust. Short-tube headers, high-flow catalytic H-pipes and cat-back systems all help a little. To really extract meaningful truck-like power, a Kenne Bell supercharger and mass air conversion will deliver the torque a truck can use. Centrifugal superchargers are available, which boost power in the upper rpm range, but they need an automatic transmission recalibration to get the most out of them. (A shift improvement kit with the Kenne Bell is highly recommended, too.)

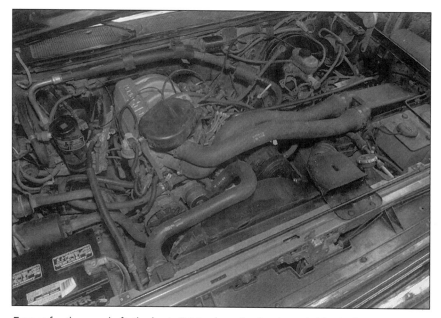

Except for the camshaft, the basic 5.0 truck engine hardware is identical to its Mustang counterpart. The quick way of warming these engines up is to port the stock heads and stick in the stock 5.0 Mustang camshaft. The trick is to maintain at least 15 inches of manifold vacuum, which keeps the MAP sensor within its calibrated range. Anything less than that idle vacuum, and mass air metering is a must.

block is likely the only portion of any concern, and then you'll really only save the block, crankshaft, and connecting rods. With so few parts being recycled, it's a wonder they call it rebuilding.

Truck Speed/Density

The 5.0 truck speed/density air metering system is quite similar to the speed/density system used in the 1986–1988 Mustangs, but uses batch fire instead of sequential fuel injection. That is, the fuel injectors fire in two groups of four, instead of squirting in the engine's firing order.

Like the Mustang speed/density engine management, the 5.0 truck system is relatively intolerant of hot rodding. It is especially needful of a reasonably strong vacuum signal while idling, 15 or 16 inches Hg. This gives the MAP (Manifold Absolute Pressure) sensor the signal it was programmed to look for, which, in turn, keeps the computer working with the right figures in its calculations.

As long as you can keep the manifold vacuum in this range while idling, the truck 5.0 will hang onto whatever idle stability it has. These engines are notorious for their lousy, and random, idle quality. Some trucks are pretty bad

about this while others are OK, and no one seems to know why. Interestingly, if your breathing modifications make it past the idle test, the next limit is fuel delivery, which is reasonably high.

Camshaft

Just in case you're considering picking up a truck short block and running it as-is in a Mustang, be advised the truck camshaft is the one major engine part that differs from the HO. It's very tame, with less than 180 degrees of duration at 0.050 inch of tappet lift, and it barely lifts the valve 0.430 inch. Such a cam will absolutely kill performance in a Mustang, so you're far ahead by installing a new aftermarket cam, or at least a 5.0 HO stocker.

Curiously, it's this small camshaft that gives truck owners a ray of hope when it comes to hot rodding. By moving up to a larger cam, but one that still maintains good idle vacuum, performance can be improved markedly. So, where can we find a speed/density friendly camshaft? In another speed/density Ford, that's where. The mid-1980s Thunderbird 5.0 (non-HO) roller camshaft works great in 5.0 trucks, building torque where the truck

engine can really use it. This cam works with the speed/density system, doesn't care about the batch-fire fuel injection, and maintains the idle quality. It's a great cam for trucks looking for a good useful power boost while maintaining great daily driving characteristics.

If more power is desired, then try the Mustang's stock 5.0 HO camshaft. It too worked on speed/density engines, although there is the chance it might give the truck idle a case of the stutters. You don't really know until you try it.

The truck ignition firing order is different than the 5.0 HOs, so you'll have to swap the spark plug wires around. The firing orders are:

Firing Orders

Truck	154263**78**
5.0 HO	1372**65**48

Boldface indicates cylinders adjacent to each other both physically and in the firing order. A danger of crossfiring exists with these; keep these wires well separated.

Truck EEC-IV batch-fires the fuel injectors, too, while the HO computer fires the injectors sequentially, in time with the firing order. This won't bother anything when changing cams, so leave the injector wiring alone unless converting to mass air metering.

Considering that the 5.0 cam is a steel roller, if you can find someone swapping out their stock Mustang cam for an aftermarket piece, their old cam should be reusable. Simply install it in your truck and go. Because of its steel construction, the roller cam is unaffected by different lifters, unlike a flat-tappet mechanical cam. Thus, you can toss in just about any 5.0 HO roller lifters you can get your hands on.

Mass Air Conversion

It's too bad Ford didn't put mass air metering on more of their trucks for our hot rodding convenience (a few California-emissions trucks did receive it). With the speed/density system fitted to nearly every 5.0 truck, the computer will tolerate only small improvements in airflow before leaning out and running

Truck manifolds draw their air from the driver side through dual hoses, and nearly all are batch-fire, speed/density engines. This gives a fair air path as built, but leaves little room for hot rodding. For a serious 302 truck hop-up program, mass air metering is required, and Ford SVO is the only game in town when it comes to converting to mass air metering.

roughly, idling with psychotic randomness and failing to make power. The answer is a mass air metering conversion kit from Ford SVO.

While not cheap, the conversion kit brings mass air metering to your 5.0 truck, allowing the huge range of 5.0 modifications Mustang owners enjoy running on pickups or Broncos. The only bad news, besides the price, is that

SVO offers mass conversion kits only for 1987–1995 5.0 trucks. They are the M-9000-T50 for manual transmission trucks, and M-9000-T51 for AOD automatics. Even though SVO lists a part number for the application in the catalog, in reality there is no direct replacement for 5.8 (351-cubic inch) trucks. This is because of the high cost of one connector necessary in the con-

version kit's wiring harness. Sales have been low enough on the 5.0 kits that SVO just doesn't want to spend the money on another connector, which it would need to do in order to support the 5.8.

That said, it is possible for someone who's quite savvy with EEC-IV to make wiring changes and get the 5.0 kits working on 5.8s, but it takes an ability to figure out what each wire does and where it should be moved—hardly an easy task.

Induction

It's interesting how Ford got the 302 truck and 5.0 HO intake manifolds mixed up. The car intake is relatively small and builds great low-end torque, which is perfect for a truck, while the truck intake has large, lazy runners that run better at higher rpm. Unfortunately, you can't swap the stock 5.0 intake onto the truck, as the truck upper faces toward the driver side, not the passenger side, and unlike the GT-40 or aftermarket intakes, the stock upper won't reverse on the lower.

Therefore, there's not much else to do except live with the truck intake manifold, or move on to the GT-40. This is fine if you're making a zippy personal-use truck out of your F-150 shortbed, but the GT-40 isn't going to help with low-end torque for towing or load hauling. In that case, you're stuck with the stocker. In fact, when it comes to truck power, a 351 really makes the difference. The light Mustangs don't need the extra torque the 351 so easily builds, but the full-framed pickups are another story.

Forced Induction

SVO offers the Powerdyne supercharger for 5.0 and 5.8 trucks, and it gives the big vehicles a nice boost in street performance, while fully supporting the engine management system with a new EEC-IV box. These kits function seamlessly from drivability, mileage, and noise standpoints, but don't expect earth-rotating performance. Centrifugal designs like the Powerdyne help only above 3,500 rpm, which is not exactly the prime truck rpm range.

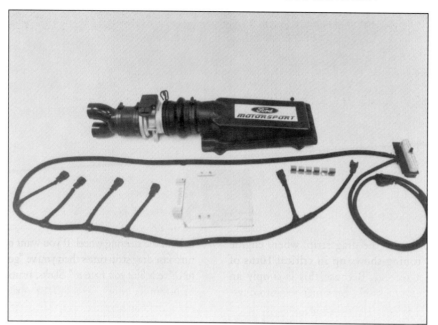

SVO's mass air metering kit will make a fair dent in your wallet, but it's the only way to support something larger than a stock 5.0 HO camshaft in a truck. Sticking with a stock 5.0 cam and a few air-flow improvers such as exhaust and an intake manifold will put off the need for mass air metering until more power is needed.

The best and easiest method of improving truck efficiency is with better exhaust parts. Short-tube headers, high-flow Y-pipes, and cats, like this system from BBK, are helpful in reducing pumping losses. Because trucks have such long exhaust systems, getting the exhaust breathing free is especially important. BBK has an especially large number of truck exhaust bolt-ons.

Also, most trucks employ automatic transmissions that shift at low rpm. With a centrifugal supercharger, the engine just gets into the 4,000-rpm range, where the blower is starting to do some good when the automatic transmission shifts. Secondly, trucks do best with tons of torque, and the centrifugal superchargers don't do anything for low-end torque, just top-end horsepower. This works okay if you run around with no to light loads in the bed, and want harder acceleration; then the SVO/Powerdyne blower gives a satisfying boost in performance when the throttle is put down and left there. If you're looking for more pulling power, however, to get a trailer over the hills or hauling heavy loads, then a centrifugal supercharger will do some good, but it isn't the great hope. Try a positive displacement blower instead. Your only real choice at press time for this was Kenne Bell, which offers a high-torque blower option with its Autorotor unit. The other real-world option is swapping to a 351W.

Exhaust

One area where the trucks can definitely be helped is with the exhaust. The slight breathing improvement of

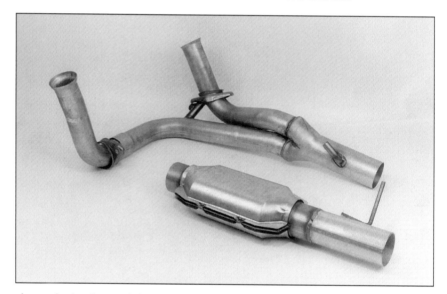

short-tube headers and larger exhaust pipes will not send the speed/density system into hysterics, yet it still helps a little with fuel economy and power. If you're looking at it purely from a financial point of view, it will take a while to pencil out, as it takes a big savings in fuel to make up the price of the exhaust parts and their installation. But if you like to play with your truck, such mods will help and are fun. Several of the larger 5.0 Mustang aftermarket manufacturers offer truck-specific headers, H-pipes, and cat-back systems.

Driving	151
Timing and Fuel	152
Electronic Tuning	152
Cooling Down	152
Short Belts	153
Head Gaskets	153

C O N T E N T S

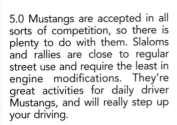

5.0 Mustangs are accepted in all sorts of competition, so there is plenty to do with them. Slaloms and rallies are close to regular street use and require the least in engine modifications. They're great activities for daily driver Mustangs, and will really step up your driving.

RUNNING THE 5.0

Whether for fun, money, or glory, many 5.0 Mustangs eventually end up on a racetrack, usually the drag strip, where engine tuning shows up in critical 10ths of a second. Because this is simply an engine book, we won't get into chassis and suspension tuning except to say that without it all the power in the world won't help. Most 5.0 races are won in the wheelwells, not under the hood. As for engines, it comes down to fuel, timing, temperature, and driving to make things happen at the track.

Numerous books have been published on Mustang handling, or should I say, the lack of it. As this subject is typically less intuitive than engine building, I recommend you read as much as possible about it. This would include the companion title to this one, *How to Tune & Modify Your Ford 5.0-Liter Mustang* by Steve Turner. It gives a broad overview of Mustang mods, including chassis, suspension, brakes, interior, powertrain, and so on.

Driving

No one talks much about it, but often the slowest thing in a 5.0 sits right behind the steering wheel. If you want to turn fast drag strip times then you've "got to drive it like you hate it." Slicks, brutal high-rpm launches, and vicious speed shifts are mandatory. Driver skill in executing those shifts, judging shift points, getting a good reaction time, and all the rest that goes with a good time slip are also mandatory. This isn't a how-to-drive book, but it's vital to consider your driving when reviewing your 5.0's performance. Seek the advice of the established racers, especially those competing in well-organized racing, like NHRA. They're the ones who know how.

And yes, if you want to go the fastest at the drags, you will break parts and spend plenty of money for that last little bit, but that's what it takes. Remember this when comparing your car to some published, or worse, locally renowned, fast time.

Slaloming and road racing require even more of the driver. Experienced,

Drag racing is usually the easiest motorsport to get into, and offers the engine enthusiast nearly unlimited opportunities to hot rod. It is easily the most popular 5.0 Mustang motorsport, and can be enjoyed with everything from a stone stock daily driver all the way up to Pro 5.0.

skilled drivers often take seconds off a beginner's time when driving the beginner's car. It's humbling, but it's not the car's fault! Pro training and practice will make you faster, so get on down to the slaloms or road course and have at it. As at any racetrack, you'll find other racers there who are ready to help. It's tons more fun than dorking around on the street, so if you want to go fast, make the effort to go to the track.

Timing and Fuel

At a bare minimum you need a timing light, a fuel pressure gauge, an adjustable fuel pressure regulator, and an ear for detonation to extract maximum performance from your 5.0. You should start by advancing the initial timing. Fourteen degrees seems to be the magic number quoted by most people, but your car might need more or less, depending on its computer calibration, compression, and cylinder head construction. You should sneak up on the timing a degree at a time until the car slows down or detonates, then back it off to the previous thing. Reading the spark plugs as outlined in Chapter 8 will also help. Be extremely wary when doing this on supercharged or nitrous-

assisted cars because it is often nearly impossible to hear the engine rattle even when running through the mufflers, and boosted 5.0s lose their head gaskets in an instant. With open exhaust, you'll never hear detonation, so you must read spark plugs to get the timing right when running unmuffled.

With timing optimized, you can do the same with fuel pressure. Simply remove the vacuum line from the fuel pressure regulator while the car is running and set the fuel pressure; stock cars can benefit from slight leaning, but try stock first! Modified cars want more pressure. Stock fuel pressure is 38 psi.

Like having a timing light, it is crucial you have a fuel pressure gauge to set your fuel pressure. If the gauge is cockpit-mounted, it will be helpful to have a friend tell you what the pressure is as you set it. Sneak up on the fuel, just like the timing, until the car slows down. Also remember that Ford's electronic fuel injection, especially the mass air metering variety, is extremely adaptable to weather conditions—unlike a carburetor—but drastic changes will still likely mandate a change. For example, a hot day will require less fuel, while a cold day needs more.

Supercharged and nitrous-boosted 5.0s follow the same theme, but require less aggressive timing, much more fuel and tuning, but here it is a matter of how much fuel and timing you take out, rather than how much you add. That's because the higher cylinder pressures accelerate combustion (so less timing is needed) and the FMU floods the engine with fuel to ward off detonation.

Electronic Tuning

Although they operate differently, electronic tuning aids such as Ford Motorsport's Extender, Extreme Performance Engine Control, and EFI Systems' Programmable Management System offer an edge at the track. While the Extender is really useful only for setting the fuel mixture, most of these tuning tools let you expand beyond simple operations like boost timing retard by giving you more control. They can also help you do away with fuel management units via larger fuel injectors. Additionally, they give you total control over fuel and timing curves, rather than just advancing the factory reference value.

Above all, the big money electronic tools give you the added benefit of data logging. This allows you to see if your fuel injectors are running at their limit, if your car is running rich or lean, and how much boost you are making at a given rpm. Data logging and the ability to react to it via electronic tuning are the best part of running a fuel-injected 5.0.

About the only downside of these systems is their complexity, not to mention cost. For casual track duty, meaning any 5.0 with license plates that sees some track action, sticking with standard nitrous or blower kits and their FMUs and stock electronics is the safest way to go.

Cooling Down

A low-tech method of eking up to 10 horsepower from your 5.0 Mustang at the drag strip is icing the intake between rounds. You should start with a wet towel to absorb the initial slug of heat, then switch to bags of ice to chill the intake. Starting with ice immediately melts the ice too quickly. Of

Far too often, easy performance "gains" are possible from simple maintenance. Treat your 5.0 like a racing business by organizing preventative maintenance and upgrades on a schedule. A small notebook or spreadsheet will do. Simple reminders like writing the next oil change mileage on the oil filter are also smart.

If you go to the drag strip, use slicks! You can't learn much if you're slipping and sliding on street rubber. Not only will you go quicker, but only a slick offers the consistency necessary to evaluate hardware changes and build your driving skills. It balls the rubber from the track under the tread, reducing traction to less than regular street asphalt. The only downside is that as you add power, the driveline needs upgrading to take the hard launches slicks make possible.

course, idling through the staging lanes and doing an extended burnout will negate much of the ice's benefit. So if you really need max power, push or tow your car up to the line and keep burnouts to a simple spin of the tires to clean the tread. Big burnouts hurt the tire anyway.

Short Belts

One of the oldest drag racing tricks is running a short accessory drive belt. You can buy short belts that bypass the Thermactor pump, power steering pump, or both. They can be worth a 10th or two and give a more positive steering feel at the top of the track. Speaking of belts, owners who drive their blown 5.0s to the track can make their first pass of the day as good as their last by leaving off the blower belt during the trip to the track. This reduces heat buildup in the blower during the road trip.

Unfortunately there are so many combinations of front engine dress that there is no way of listing the belt sizes that are going to work. So many underdrive pulleys are being used, each from a company with its own ideas on pulley diameter, plus the various combinations of front engine dress available from Ford that even the pros have to wade through several belt changes until they find the one that works. The best advice is to work with your local shop until you find the right short belt, then don't lose it!

Head Gaskets

The 5.0 liter engine is pretty tough, but when things go wrong at the track, like detonation from overleaning or over advancing, the head gasket is usually the first thing to go. Of course, this is far better than the days of melting pistons and rebuilding the whole engine— which 4.6 owners have discovered all

over again. In light of that, changing head gaskets isn't so bad. You can go back to the bad-old days by O-ringing the block or using O-ring-style head gaskets, which leave a more difficult escape route for cylinder pressure, thus making the piston a target once more. This is fine if you don't mind melting down the engine just to win that $50,000 purse, but that isn't likely in a 5.0 race, much less at test 'n' tune night.

Whether of not you hear the rattle of detonation, if it was severe enough, you've probably weakened or blown a head gasket. Of course, naturally aspirated cars are less susceptible to blowing head gaskets than supercharged or nitrous-injected 5.0s, but get crazy with any combination and the gasket will fail.

Typically you know a head gasket is gone when the battery tray is filled with coolant. This is because the cylinder pressure created by detonation is much

Get in the habit of using the best fuel available. Unleaded race gas is readily available in well over 100 octane, so even having catalytic converters is not an issue. Race gas, or pump gas doped with octane boosters, goes a long way to holding off detonation. You can also raise the ignition timing to gain more power. This is a commonly overlooked and inexpensive advantage.

Cooling the engine between rounds is worthwhile. The towel and ice method will chill the intake; you can extract more heat by wetting the radiator. Drenching the radiator is not necessary or preferable. A light mist from a garden sprayer is best. The idea is to evaporate a thin layer of water on the radiator core. The change of state from liquid to vapor that takes place during evaporation is what provides the cooling effect. A heavy coat of water is more like a layer of insulation.

higher than is present even in a supercharged cylinder. Such uncontrolled combustion is usually strong enough to lift the heads off the block, stretching the head bolts and letting combustion gases rip through the now-vulnerable gasket. In the process of lifting the head and setting it back down, some of the gases enter the cooling system via the cylinder head water jackets, pressurizing the cooling system and causing coolant to blow out the radiator overflow bottle into the battery tray.

Depending on how badly the engine detonated, or more precisely, how long you kept your foot in it, a head gasket can be blown in varying degrees. A mildly blown gasket may just weep a little water into the cylinders, a moderately blown gasket will weep a little coolant into the cylinders and the oiling system, and a badly blown gasket can fill the cylinders up with coolant, causing it to

hydraulically lock—a costly proposition.

With a mildly blown gasket, you can simply purge the system and pour in water as needed. People have driven around for months with mildly blown gaskets, provided you don't race the car or get back into the boost or nitrous. You can still limp home on a moderately

blown gasket, but you'll likely want to change the gaskets and oil as soon as possible. It's probably a good idea to leave the radiator cap on the first notch (not sealed) to allow cylinder pressure to vent through the cooling system.

If you really waste the gaskets and the car feels like it's going to be hard to

All racing, especially drag racing, encourages development to faster and faster performance. That's great, but remember, as the horsepower goes up, so does the parts breakage, and occasionally it can be character building. Don Walsh of D&D Performance and Ford SVO towed from Michigan to California for a 5.0 race, only to have a simple part let go at the starting line of the first round. All that money and effort went into the puddle of ATF Don is staring disgustedly into here. It's part of racing, and something to consider before modifying your street driver into a racer.

If your blower installation uses a drive belt separate from the engine's serpentine belt, drive it to the track with the blower belt removed. This keeps the blower from building up heat before the racing begins. Pete Misinsky taught us this one; here he's reconnecting the belt to his SN-95's supercharger. The long bungee cord keeps the radiator hose away from the blower belt.

start after you pull it into the pits—don't start it! Some of the cylinders are likely filled with water and starting would cause catastrophic damage. In this instance, remove the plugs, crank the engine over until most of the water pumps out the spark plug holes. Then you can put the plugs back in, refill the cooling system and limp home. Again, take it easy until you replace the head gaskets.

When you replace your head gaskets, you should thoroughly clean the head and block surfaces. Once the areas are prepped, use a high-quality aftermarket head gasket designed for your performance application. Also consider using aftermarket fasteners like those sold by ARP. These help your gaskets survive mild detonation by exerting more clamping force on the gaskets. While putting the rest of the engine together, replace the thermostat, as the hot gases forced into the cooling system by detonation often cause a thermostat to lock up.

If you have compressed air, a leak-down tester is a big help at the track. It is especially useful for pinpointing those tough-to-diagnose conditions that aren't quite obvious. Here Paul Silva uses his to determine an exhaust valve leak. His ET and miles per hour were a bit off, but he knew he could make a few more passes before having to pull the head. He also knew what to expect once the head came off.

Mustang power steering is too light at the race track, especially if you're running skinny front tires. Bypassing the pump with a shorter belt is a good way of getting around this. The steering is reasonably weighted without the power assist, and a bit more power is available at the flywheel. Obviously there's no need for the air conditioning under the power steering pump, either.

APPENDIX

5.0 Mustang Parts Sources

The following sources for 5.0 parts will get you started. It is, however, far from complete, and its reliance on mail order parts houses should not suggest you ignore your local speed shop. Supporting your local speed shop as a matter of habit pays off for those times when you really need it.

Anderson Ford Motorsport
PO Box 638
Clinton, IL 61727
(271) 935-2384
Mail order parts

BBK
1605 Railroad Street
Corona, CA 91720
(909) 735-2400
Exhaust, superchargers, mail order parts

Canton Racing Products
2 Commerce Drive
North Branford, CT 06471
(203) 484-4900
Oil pans

Charlie's Mustangs
766-A North 9th
San Jose, CA 95112
(408) 275-6511
All parts, speed shop, mail order parts

Crane Cams
530 Fentress Boulevard
Daytona Beach, FL 32114
(904) 258-6174
Camshafts, valvetrain giant

DSS
960 Ridge Avenue
Lombard, IL 60148
(630) 268-1630
Machine shop, strokers, main stud girdle

Ford Special Vehicle Operations (SVO, or Motorsport)
to order a catalog write to:
PO Box 51394
Livonia, MI 48151
(810) 468-1356 (technical hotline)

Holcomb Motorsports
900 Hardin Road
Lumberton, NC 28358
(910) 739-0747
Mail order parts

MPG Head Service
3881 South Jason
Englewood, CO 80110
(303) 762-8196
Ford cam specialist, machine shop

Nowak and Co.
249 East Emerson, Unit F
Orange, CA 92665
(714) 282-7996
Machine shop, pistons, strokers

Mustang Parts Specialties
53 Commercial Drive
Statham, GA 30666
(770) 725-7862
Late-model Mustang wrecking yard, all parts sales

Nitrous Oxide Systems
2970 Airway
Costa Mesa, CA 92626
(714) 545-0580
Nitrous systems

Panhandle Performance
106 West Peachtree Drive
Lynn Haven, FL 32444
(850) 265-9818
Machine shop, parts

Paxton Automotive Corp.
1250 Calle Suerte
Camarillo, CA 93012
(805) 987-8660
Novi 2000 supercharger, fuel systems

Powered by Ford
1516 South Division Avenue
Orlando, FL 32805
(407) 843-3673
Machine shop

Steeda Autosports
2241 Hammondville Road
Pompano Beach, FL 33069
(954) 960-0774
Parts, machine shop, all services

Tommie Vaughn
1145 North Shepherd
Houston, Texas 77008
(713) 869-4661
Mail order parts

Trick Flow
1248 Southeast Avenue
Tallmadge, OH 44278
(330) 630-1555
Cylinder heads, valvetrain parts

Vortech Engineering, Inc.
8353 Bonsai Avenue
Moorpark, CA 93021
(805) 529-9330
Superchargers, fuel systems

Windsor-Fox
PO Box 2663
Apple Valley, CA 92307
(760) 946-3835
351 engine swap specialist, wiring, electronics

INDEX

5.0 HO engine, 1986–1993, 8–16
  1994–1995, 7, 15–17
  1996, 17
  Camshaft changes, 9, 12
  Compartment, 10, 11
  EFI, introduction of, 9
  General description, 8
  Mustang Cobra, 1993, 13, 16
  Mustang-based, 8, 9
  Pistons, forged vs. hypereutectic, 12
  Power ratings, 15, 16
  Speed/density vs. mass air metering, 12–15
ACCEL, 62, 64, 66
Aftercoolers, 90
Air filters, 33, 92, 93
Air inlet, low restriction, 93
  Power Pipe, 93
Anderson, Rick, 93
ARP, 111, 113, 115, 155
Attwood, Bob, 36
Autologic, 28, 37
Battery, 66
BBK, 22–25, 35, 38, 75, 76, 84, 85, 90–92, 95, 96, 150
Bell, Corkey, 98
Blue Thunder, 105, 106, 113
Blueprinting, 108
Boost retards, 93
Brown, Kenny, 96
Bypass kits, 93
C&M Racing Systems, 28
Camshafts, 9, 12, 134–146, 148
  With nitrous oxide, 141
  With normal aspiration, 138, 139
  With superchargers, 139, 140
  With turbocharging, 140, 141
Camshafts, popular, 141–143
Camshafts, specifications, 142, 143
Camshafts, terminology, 134–137
  Cam card, 135
  Duration, 135
  Lobe center, 135, 136
  Lobe lift, 135
  Straight up, 136, 137

Valve lift, 135
Cap and rotor, 62, 63
Cartech, 91, 95, 98, 99
Coast High Performance, 104–106
Cold/Ram air, 45
Comp Cams, 145
Compucar, 80
Connecting rods See Short-block preparation and Strokers
Crane Cams, 9, 63–65, 134, 143, 145
Crankshafts, 9 See also Short-block preparation and Strokers
Crower, 105, 106, 113
Cylinder heads, 118–133
Cylinder heads, other, 125–127
  Australian Cleveland, 125, 125
  C302, 126, 127
  Cleveland, 126
  N351 Sportsman, 126
  Yates, 127
Cylinder heads, porting, 129–132
  CNC porting, 131
  Extrude honing, 131, 132
  Port matching, 132, 133
Cylinder heads, preparation, 127–129
  Combustion Chambering (CCing), 127
  Milling, 127
  O-ring/loc wire, 127, 128
  Valve job, 128, 129
Cylinder heads, screw in studs/guide plates, 133
Cylinder heads, stock, 119–125
  Avenger/Canfield, 125
  Brodix, 125
  Edelbrock Performer, 121, 122
  Edelbrock Victor Jr., 121, 122
  Edelbrock Victor, 121, 123
  GT-40, 119, 120
  Holley, 125
  J302, 120
  Street Heat, 123, 124
  Twisted Wedge, 122–124
  Windsor Jrs., 121
  Windsor, 120, 121

Deputy, Gene, 98
Devine, Bill, 98
DFI, 18, 29, 31, 82, 98
Distributors, 64–66
Drive belts/pulleys, 94, 95
Drive gear, 66
Duttweiler, Kenny, 97, 98
Dyno testing, 45
E7TE heads, 9, 86, 119
Eagle, 105, 106, 113
Eaton, 90
Edelbrock, 39, 41, 42, 75, 121, 123
EEC-IV, 12, 13, 15, 17–45, 59, 60, 66, 68, 74, 148, 149
  Carburetion, replacing with, 30, 31
  Computer chips, 26–28
  Description of, 19–21
  Electronic Control Module (ECM), 19
  Electronic Control Unit (ECU), 19, 73
  EPEC, replacement with, 29, 30
  FADEC (Full-Authority Digital Engine Control), 18
  Fuel Management Unit (FMU), 19, 28, 29, 70–73, 91, 92
  Piggyback devices, 28, 29
    Extender (SVO), 29
    Interceptor, 28
    PMS, 27, 28
  Sequential Electronic Fuel Injection, 18
EEC-V, 18
EFI Systems, Inc., 28
EGR spacer, 22–24 See also Throttle body
Electrical specifications, Mustang, 66
Electromotive, 18, 28, 29
Electronic fuel injection (EFI), introduction of, 7–9
EPEC, 27, 28, 82, 86 See also EEC-IV
Exhaust, 46–58, 150
  Cat-back, 57, 58, 93
    Borla, 57, 58
    Flowmaster, 57, 58
    Installing, 58
    Pacesetter, 58

Walker, 58
Race, 48
Stock, 46–48, 54
Street, 48
Fel Pro, 28, 31
Fuel Management Unit (FMU) See
   EEC-IV
Forced induction requirements, 63
Ford Explorer, 14–17
Ford Motorsport, 8, 13, 17, 78
Ford Thunderbird, 14–16
Fuel pumps, 67, 68, 92
Fuel system, 67–73, 82, 83
   Definition of terms, 68–70
GT-40, 13, 14, 16, 41, 75, 119, 120,
   149
Guido, Sam, 29
H-Pipes, 56
Haltech, 29
Headers, coatings, 54
Headers, long-tube, 54–56
Headers, short-tube, 48–55
   Bolt vs. stud, 55
   Build quality, 54, 55
   Equal vs. unequal primaries, 49
   Flange style, 49, 54
   Installing, 50–53
   Pipe diameter, 48, 49
   Spark plug access, 49
Holley, 40, 42, 43, 64, 75, 125
HP Motorsports, 95, 96
Ignitions, aftermarket, 63–65
   ACCEL, 64
   Crane, 64
   Holley, 64
   Installing, 65
   Jacobs Electronics, 65
   Mallory, 64
   MSD, 54
Ignition, 59–66
Ignition, capacitor-discharge, 59, 60,
   63
Ignition, inductive, 59, 60
Ignition, maintaining, 60–63
Ignition, setting timing, 59, 62
Induction, 32–45, 149, 150
Injectors, 92
Intake air silencer, 33
Intake manifolds, 15, 39
   Box intakes, 43
      Hartmann, 43
      Ron Anderson Power Box, 43
   Cowl induction, 43
      Roush Induction System, 44
   Installation tips, 44

Long runner, 39–43
   BXR, 40, 43
   Cut and weld, 40
   Edelbrock Performer RPM, 42
   Edelbrock Performer, 39, 41,
      42
   Edelbrock Victor 5.0, 42
   Extrude honing, 40, 41
   GT-40, 41
   Holley SysteMAX I & II, 40, 42,
      43
   Vortech/Saleen, 39, 42
Intercoolers, 90, 96
Jacobs Electronics, 61, 62, 65, 82
JBA, 49–54
Keith Black, 12, 114, 116
Kenne Bell, 35, 37, 71, 75, 76, 84,
      85, 89–91, 93, 95, 147, 150
Kuntz and Company, 66
Lifters, 139, 143, 144
Machining engines, 108
Mallory, 64, 66
Manifold Absolute Pressure (MAP),
      12, 13, 15, 148
Mass air metering, 12–15, 20, 21,
      26, 33–37
   Bored stock, 37
   Kenne Bell, 35, 37
Mass airflow (MAF) meter See
      Mass air metering
McClure Motorsport, 94, 95
MSD, 12, 54, 59, 61, 64, 66, 98
Mustang Cobra, 13, 16, 38
Mustang GT, 14
Mustang, Fox-4, 16
Mustang, Fox-bodied, 16
Mustang, SN-95, 16, 43, 80
Nitrous oxide, 78–83, 141
   Fuel system upgrades, 82, 83
   System description of, 79, 80
   Theory of operation, 79
   Wet vs. dry, 80, 81
Nitrous oxide, accessories, 81, 82
   Bottle gauge, 81
   Bottle warmer, 81
   Nitrous controller, 82
   Nitrous retard, 82
   Progressive timer, 82
   RPM switch, 81
Nitrous Oxide Systems (NOS),
      80–83
Nitrous Works, 80
Nowak and Company, 104–106
Nowak, Dan, 104
Octane boosters, 93

Omega, 145
Part numbers, reading, 13
Paxton, 72, 74, 76, 85–87, 91, 94
Performance Parts, 62
Phenolic spacers, 42, 45
Pistons, forged vs. hypereutectic,
      12 See also Short-block prepa-
      ration and Strokers
PMS, 82, 86
Port matching, 44, 45
Power adders, 74–77 See also
      Nitrous oxide, Turbochargers,
      and Superchargers
   Convenience, 76
   Cost, 76, 77
   Future increases, 76
Power adders
   Comparison, 77
   Kits, 74, 75
   Racing, 75
   Street, 75
Powerdyne, 76, 88, 89, 149, 150
Probe, 105, 106
Pushrods, 144
Racing, 151–156
   Cooling down, 152–154
   Drive belt, short, 153, 155
   Driving, 151, 152
   Electronic tuning, 152
   Fuel, 152, 154
   Head gaskets, 153–155
   Timing, 152
Radovich, Craig, 85
Regan, Mike, 94
Robert Yates Racing, 127
Rocker arms, 139, 140, 144, 145
   Adjusting, 145
   Installing, 145
Rocker geometry, 144
Roush Racing, 43, 44
Roush, Jack, 43
Saleen, 39, 42, 77, 107
Shelby, Carroll, 7
Short-block preparation, 108–117
   Balancing, 111, 112, 115
   Boring, 109, 110
   Cleaning parts, 108
   Connecting rods, 113
      Aftermarket, 113, 114
   Cost, 117
   Crank kit, 116
   Crankshafts, 110, 111
   Crate engines, 115, 116
   Deburring/shot peening, 113
   Decking, 110

Head bolts/studs, 115
Honing, 110
Knife-edging, 112
Lightening, 111
New vs. rebuilt, 116, 117
Oil pans, 112, 113
Oiling, 112
Pistons, 114
Pistons, shape and deburring, 114, 115
Seal, rear main, 112
Sonic checking, 109, 110
Stock vs. modified, 117
Smith, Rick, 123, 124
Spark plug wires, 60–62
Spark plugs, 60, 61, 83
Special Vehicle Engineering (SVE), 8
Special Vehicle Operations (SVO), 8
Special Vehicle Team (SVT), 8, 13
Speed/density air metering, 12–15, 21, 26, 31, 148, 149
Speed/density, fuel injection, 12–15
Spetter, Job, 97, 98
Starters, 12
Strokers, 103–107
Blocks, 104
Connecting rods/pistons, 105, 106
Crankshafts, 104
Damper/flywheel, 104, 105

Tradeoffs, 105, 106
Tuning, 106, 107
Summit Racing, 123, 124
Superchargers, 84–96, 139, 140
Accessories, 91
Braces, 95, 96
Hints, 86
Superchargers, centrifugal, 84–89
ATI ProCharger, 89, 90, 96
Paxton Novi 2000, 85–87
Paxton SN-93, 87
Paxton VR4, 87
Powerdyne, 88, 89
Vortech Mondo, 88, 96
Vortech V1, 88, 94, 95
Superchargers, positive displacement, 84–87, 89–91
BBK Performance, 84, 85, 90–92, 96
Kenne Bell, 89–91
SVO, 13, 17, 38, 104, 105
Tailpipes, See Exhaust, cat-back
Throttle body, 37–39 See also EGR Spacer
Accufab, 38, 39
BBK/Edelbrock, 35, 38
SVO, 38
Throttle body installation, 22–25
Throttle Position Sensor (TPS), 12, 20, 22–25, 30, 37

Trick Flow Specialties, 122, 123, 124
Trucks, 147–150
Camshaft, 148
Engine, basic, 147, 148
Exhaust, 150
Induction, 149
Induction, forced, 149, 150
Mass air conversion, 148, 149
Speed/density, 148, 149
TRW, 114, 116
Turbo People, 97
Turbochargers, 97–102, 140, 141
Turbochargers, kits, 98–102
Cartech, 98, 99
DDMI, 99, 100
INCON Systems, 99–101
Turbo Technology, 101, 102
Turbonetics, 97, 98
Valve seat replacement, 130
Valvetrain See Camshafts/Valvetrain
Vortech, 39, 42, 72, 76, 84, 88, 91, 94–96
Wallis, Doug, 28
Wesley, Mike, 28
Wet manifolding, 45
Wheeler, Jim, 88
Will Burt Street Heat, 49, 123, 124
World Products, 120, 121
X-Pipes, 56, 57